TSQ Transgender Studies Quarterly

Volume 7 ∗ Number 3 ∗ August 2020

Trans* Studies Now

Edited by Susan Stryker

COMMENTARY

BOOK REVIEWS

Introduction

Trans* Studies Now

SUSAN STRYKER

This issue of *TSQ*, "Trans* Studies Now," already somewhat dated by the COVID-19 pandemic and its consequences, is a child born of necessity. A planned issue experienced unavoidable delay, and given that we needed to pull together another one in short order, I gathered an assortment of work I found readily at hand. It offers less than a full-fledged "state of the field" and more of a casual snapshot that documents something about the moment, when questions abound about what trans* studies has become and what it's doing, both in the academy and in the wider world, what it sees as it looks back and where its futures might lie.

Self-styled "writer, critic, and sad trans girl" Andrea Long Chu had a break-out year in 2019, including the publication here (with coauthor Emmett Harsin Drager) of "After Trans Studies," which turned out to be the most-read article of the year for *TSQ* and among the top ten most-read journal articles of 2019 for Duke University Press overall (Duke University Press 2019). In recognition of that accomplishment, we've organized a special section of this issue, "After Andrea Long Chu," to allow several authors to respond to various dimensions of Chu's work. Cassius Adair, Cameron Awkward-Rich, and Amy Marvin's "Before Trans Studies" offers a measured rebuttal of Chu and Harsin Drager's *TSQ* article, while Jack Halberstam, in "Nice Trannies," accords Chu's self-consciously pugnacious and deliberately provocative style the sincerest form of flattery by delivering a bare-knuckled counter-punch of his own. Jules Joanne Gleeson's review essay of Chu's debut book, *Females*, situates that work in Chu's rapidly expanding oeuvre as a public intellectual, while longtime trans activist Riki Wilchins uses Chu's *New York Times* opinion piece about her impending genital surgery to reflect on what transgender studies doesn't—but might—tend to say about the phenomenological experience of being a post-op trans woman in the contemporary United States.

TSQ: Transgender Studies Quarterly * Volume 7, Number 3 * August 2020 **299**
DOI 10.1215/23289252-8552908 © 2020 Duke University Press

The section "Institutionalizing Trans⋆ Studies" takes the pulse of recent field-building efforts on behalf of an interdisciplinary transgender studies and possibilities for imagining trans studies otherwise in relation to other interdisciplinary formations. Cáel M. Keegan draws from a spate of his own recent work on field formation to further reflect on how trans studies is "against queer theory," not in the sense of being opposed to it but in the sense of being positioned fricatively adjacent to it. My own contribution to the issue recounts the fraught history of attempting to institutionalize trans studies at the University of Arizona. Madi Day offers an important reminder in "Indigenist Origins" that trans studies has many genealogies, not all of them rooted in settler colonialism, as they discuss the establishment of the first queer and trans Indigenous studies program in Australia. Members of the editorial collective of the *Somatechnics* journal discuss the intersections and shared history of trans studies and their own interdisciplinary investigations into the technicity of all embodiment.

"(Un)Disciplining Trans⋆ Knowledges," on how established fields do and don't accommodate trans studies scholarship, is kicked off by Grace Lavery's "Egg Theory's Early Style," which weaves together many of the themes touched on by other essays in this section while advancing sophisticated arguments about, among other things, a cis-centric queer theory's inability to imagine transition. Robin Dembroff analyzes the worrisome rise of antitransgender perspectives in analytical philosophy in "Cisgender Commonsense and Philosophy's Transgender Trouble," while Travers offers an account of the "masculinity contest culture" that contributes to a transmisogynistic bias against trans femininity and trans womanhood, both beyond and within trans studies. Ian Khara Ellasante asks the important and related question of whether trans studies is equipped to offer an affirmative intellectual, political, and spiritual home for many kinds of trans⋆ difference in "Dear Trans Studies, Can You Do Love?" Joshua Aiken, Jessica Marion Modi, and Olivia R. Polk explore the growing nexus of black studies and trans studies in three interrelated "gestures" toward a common set of texts in "Issued by Way of the 'Issue of Blackness,'" which takes the 2017 black trans studies issue of *TSQ* as its point of departure.

A section of conference reports profiles three recent trans studies symposia. In "Empire and Eugenics: Trans Studies in the United Kingdom," Ezra Horbury and Christine "Xine" Yao contextualize their efforts to convene a trans studies symposium at University College London within (and in response to) the antitrans moral panic currently running rampant in the United Kingdom. Nicole Seymour reports on the 2019 "Trans ± Sex: Rethinking Sex/Gender in Trans Studies" symposium at the University of Arizona in her contribution, "Bad Dads and Precarious Grads." Pamela L. Caughie and Emily Datskou document the transfeminist digital humanities praxis that informed their construction of the

Lili Elbe Digital Archive, which culminated in a remarkable symposium at Loyola University Chicago that simultaneously showcased the archive and enacted their values in a project that revolved around the legacy of a transfeminine person. In a related section titled "How to Do Things with Trans*," McKenzie Wark curates and introduces work by Marquis Bey, Kay Gabriel, and K. K. Trieu from the "Trans | Acker Symposium" she organized at the New School, all of which exemplifies how critique and commentary from trans* perspectives—rather than about transgender topics—can offer fresh readings of literary works and the worlds in which they have been produced, specifically in this case the work of postmodern novelist Kathy Acker. The issue concludes with a commentary from medical anthropologist Sahar Sadjadi, MD, on puberty-blocking pharmaceuticals and book reviews by James McMaster, D-L Stewart, and Nicole Erin Morse.

In keeping with the theme of "trans studies now," this issue of *TSQ* offers the perfect opportunity to announce changes to the journal's editorial structure. This will be the last issue for which I will have primary editorial responsibility, as I step back from hands-on involvement at that level and step up to a new position as executive editor. Francisco Galarte will continue as coeditor and will move the journal's editorial office with him to the University of New Mexico, where he is now assistant professor in the departments of American studies and women's, gender, and sexuality studies. Joining him on the coeditorial team will be Abraham Weil, assistant professor in women's, gender, and sexuality studies at California State University, Long Beach, who has served as managing editor of *TSQ* since its founding, as well as two new coeditors: Jules Gill-Peterson, associate professor of English and gender, sexuality, and women's studies at the University of Pittsburgh, and Grace Lavery, associate professor of English at the University of California, Berkeley. The four of them will each have primary responsibilities for supervising the production of one issue per year, along with developing a consensus among themselves as to the overall direction of the journal. I will no longer have a public-facing role and will instead serve as primary point of contact with the press, tiebreaker in case of editorial deadlock, general in-house sounding board, and resident "granny tranny." As I rotate entirely off the editorial team at the end of 2023 when I will have completed ten years of editorial service, Francisco Galarte will step into the executive editor role and will in turn be followed in that position by each of the other coeditors in succession, as new coeditors cycle onto the editorial team and the most senior member cycles off. In this way, we feel we can both foster continuity and preserve institutional memory, while opening the journal's editorial vision to fresher and broader perspectives and connecting it more effectively to emerging scholarship and issues.

In this moment of editorial transition, as I look back at what this journal has accomplished and reflect on trans* studies now, I am struck most deeply and obviously by the change in the political climate in which we do our work. The year we launched *TSQ*—2014—was the year of the so-called tipping point, when Laverne Cox appeared on the cover of *Time* magazine, *Transparent* started streaming on Amazon, the Obama administration was actively defending trans-gender civil rights and health-care access, and liberal society seemed poised to offer at least the whitest and most normative trans people a seat at the table of social inclusion. It was the year the trans studies initiative at the University of Arizona hired its first three tenure-track lines. We in the field knew even then that the gains represented by those fragile beginnings were unevenly distributed and tied to a neoliberal politics of identity management, one that celebrated a patriotic "transnormative" citizenship while reproducing sharp violence against the most marginalized trans people and enacting "slow death" for most of the rest. From the outset, *TSQ* has offered its assessment of the political economy and the bio/necropolitical conditions in which trans lives transpire, even as we grasp to make sense of and respond to the heightened precarity of our lives as the neoliberal paradigm unravels and something worse tries to elbow its way into power.

That same year, 2014, witnessed mass resistance to homicidal antiblack police violence in Ferguson, Missouri, and the rapid expansion of the nascent Black Lives Matters movement in defiance to a rash of police killings of unarmed black men all across the United States. In this context there was a heightened sense of urgency—all the more pressing now—regarding the need for a deeper analysis of the relation of transness to whiteness, blackness, racism, and misogyny, especially in light of the bifurcated realities of Caitlin Jenner's peaking celebrity, the accelerating wave of violence against black, brown, and indigenous trans women and transfeminine people, and the logical conundrums posed to domi-nant racial imaginaries by Rachel Dolezal's claims of transracial identity. Over the years, *TSQ* has become an important venue for promulgating work in black trans studies and trans-of-color scholarship that has profoundly reshaped the field as it existed in the 1990s and 2000s. Alongside long-running efforts to carve out trans speaking positions in the games of power-knowledge, resist pathologizing med-ical frameworks that reduce the meaning of our lives to a symptom, and attend to feminist struggles over the consequences of sexual difference, the field increas-ingly foregrounds the recognition of gender as always-already racialized, expe-riences of fugitivity and fungibility as varieties of transness that transpire along axes not reducible to gender, and the unmarked whiteness of notions of bodily plasticity and capacity for transformation that have long been central to trans aesthetics and analytics.

While the journal's critical attention to intersections of transness and ethnicity/race have drawn particular force from the political intensities that have characterized life in the United States in the Obama and Trump years, it speaks as well to our determination to decenter the Northern, white, anglophone bias of trans scholarship. To that end, *TSQ* has featured a recurring content section featuring translations ever since its launch in 2014, solicited work in languages other than English and made ad hoc arrangements to support translation, aimed without always succeeding to have work by scholars outside the United States or on non-US topics constitute half of each issue, and offered special issues on decoloniality, translation, Asian trans studies, and "trans studies in las Américas." Given that racialized gender is a crucial component of the heteropatriarchal capitalist world system for ordering bodies and lives, that it is part of settler colonialism, and that trans-ing gender transpires along contested vectors of flight from and capture by these apparatuses, it behooves us to understand with as much sophistication and clarity as we can muster how these operations of ordering and transiting function in different locations at different scales, how *trans-* itself functions as a logical operator within schemes of power, creating switch points for strategies of evasion and control.

The publication in 2014 of Sheila Jeffreys's *Gender Hurts: A Feminist Analysis of the Politics of Transgenderism* appears in retrospect to mark an inflection point in the resurgence of a transphobic feminist discourse that had seemed on the wane for nearly a quarter century, and one to which trans studies has been perhaps too slow to respond, effectively dismissing it as an increasingly anachronistic and revanchist form of nostalgia best left to wither and die. *TSQ* did publish a special double issue titled "Trans/Feminisms," specifically in response to Jeffreys's book, but chose to showcase transfeminist work that refused to cede feminism to transphobes, rather than addressing so-called gender-critical feminism more directly. However noble that gesture may have been, it appears increasingly naïve in light of transphobic feminism's increasingly close association with reactionary ethnonationalism. Transphobic feminism's strangest bedfellow is the conservative global movement against "gender ideology" that positions transgender as an especially potent threat to "traditional values" or even—as in Pope Francis's characterization of transgenderism as more dangerous than nuclear weapons, given its perverse destruction of biological reproductive capacity—to the continuation of human life. It scarcely matters if the transgender figure imagined by transphobic feminism and antigender ideology is a phantasm, like the anti-Semitic figure of the Jew, when it nevertheless serves the ideological purpose of uniting disparate social groups with disparate interests in service to a dominant mode of power that is detrimental to our very existence. Trans studies has the deepest imaginable stake, now and in the near term, in monkey wrenching this disquieting development as it continues to unfold.

Looking back over the seven volumes of *TSQ* that have been published since 2014, I see resources for living, even when they attend to matters of violence and death. There is work on cultural production and artistic expression, work that recovers and reinterprets trans histories, work that critiques institutions and social policies and proposes better ones, work that intervenes in environmental practice, work that enacts new aesthetics, ontologies, epistemologies, cosmologies, and metaphysics. To cite my own contribution to this issue, I see the development of trans studies and the platform it is offered in *TSQ* as one small piece of infrastructure that might not only help keep actual trans people alive, but:

> for using transness to learn and teach how we might better decenter human privilege in our cohabitation with the nonhuman world, extract all of our bodies from the coloniality of gender, untether ourselves from the racializing biopolitical assemblages that fasten on the flesh of us all in different ways, and heal from the wounded attachments to identity categories through which we live but that can thwart our collective work, in this moment of political, economic, and ecological crisis that demands our undivided attention.

In the words Paisley Currah and I chose as *TSQ*'s marketing tag line and motto when we launched it in 2014: "We're changing gender." The work in this journal changes gender. And changing gender is part of changing the world in ways that help us live in it, or die trying.

As I wrote this introduction in mid-February 2020, COVID-19 seemed a distant concern, Bernie Sanders was leading the race for the Democratic Party's nomination, an online controversy about *TSQ*'s "Trans Pornography" issue was months in the future, and George Floyd was still alive. By the time I made final copyedits in the summer of 2020, "Trans* Studies Now" had already become "Trans* Studies Then," and the choice of Gordon Matta Clark's deconstructed house as a cover image seemed more apt than ever. Who knows what the world, higher education, the field of trans* studies, and this journal will look like by the third quarter of 2020 when this issue sees print, around the time of what promises to be a contested US presidential election, in the midst of the pandemic and all its economic fallout, a hopefully ongoing antiracist uprising demanding abolition of policing and prisons, and the journal's revamped editorial structure? All we can do is work in the present and hope for the best.

While I have no better sense than anyone else of what 2020 will hold in store, I do know that as of this issue, *TSQ* has accomplished one of the goals Paisley and I set for ourselves when we launched the journal, which was to turn over a financially sound and thriving publication to a trans-of-color majority in the lead editorial positions, a majority of whom originated from or worked on topics outside the United States, by the time we ourselves stepped aside. That might not be enough, but it's not nothing. In closing, I'd like to celebrate

Francisco's continued leadership and Abraham's advancement now that he's joined the ranks of the professoriat, while welcoming aboard Jules and Grace, two exciting and accomplished scholars already making powerful contributions to the field. The journal is in exceptionally good hands, and I look forward to seeing what they and our contributors make of it.

Susan Stryker, executive editor of *TSQ*, is professor emerita of gender and women's studies at the University of Arizona and Barbara Lee Distinguished Chair of Women's Leadership at Mills College.

Reference

Duke University Press. 2019. "The Most Read Articles of 2019." December 23. dukeupress.word press.com/2019/12/23/the-most-read-articles-of-2019/.

Before Trans Studies

CASSIUS ADAIR, CAMERON AWKWARD-RICH, and AMY MARVIN

Abstract In conversation with Emmett Harsin Drager and Andrea Long Chu's "After Trans Studies," this collaborative essay also turns to questions of field formation and the ethos of trans studies. Situating the growth of the field in the material conditions of precarity under which trans knowledge-workers work, the authors argue that trans studies can't be "over" because, in fact, it isn't yet here. Rather than viewing this as only a dismal proposition, however, they insist that the tenuousness of trans studies provides us with the opportunity to envision and enact more sustaining ways of being "in the field."
Keywords trans studies, discipline, queer studies, field, academy

Perhaps analogous to the way that trans people—our lives, our literatures, our activism—are iteratively "discovered" by the media, trans studies, with its institutional life, its laborers, and its literature, is iteratively discovered by academia, including by trans studies scholars themselves. As a result, trans studies is always just now arriving. First because there is an essay and a handful of scholars, then an anthology or three, then a hiring initiative and an interdisciplinary journal, then, it seems, the field is "flourishing."[1] Now there are articles and books and a cluster hire in Arizona and a handful of tenure-track jobs in California that go by the name "trans studies." An abundance of small beginnings! But given that the first seeds were sown decades ago, of course one might take a look at a field full of tiny tentative plants and see only weak growth. Maybe, then, it makes sense to declare the field a failure, leave it fallow.

We would like to propose that, actually, the "field" of trans studies has not yet happened. Further (to stretch this metaphor), we contend that the field has not yet happened, not because its seeds were flawed from the beginning but because the sprouts have been struggling to survive in the poison soil of the contemporary university system. Trans knowledge laborers have largely remained contingent or have been outright discarded. The production of "very good monographs" (though, we think, there are many good monographs) has, until

TSQ: Transgender Studies Quarterly * Volume 7, Number 3 * August 2020 **306**
DOI 10.1215/23289252-8552922 © 2020 Duke University Press

recently, been constrained because trans books have largely been tasked with discovering/defending the existence of trans life to skeptical editors/reviewers. Furthermore, the relative lack of tenured/tenure-track trans studies faculty ensures that the institutional skepticism toward trans studies as a unique knowledge practice will endure. Graduate students and faculty alike must iteratively discover on our own that there is much more to trans studies than we have been led to believe by our various gender studies or queer theory classes: this was certainly the case, it is worth noting, for the three of us.

But if this sounds like a dismal proposition, it need not only be that. In fact, the tenuousness of trans studies at the end of the university ought to lead us to value knowledge work differently than even other "identity knowledges" have (Wiegman 2012: 3). After all, if trans studies is not a project of making possible trans thought in, adjacent to, and hostile to the academy, then what are we all doing here?

All of this is to say that, although we are most directly responding to a recent entry into the field's self-accounting, we hope this essay will be read in conversation with the much longer history of inquiries into "what are we all doing here." These include but are not limited to: Jay Prosser's *Second Skins* (1998); Viviane Namaste's *Invisible Lives* (2000); Susan Stryker's "(De)Subjugating Knowledges" (2006a) and "Transgender Studies: Queer Theory's Evil Twin" (2006b); b. binaohan's *decolonizing trans/gender 101* (2014); Regina Kunzel's "Flourishing of Transgender Studies" (2014); Treva Ellison, Kai M. Green, Matt Richardson, and C. Riley Snorton's "We Got Issues: Toward a Black Trans*/ Studies" (2017); Kai M. Green and Marquis Bey's "Where Black Feminist Thought and Trans* Feminism Meet" (2017); Cáel Keegan's "Getting Disciplined: What's Trans* about Queer Studies Now?" (2020); and so on.

Importantly, "the field" represented by even the small list above is obviously not a unitary one: the genealogies of trans studies can be variously traced through black and woman of color feminist theory, disability studies, postcolonial theory, queer theory, poststructural feminisms, indigenous studies, and trans community organizing and cultural production. While in this essay we aim to disrupt a dominant field imaginary by foregrounding trans precarity as a condition of trans studies' formation, we want to note that the field imaginary we engage here is that of a decidedly white trans studies. To some extent, our terrain has been dictated by the piece to which we are responding; however, we hope that rather than reinforcing the terms of white trans studies as trans studies per se, our engagement will reaffirm the field's necessary cross-pollination with black feminist theory, woman of color feminisms, and disability studies in particular, whose ongoing conversations about care labor, pedagogical labor, and the politics of citation undergird our thought.[2]

Before continuing further, it is worth pausing to explain the essay at hand. "After Trans Studies" is a conversation between Andrea Long Chu and Emmett Harsin Drager (2019) that rallies behind the self-defined polemic that "trans studies is over," or at least approaching the crossroads of a necessary major overhaul (103–4). To set out this bold new path of trans studies after trans studies, or (dare we say) post-post-post-transsexual studies, Chu and Harsin Drager raise concerns that the current practice of trans studies lacks proper field definition and unacceptably constrains conversations about trans (and especially what they call "transsexual") lives.

Harsin Drager and Chu find that trans studies has failed to distinguish itself from queer theory, insofar as it lacks a distinct set of theories and prestigious theory battles to call its own. Chu, in particular, calls for the production of theory through strife, calling up a metaphor of field development as an elite battle, or "a small number of very good monographs that we can really yell at each other over" that cultivates real disagreement (104). Both authors insist this disagreement has been foreclosed because of dogmas within the field, dogmas that they do not ever really name but one of which implicitly might be something like "trans is a good [read: politically radical] object." That is, Harsin Drager and Chu agree that trans studies has served as a constraining "church" sacrificing rigorous inquiry to "warmed-over pieties," in part by imposing a feel-good "gender affirming" approach, which, they argue, precludes potentially controversial claims about trans lives and bodies (104). The picture they give is of trans studies as a wobbly church that must be shaken from its dogmatic slumber. Only the din of elite battle, in this view, will awaken its clergy from the paralyzing combination of queer theory and hugboxing.

Further, Chu and Harsin Drager tie the failed development of trans studies to the continued inability of the field to address the figure of the transsexual and the conversations of transsexuals. In this account, the field's capitulation to the methods of queer theory has decentered the transsexual and relegated her to the medicalized, problematic, backward shadow of true affirmative transgender progress (110). Trans studies' apparent sacrifice of the transsexual to the demands of queer theory has led to a further silencing of everyday transsexual life beyond the demands of antinormative politics and theory, and has collapsed the ability to "speak candidly about our lives as transsexuals" (113). Candidness beyond trans studies' enforced political optimism, by contrast, would enrich the field's articulated critical trans affects by adding bitterness, satire, and disappointment to the mix (105–6). Ultimately, the authors conclude that trans studies is over, has been over for transsexuals since its beginnings, and must give up its attachments to antinormativity to be transformed into something other than a failed derivation of queer theory.

Although we agree with some of this conclusion, we were inspired to write this essay out of a question about the assumptions that ground the thinking that leads there. In particular, the idea of being "after" trans studies invokes a rise to power and consolidation that seems to us to have not occurred, or at the very least to be so unevenly distributed that it is thinkable for trans studies to be "over" in some places but simultaneously absent or antagonized in other places.[3] So where is this vision of trans studies coming from? What must these authors themselves disavow or ignore (or simply not know) for this vision to so cohere that they can insist that there are dogmas we all know well enough to leave them virtually unnamed? And, most importantly, what are the material conditions that have produced this situation in which the five of us—and, implicitly, the wider cohort of late-stage grad students and recent graduates who have, will, or currently do labor under the sign of "trans studies"—can have such noncompatible views of what constitutes the field space? That is, how is it possible that, from one point of view, we can be "after trans studies," whereas, from others, it seems that we are still hanging out in the "before" or to the side of the time of institutionalization?

Rather than—or in addition to—being evidence of constraining intellectual trends and political desires, we see the limits of existing trans studies as being shaped by the political, economic, and institutional conditions into which it emerged and continues to emerge. Put bluntly, the "great failure" of trans studies is that we can't all afford to write. To point out gaps in the intellectual project of trans studies and to pin these gaps on the attachments of its laborers without engaging with the simple fact that most trans intellectuals are not afforded the time, money, and energy to participate in it seems to miss the whole ballgame. These are not abstract concerns about intellectual style but material questions: questions about who gets jobs, who gets read, who gets cited, who reviewers demand you cite, who has access to the university in the first place, and so on. Besides the obvious point that an academic field only exists insofar as it has people doing the work of cultivating it (teaching courses, training grad students, publishing, organizing conferences, reviewing journal articles, etc.), relegating talk of money and time to a footnote is precisely what grants Chu and Harsin Drager's argument for a return to "the transsexual" the appearance of newness or controversial polemic: there are plenty of transsexual scholars, but they work and have worked under the conditions of precarity.

After all, the issue that Chu and Harsin Drager invoke as somehow verboten within the field—the very real friction between forms of transness (transsexuality) that strive to embody the norm through nonnormative means, forms that strive to expand what might be considered in a colloquial sense "normal," and those that really do seem to be derived from a commitment to anti- or nonnormativity and the consequences of those tensions for trying to make any coherent trans politics/epistemology/theoretical stance—is literally the debate that runs through trans discourse of at least the last half-century. That is, it was not only Jay Prosser who warned us and continues to warn us about the subsumption of trans epistemologies to queer/poststructural feminist ones—so did Viviane Namaste (2000, 2009), C. Jacob Hale (1997, 1998), Trish Salah (2007, 2009), Henry Rubin (1998a), Talia Bettcher (2014), and every 1990s trans community newsletter (OK, OK, we exaggerate, a little). Prosser is merely the trans thinker on this question who is regularly taught, perhaps in part because *Second Skins* is a text that fits nicely into the "debate" format through which transness often shows up on gender studies syllabi.

Our corrective to the absence of this strain of thinking in contemporary trans studies, then, is not to insist that it hasn't happened. Rather, we wish to cite a genealogy of trans studies that is decidedly political and (most importantly for our argument) decidedly material, unafraid to critique queer theory and its subjectless critique to foreground the lived experiences of sex workers and other trans laborers. Viviane Namaste (2000, 2005), for example, stands out: her work throughout the aughts and beyond centers transsexuals while explicitly pushing against the tethering of research on transsexuals to the methods of queer theory and women's and gender studies departments more broadly. Namaste's (1998) humorous video, "How to Become an American Transgender Theorist (a Recipe)," for example, parodies the limitations and stagnation caused by the dominance of American academic queer theory over understanding transsexual lives.

In the video and in her writings, Namaste considers queer theory a form of imperialism that decides whether other modes of life are properly queer, and hence liberatory rather than problematic, conveniently ignoring the ways its own practice often becomes a largely shallow enterprise. Namaste's critique of imperialism links with a critique of upper- and middle-class transgender politics, especially when transgender theory and organizing leaves out transsexual sex workers, prisoners, drug users, and poor people more broadly. For Namaste and other trans thinkers and activists such as Mirha-Soleil Ross, contesting the erasure of trans people by queer theory is not a matter of recentering the abstract figure of the transsexual but rather of ameliorating the material conditions that cause economically disenfranchised trans people to be erased from knowledge production and barred from institutions more broadly, including contesting larger political structures such as global capitalism (Namaste 2005).

The field of transsexual critique continues to expand as we consider more scholars. Salah (2013), for example, has argued that Sandy Stone's (1992) "post-transsexual" move (later renamed "transgender," as Salah points out) gave too much ground to Janice Raymond's ([1979] 1994) specifically antitranssexual project. Salah navigates tensions between Namaste, Prosser, queer theory, and antinormative-focused trans studies to develop a space beyond antitranssexual politics and cultural production while also not completely dismissing "queerly-identified" trans people as irreconciliably traitorous to the transsexual cause (2009, 2007). Salah (2013: 181), turning to the politics of cultural production while also refusing to totally reduce aesthetics to politics, also acknowledges the collective labor involved on the part of trans people, many who are sex workers, to create counter-publics beyond "queer or feminist economies of prestige." In doing so, Salah acknowledges the work involved in creating transsexual spaces and the cultural production that contests those spaces' erasure.

Namaste and others frame the transsexual as a situated group of people, a heterogenous group of racialized, class-oppressed, disabled, and otherwise marginal figures who should be thought of as a group, not by the fact of their genders but by their shared need to surmount serious deficits of institutional access. Contrary to Chu and Harsin Drager's generalized transsexual, which attempts to focus on a transsexual who simply has conversations like "we" do (a telling use of "we"), Namaste centers on transsexuals who have a specific marginalized relationship to class status, and who have a need to smash the institutionalized barriers that stand in their way through collective counter-publics. This emphasis on situated material needs is missed by Harsin Drager and Chu's call to the transsexual "we," and especially the call for trans studies as a field of theory battles. Is a call for restricted elite monographs to be yelled over really a call to bring the transsexual voice and transsexual theory, and ultimately a more robust trans studies, into development? We worry that, whatever voices emerge from this practice, this method of knowledge making does little to challenge and change the material conditions of the academy that has vanished "the transsexual" in the first place. Insofar as there has been something that we might call "transsexual theory," in other words, its aim has been to transform or even wholesale resist institutionalization—not to argue that our existing institutions should have more fights.

Furthermore, while there might be work that invokes trans as queer again, we think that there is no good reason to call this "trans studies." In fact, it is arguably one of the discourses that has been a block to trans studies' arrival. Harsin Drager, that is, is onto something when they note that many of the "most cited texts about trans people . . . have been the work of non-trans (i.e., cis) scholars recycling the same citations, concepts, and metaphors" (Chu and Harsin Drager 2019: 104). However, the problem is not that these scholars are cis, but that they might not actually represent "the field." If there is a force making queer and trans studies synonymous with one another, it is not, in our eyes, the attachments of trans studies scholars to being politically good objects. Rather, it is the fact that those making hiring decisions often view these fields as interchangeable. For example: in the 2018–19 cycle there were thirteen tenure-track job ads listed on the Women/Queer Studies wiki that in some way mentioned trans studies (Academic Jobs Wiki n.d.). Of these, only 2.5 did not either collapse trans studies into queer/ sexuality studies or simply include trans studies (or, in one case, "intersectional expertise in . . . transgenderism," whatever that means) among a long list of useful et ceteras to the desired candidate's primary focus. Put yet one more way—if there is something we should be bitter about, it is not what "trans studies" is or might become, but the way it is marketed and, more broadly, the university-as-market.

Here, we arrive at our most fundamental difference with Chu and Harsin Drager, we think. It is not only that we do not recognize the unstated dogmas that Chu and Harsin Drager feel we are beholden to as trans studies' own; also, we do not recognize their model of field-space as our own. What they are after, it seems, is not only different ideas but also a different "emotional habitus," one in which various kinds of intragroup bad feeling (anger, strife, bitterness, true disagreement) are not only more tolerable but are understood as central to intellectual advancement (Gould 2009: 32). "Why," Chu and Harsin Drager (2019: 104) want to know, "are we so nice to each other?" To which we respond: given that trans studies inevitably unfolds within the context of a world in which trans people are overwhelmingly poor, discarded, fucked over and fucked up, regarded as unreliable narrators, and so on, why would we want our small corner of the small corner of/adjacent to the university to be a battleground rather than a shelter?

In positing that trans studies hasn't yet happened, then, we do not mean that trans individuals (including the aforementioned, undercited "transsexual" materialists) have been absent from intellectual life. What we mean instead is that there is not yet a trans studies that has been able to organize itself around the sustenance and survival of trans life. As such, we must amend our own cheeky polemic—that trans studies has not yet happened, and thus cannot be over—to acknowledge that, precisely to the extent that trans work in the academy has been a battle/field, trans studies has already happened.

We know this because there have been casualties. In the drafting of this essay, we found ourselves evoking the figure of the "lost trans scholar," a person whose contributions to a larger genealogy of trans studies have been foreclosed on. Among this number: people who left the academy as students or faculty members owing to hostile conditions or inadequate compensation; people who work in the academy but under conditions in which they do not have sufficient support for trans-related research or teaching; people who are in the academy and attempt to work in trans-related areas only to experience such significant ideological pushback or emotional cost that they burn out and devote their energy elsewhere; people who were in the academy and published trans work who, for reasons of inadequate cultural memory or a too-narrow field imaginary, are not frequently cited and have fallen off gender and women's studies syllabi; people who are creating art and writing related to trans studies but whose work is taught as "objects" rather than as theoretical interventions, or does not enter the academic conversation at all.[4] (Two of us, it bears stating, could be counted within that number.) By "lost," then, we do not mean to suggest that such people are not actively making trans knowledge and culture—they/we are. However, we do mean to suggest that their absences from the university and from standard genealogies of trans studies are meaningful; we cannot know what trans studies might have been (and might yet be) had trans academics labored under less hostile conditions.

To the best of our knowledge, these casualties have not been due to individuals' refusal to genuflect to field dogmas. Those of us who have failed to achieve the (purported) economic security of an academic trans studies position do not believe that this failure occurred because we are, for example, too skeptical of antimedicalization frames. No, we did not get jobs in trans studies because there were so few to be had, so few that any particular trans studies scholar has to be preternaturally talented—or perhaps simply famous—to fill those slots. This is not a field-specific pathology or a personal whine; it is to say that trans studies feels less "over" if you belong to one of the decades of trans studies scholars who did not benefit from the (mythical) moment when it presumably "happened," nor if you belong to future cohorts of trans students who we, as some ragtag gender-freak version of a beloved community, might be nurturing, teaching to think about knowledge production as less of a zero-sum game.

Field, after all, is a concept and a space that might support warfare, but it need not. While a field might be a battlefield or a hunting ground, or might be an athletic field ("a field of play"), it most often is simply an open space populated by flora and fauna, a space that might be cultivated, made habitable, or left alone. From the *Oxford English Dictionary*, at least, it isn't clear that these more literal meanings of *field* as an open space preceded *field* as an area of inquiry, but it does seem true that these three meanings suggest three very different kinds of engagement that are possible within a field—warfare, play, cultivation. All of these suggest collective action, all of these are ways of being together, but they are obviously oriented toward very different ends. If warfare is the primary model we inherited (and to which some wish to return) and play (by which we mean to invoke both "sometimes pleasurable engagement" and "forms of uncompensated activity") seems to better reflect what the academic humanities presently are, then cultivation can model what they might yet be.

Following José Muñoz (2009: 1), if trans studies "is not yet here," then we have the ongoing opportunity to "think and feel a then and there," to "dream and enact . . . other ways of being in" and adjacent to "the world" and the university. We desire a trans studies that yearns toward collaboration and solidarity, orientations that demand practices of care and communal cultivation. That is, we see the ideal trans studies as primarily a collective practice, not necessarily tethered to a telos of novel theory (although novel theory should certainly be welcome). We desire the creation of a space in which trans thought can unfold, in which trans students might learn ways to live as trans in the world, and in which disagreement occurs, but not for its own sake.[5] Such cultivation is complicated when the people doing the work are so dispersed, consumed, crushed (and, of course, also doggedly persistent) in so many small ways that their contributions go unnoticed or forestalled. Yet that complication is not, in the end, sufficient to dismiss hope as "a critical affect and a methodology" of field formation (2). As Muñoz reminds us, "Both hope and utopia, as affective structures and approaches to challenges within the social, ha[ve] been prone to disappointment, making this critical approach difficult . . . [but] the eventual disappointment of hope is not a reason to forsake it as a critical thought process, in the same way that even though we can know in advance that felicity of language ultimately falters, it is nonetheless essential" (9–10).

In our utopian turn toward an alternative meaning of "field," we also desire modes of scholarship that turn away from the contextless battle of independent hero-scholars to the more fragile and multiplicitous work of growing trans life. We emphasize the care involved in sustaining community, including communities of thought, as we work alongside one another and challenge each other to do better rather than allowing the inequalities of the academy to be obscured. We align ourselves against any model of trans studies, but also trans activism and trans "representation" more broadly, in which a select few, not in conversation with or dependent on larger communities, are given a false mantle to define or even "save" all other trans people. We believe that emphasizing care in this context calls us to be more attentive toward our dependency on others, our responsibilities to each other in the context of material differences, and the important but devalued work of supporting friends, building spaces, teaching, and cultivating connections.

We do not believe that emphasizing care and hope leads to the sort of dogmatic, fragile church of agreement that Chu and Harsin Drager attribute to trans studies. Instead, borrowing from the field imaginaries emergent in disability studies, we hope that emphasizing the work of care in the context of real fragility and dependency can allow us to disagree, express negative feelings, and even sometimes express a thoughtful bitterness and satire that promotes self-reflection about disconnection, failure, and conflict. Indeed, we suggest that there is no particular reason that the most important field questions need revolve around determining what "true" trans phenomenology is; even asking if an ethics of care can organize a field of thought is itself an interesting intellectual project, one around which a future trans studies might organize.

We recognize the risks of this proposition: emphasizing care means that we should also beware the "revolving door" of its practice, in which cultivation goes unrewarded, and people are continuously kicked out the door after their care labors have been sucked dry by vampiric institutions. This is not a call to pump more hours of unreciprocal care into soul-crushing academic departments, impossibly underresourced classrooms, or other dead-end labors. Rather, we call attention to care to also call for giving critical attention to—and attacking—the material conditions that give rise to this "revolving door." Someone, after all, needs to imagine what intellectual life can look like outside extraction; trans studies, the precursors of which were literally medical studies of trans people as sites of knowledge extraction, seems as good a site as any for this work. Indeed, such imagining is already beginning: Hilary Malatino and Aren Aizura's 2019 seminar "We Care a Lot: Theorizing Queer and Trans Affective Labor," cotaught at the Society for the Study of Affect Summer School, is simply one recent example. As trans people, we know—along with marginalized people across many identities—how it feels to try to do care work at the end of the world. This is a form of knowledge that we can cultivate together, no monographs necessary.

Thus what is this not-yet-here trans studies, a trans studies of the then and there? To us, another way of asking that question is, What are the necessary conditions that will make trans life more livable in the here and now? For some of us, that would mean the immediate end to the contingent nature of our knowledge production and pedagogical labor in the form of the radical expansion of benefits-eligible, living-wage positions within the academy. For others, it would mean the end of the wealthy North American university's expansion into our neighborhoods as landlord, segregator, speculator, and evictor (New York University in New York City [*Washington Square News* 2017] and the University of Michigan in Detroit [Alvarez 2019; Mihaylova 2019]). While the former may seem less radical, we don't see these as inherently contradictory dreams, as we should be able to demand educational justice that doesn't come with an attendant reinvestment in the university-as-hedge-fund. But because it feels contradictory to both lament the casting-out of people from the university and to question the validity of academic institutions per se, we must acknowledge that this is tricky work, a hard needle to thread; it requires, above all, not lockstep agreement among different types of people but a feeling of trust. Institutional access for trans people continues to be completely broken in the academy, resulting in a highly skewed contribution, whether or not their voices are transsexual ones. Many trans people have been erased from the narrative of trans studies, and many others have been excluded. It's possible that there is no "trans studies" as a social and intellectual practice that doesn't eventually require an abolitionist stance toward higher education. Therefore, it is critical that trans studies produces not the tools for career advancement but an ethic of solidarity, an orientation toward each other, even as it conserves our bitterness toward the conditions that harm or abandon us.

Like Chu and Harsin Drager, we *are* bitter and see, undoubtedly, some critical uses for a bitterness that seeks to describe how and why the world fails to accommodate our desires. However, by Chu's own account of "real bitterness, the bitter disappointment of finding out the world is too small for all our desires, and especially the political ones," there must have first been desire, or even hope, to disappoint (Chu and Harsin Drager 2019: 106). In fact, hope, as Snorton (2009) has argued, might be understood to make transition and trans life possible in the first place; if dysphoria, dissonance, and unease alert us to the need to change, ultimately it requires wild, naive hope to see change through. To live and think as trans in this world, we cannot assume, in advance, that the world will not accommodate our desires. We must again and again find out.

Cassius Adair is an independent scholar and public radio producer based at Virginia Humanities, a state humanities council in Charlottesville, Virginia. His scholarship appears in *American Literature, TSQ, American Quarterly,* and *Frontiers,* and his essays and audio pieces can be found in various magazines and on National Public Radio member stations. Adair holds a PhD in English language and literature from the University of Michigan. He is currently working on two books: a monograph about transgender people and digital history and an edited collection of speculative fiction about academic life.

Cameron Awkward-Rich is the author of the poetry collections *Sympathetic Little Monster* (2016) and *Dispatch* (2019), and his critical writing can be found in *Signs, Science Fiction Studies, American Quarterly*, and elsewhere. He is an assistant professor of women, gender, and sexuality studies at the University of Massachusetts Amherst.

Amy Marvin is a feminist philosopher who received her PhD from the University of Oregon; her dissertation is on the politics of humor. Her work can be found in *Hypatia* and in the inaugural issue of *Feminist Philosophy Quarterly* (under Amy Billingsley). She was a coorganizer of the "Trans* Experience in Philosophy" conference, and her essay "Transsexuality, the Curio, and the Transgender Tipping Point" is forthcoming in *Curiosity Studies: Toward a New Ecology of Knowledge*. She enjoys gradually baking better and better breads.

Notes

1. For a (partial) list of announcements of trans studies' arrival, see Wilson 1998; More and Whittle 1999; Stryker 2006a; Joselow 2016; and Kunzel 2014.

2. For example, Hartman 2016; Piepzna-Samarasinha 2018; Price 2015; Erevelles 2011; Bailey and Trudy 2018; Cite Black Women Collective n.d.; Ahmed 2017; and Gutiérrez y Muhs et al. 2012.

3. We think of "places" here both in reference to institutional/social location and with respect to the uneven distribution of trans work across the global community of scholars. We also note the inadequacy of anglophone "trans studies" to engage non-Western forms of gendering in its scholarly practice, leaving much crucial transnational work not yet done; we here return to our point above about the racial (and, we should add, spatial) boundedness of the trans studies genealogy debates that rinse and repeat themselves every so often in the North American academy.

4. A very partial, off-the-top-of-our-heads list of work by those we might count among this expansive category of the lost includes Gan 2007; Bellwether 2010; Beemyn and Rankin 2011; Singer 2006; Prosser 2004; Rubin 1998a, 1998b; binaohan 2014; Perkins 1983; Escalante 2016, 2018; Brager and Lavery 2017; Janssen 2017; Ziegler 2008; and Bess 2018. We invite you to consider who else you might include here. Importantly, we might consider as "lost" even Stone and Stryker, insofar as Stone is remembered within the field almost entirely for an essay she wrote as a graduate student and Stryker was in nonacademic/contingent positions for over a decade.

5. In fact, this model of field-space is alive in many trans pedagogy publications, which orient trans studies (and attempt to orient women's/gender/queer studies broadly) to questions of how to enable the thriving of trans students. See, for example, Clarkson 2017. Further, trans knowledge work outside the university enables the circulation of trans writing in critical relation to the literary/academic market. Exemplary among these is Jamie Berrout's (n.d.) editorial practice through the Trans Women Writers Collective, which prioritizes making trans writing possible by circumventing institutional barriers inherent to publication. These two models might feel in conflict with one another but actually, we think, exist in a reciprocal relationship in the larger ecosystem of trans thought.

References

Academic Jobs Wiki. n.d. "Womens/Gender/Queer Studies 2018–2019." academicjobs.wikia.org /wiki/Womens/Gender/Queer_Studies_2018-2019 (accessed March 26, 2019).

Ahmed, Sara. 2017. *Living a Feminist Life*. Durham, NC: Duke University Press.

Alvarez, Sarah. 2019. "The University of Michigan Invested Big in Detroit. Now Come the Evictions." *Bridge Magazine*, July 12. www.bridgemi.com/detroit/university-michigan -invested-big-detroit-now-come-evictions.

Bailey, Moya, and Trudy. 2018. "On Misogynoir: Citation, Erasure, and Plagiarism." *Feminist Media Studies* 18, no. 4: 762–68.

Beemyn, Genny, and Susan Rankin. 2011. *The Lives of Transgender People*. New York: Columbia University Press.

Bellwether, Mira. 2010. *Fucking Trans Women #0*. payhip.com/b/hRtK.

Berrout, Jamie. n.d. The Booklet Series. Trans Women Writers Collective. www.patreon.com /transwomenwriters/overview (accessed April 27, 2020).

Bess, Isobel. 2018. *Deep New Unstable Against*. Bandcamp. isobelbess.bandcamp.com/album/deep
-new-unstable-against.

Bettcher, Talia Mea. 2014. "Trapped in the Wrong Theory: Rethinking Trans Oppression and
Resistance." *Signs* 39, no. 2: 383–406.

binaohan, b. 2014. *decolonizing trans/gender 101*. n.p.: Biyuti.

Brager, JB, and Cee Lavery. 2017. "My Gender Is Saturn Return." *GUTS Magazine*, November 22.
gutsmagazine.ca/my-gender-is-saturn-return/.

Chu, Andrea, and Emmett Harsin Drager. 2019. "After Trans Studies." *TSQ* 6, no. 1: 103–16.

Cite Black Women Collective. n.d. "Cite Black Women." www.citeblackwomencollective.org.

Clarkson, Nicholas L. 2017. "Teaching Trans Students, Teaching Trans Studies." *Feminist Teacher*
27, nos. 2–3: 233–52.

Ellison, Treva, Kai M. Green, Matt Richardson, and C. Riley Snorton. 2017. "We Got Issues:
Toward a Black Trans*/Studies." *TSQ* 4, no. 2: 162–69.

Erevelles, Nirmala. 2011. *Disability and Difference in Global Contexts: Enabling a Transformative
Body Politic*. New York: Palgrave Macmillan.

Escalante, Alyson. 2016. "Gender Nihilism: An Anti-manifesto." *LibCom*, June 22. libcom.org
/library/gender-nihilism-anti-manifesto.

Escalante, Alyson. 2018. "Beyond Negativity: What Comes after Gender Nihilism?" *Medium*,
March 15. medium.com/@alysonescalante/beyond-negativity-what-comes-after-gender
-nihilism-bbd80a5fc05d.

Gan, Jessi. 2007. "'Still at the Back of the Bus': Sylvia Rivera's Struggle." *Centro Journal* 19, no. 1:
124–39.

Gould, Deborah B. 2009. *Moving Politics: Emotion and Act Up's Fight against Aids*. Chicago:
University of Chicago Press.

Green, Kai M., and Marquis Bey. 2017. "Where Black Feminist Thought and Trans* Feminism
Meet: A Conversation." *Souls* 19, no. 4: 438–54.

Gutiérrez y Muhs, Gabriella, Yolanda Flores Niemann, Carmen G. González, and Angela P. Harris,
eds. 2012. *Presumed Incompetent: The Intersections of Race and Class for Women in Academia*. Boulder: University Press of Colorado.

Hale, C. Jacob. 1997. "Suggested Rules for Non-transsexuals Writing about Transsexuals, Transsexuality, Transsexualism, or Trans _____." *Sandy Stone: Would You Like Theory with
That?* sandystone.com/hale.rules.html.

Hale, C. Jacob. 1998. "Tracing a Ghostly Memory in My Throat: Reflections on Ftm Feminist Voice
and Agency." In *Men Doing Feminism*, edited by Tom Digby, 99–129. New York: Routledge.

Hartman, Saidiya. 2016. "The Belly of the World: A Note on Black Women's Labors." *Souls* 18, no.
1: 166–73.

Janssen, Ephraim Das. 2017. *Phenomenal Gender: What Transgender Experience Discloses*. Bloo-
mington: Indiana University Press.

Joselow, Maxine. 2016. "A Push for Transgender Studies." *Inside Higher Ed*, June 22. www
.insidehighered.com/news/2016/06/22/u-arizona-emphasizes-transgender-studies.

Keegan, Cáel. 2020. "Getting Disciplined: What's Trans* about Queer Studies Now?" *Journal of
Homosexuality* 67, no. 3: 384–97.

Kunzel, Regina. 2014. "The Flourishing of Transgender Studies." *TSQ* 1, nos. 1–2: 285–97.

Mihaylova, Magdelena. 2019. "Students to University of Michigan: Stop Funding Detroit Evictions." *Bridge Magazine*, July 19. www.bridgemi.com/talent-education/students
-university-michigan-stop-funding-detroit-evictions.

More, Kate, and Stephen Whittle, eds. 1999. *Reclaiming Genders: Transsexual Grammars at the Fin de Siècle*. New York: Cassel.

Muñoz, José Esteban. 2009. *Cruising Utopia: The Then and There of Queer Futurity*. New York: New York University Press.

Namaste, Viviane. 2000. *Invisible Lives: The Erasure of Transsexual and Transgendered People*. Chicago: University of Chicago Press.

Namaste, Viviane. 2005. *Sex Change, Social Change: Reflections on Identity, Institutions, and Imperialism*. Toronto: Women's Press.

Namaste, Viviane. 2009. "Undoing Theory: The 'Transgender Question' and the Epistemic Violence of Anglo-American Feminist Theory." *Hypatia* 24, no. 3: 11–32.

Namaste, Viviane, and Lynne Trépanier Réalisé. 1998. "How to Become an American Transgender Theorist (a Recipe)." YouTube video, 07:51 min. Posted December 7, 2008. www.youtube.com/watch?v=9NX2OkvLzmU.

Perkins, Roberta. 1983. *The "Drag Queen" Scene: Transsexuals in Kings Cross*. Boston: Allen and Unwin.

Piepzna-Samarasinha, Leah Lakshmi. 2018. *Care Work: Dreaming Disability Justice*. Vancouver, BC: Arsenal Pulp.

Price, Margaret. 2015. "The Bodymind Problem and the Possibilities of Pain." *Hypatia* 30, no. 1: 268–84.

Prosser, Jay. 1998. *Second Skins: The Body Narratives of Transsexuality*. New York: Columbia University Press.

Prosser, Jay. 2004. *Light in the Dark Room: Photography and Loss*. Minneapolis: University of Minnesota Press.

Raymond, Janice G. (1979) 1994. *The Transsexual Empire: The Making of the She-male*. New York: Teachers College Press.

Rubin, Henry. 1998a. "Phenomenology as Method in Trans Studies." *GLQ* 4, no. 2: 263–81.

Rubin, Henry. 1998b. "Reading like a (Transsexual) Man." In *Men Doing Feminism*, edited by Tom Digby, 305–24. New York: Routledge.

Salah, Trish. 2007. "Undoing Trans Studies: Review Essay on J. Butler's Undoing Gender and V. Namaste's Sex Change, Social Change." *Topia: Canadian Journal of Cultural Studies*, no. 17: 150–55.

Salah, Trish. 2009. "After Cissexual Poetry." In "Contemporary Queer Poetics," edited by Julian Brolaski. Special issue, *Aufgabe: Journal of Poetry*, no. 8: 282–98.

Salah, Trish. 2013. "Notes towards Thinking Transsexual Institutional Poetics." In *Trans/acting Culture, Writing, and Memory: Essays in Honour of Barbara Godard*, edited by Eva C. Karpinski, Jennifer Henderson, Ian Sowton, and Ray Ellenwood, 167–89. Waterloo, ON: Wilfrid Laurier.

Singer, T. Benjamin. 2006. "From the Medical Gaze to *Sublime Mutations*: The Ethics of (Re)Viewing Non-normative Body Images." In *The Transgender Studies Reader*, edited by Susan Stryker and Stephen Whittle, 601–20. New York: Routledge.

Snorton, C. Riley. 2009. "'A New Hope': The Psychic Life of Passing." *Hypatia* 24, no. 3: 77–92.

Stone, Sandy. 1992. "The *Empire* Strikes Back: A Posttranssexual Manifesto." *Camera Obscura*, no. 29: 150–76.

Stryker, Susan. 2006a. "(De)Subjugated Knowledges: An Introduction to Transgender Studies." In *The Transgender Studies Reader*, edited by Susan Stryker and Stephen Whittle, 1–17. New York: Routledge.

Stryker, Susan. 2006b. "Transgender Studies: Queer Theory's Evil Twin." *GLQ* 10, no. 2: 211–12.

Washington Square News. 2017. "NYU's Role in Gentrification." *Washington Square News*, February 6. nyunews.com/2017/02/06/nyus-role-in-gentrification/.

Wiegman, Robyn. 2012. *Object Lessons.* Durham, NC: Duke University Press.

Wilson, Robin. 1998. "Transgendered Scholars Defy Convention, Seeking to Be Heard and Seen in Academe; A Growing Movement Demands Protection in Anti-bias Policies and Attention for Their Ideas." *Chronicle of Higher Education*, February 6. Retrieved from Nexis Uni.

Ziegler, Kortney Ryan, dir. 2008. *Still Black: A Portrait of Black Transmen.* San Francisco: Blackstarmedia.

Nice Trannies

JACK HALBERSTAM

Abstract Is trans studies over? Some scholars claim it was over before it began, swallowed whole by queer studies. Rather than doubling down on a small territorial struggle, this essay tries to make sense of the appeal of such claims on the one hand and the futility of them on the other. Offering a reading of Andrea Long Chu's recent book *Females* and situating that book within its rather narrow North American context, this essay offers a different view of the present, past, and future of trans studies.

Keywords trans studies, oedipal struggles, queer studies, Valerie Solanas

> It's only comrades and friends that can yell at each other like this.
> —Nikita Khrushchev, *The Death of Stalin*

"Let's face it," writes provocateur Andrea Long Chu in a recent, much-circulated essay in *TSQ*, "trans studies is over." And just to make this punchy opening carry a bit more clout, she adds, "If it isn't, it should be" (Chu and Harsin Drager 2019).

Declarations that entire fields of thought are "over"—or that they simply never began in the first place, or that they are self-cannibalizing, or that they are wrong, or stupid, too limited or too expansive, that they went down the wrong path long ago or never found the path, that they wore the wrong clothes, have no clothes, are boring, have left no trace, are full of blind sheep, use too much jargon, are too political, lack a politics, exclude too many, lack clear membership, depend on identity politics, ignore the very people who are the subjects of the discourse, preach to the converted, want to be right, behave badly, posture as radical, make too much noise, say nothing, mean well, et cetera ad nauseum—have tended to be the well-tended pasture of the enraged right wingers. Such declarations are bad enough when one or two of these reasons for being declared dead and dusted are provided; they are especially annoying when all these reasons are given at once.

TSQ: Transgender Studies Quarterly ∗ Volume 7, Number 3 ∗ August 2020
DOI 10.1215/23289252-8552936 © 2020 Duke University Press

Usually, treatises on the death of this or the end of that (think Francis Fukuyama's *End of History* [(1992) 2006] or Daniel Bell's *End of Ideology* [1965] or Allan Bloom's *Closing of the American Mind* [(1992) 2002]) want to add a punctuation point to a set of rapid developments and acquiesce to the status quo. They want to declare change, transformation, and the new as resolutely over while indulging in nostalgia for earlier, more dynamic moments.

Declarations of the death of this or that are also all too often very popular. They are full of verve; they thrive on bold if caricatured assertions, and they make for excellent and dynamic reading. But like certain orange-skinned, comb-over real-estate moguls turned presidents, they age poorly. And more than that, the judgment-laden polemics about the end of everything make for poor theory and leave only scorched earth in their wake. I personally appreciate a good polemic, and I have made my own disciplinary critiques, but, be that as it may, I am not fond of the "X studies is over" statement, especially when thousands of graduate students might be at any given moment clinging to the raft of X studies and planning on trying to have a career in X studies.

OK, true: back in the early aughts I did say that the discipline of English was "dead." But pointing out the zombie status of a dead colonial discipline is different from declaring a marginal area of study to be "over" or, worse, redundant. While disciplines like English, history, anthropology, and philosophy have, after all, cohered around nationalist or colonial projects of rule and have produced massive ideological structures of domination, inter- or antidisciplines like queer studies, ethnic studies, and trans studies have challenged received wisdom, shaken up the foundations of knowledge production, and, often, tethered themselves to social justice projects. Never mind these massive distinctions between hegemonic areas of study and minoritarian projects; Chu comes along to issue her jeremiad to a field that, mostly through the heroic efforts of Susan Stryker, is finally picking up steam. Chu's opening statement, in her dialogue on "the state of trans studies today" with Emmett Harsin Drager, reads in full:

> Let's face it: Trans studies is over. If it isn't, it should be. Thus far, trans studies has largely failed to establish a robust, compelling set of theories, methods, and concepts that would distinguish itself from gender studies or queer studies. Stryker (2004) once wrote that trans studies was "queer theory's evil twin." She was wrong: Trans studies is the twin that queer studies ate in the womb. (The womb, as usual, was feminism.) What everyone knows is that queer theory has never had any qualms about arrogating gender as one of its primary sites of inquiry, and reasonably so, since trying to study sexuality without studying gender would be manifestly absurd. Queer has, from the get go, described both gender and

sexual deviance, and what's more, gender as sexual deviance and sexuality as
gender deviance. From this perspective, trans studies is just an embarrassing
redundancy—junk DNA. (Chu and Harsin Drager 2019: 103)

Let's face it, Oedipal dynamics are alive and well in trans studies. The state of trans
studies today is, at least in part, a set of tedious reversals that promise not change
or something new but only what Eve Sedgwick (2003: 147) once called "the stifling
reproductive logics of oedipal temporality." In the dialogue that follows, Chu's
drag performance as a reincarnation of Allan Bloom ([1992] 2002) (he who once
pronounced, "We are like ignorant shepherds living on a site where great civili-
zations once flourished" [239]) is tempered by Harsin Drager's "optimism about
the future of trans studies" (Chu and Harsin Drager 2019: 114). Despite that
optimism, Harsin Drager decries "an obsession with resistance and radicality"
(107) in earlier scholarship and advocates (for very different reasons than Chu) for
a return to the much-maligned, medically conceived category of the "the transsexual." For both theorists, trans studies in the future must be the critique of its
past. For both, the category of the "transsexual" is a clearly bounded entity, often a
trans woman, who steadfastly refuses the role of rebellion that has been projected
onto her while, with equal resolve, she represents herself as the most maligned, the
most marginalized, and the most radical of all!

If earlier trans studies scholars, in other words, said, in effect, "Let's move
on from the medically produced category of the transsexual," younger scholars
want to return to it. If earlier scholars proposed moving beyond identity by
turning trans into "transing," young theorists find "transing" to be an ugly ter-
minology with zero impact. If some older theorists jousted with norms that, far
from being mere imaginary standards that nobody met, were often damaging to
people's sense of sanity, now we must say that "norms, as such, do not exist." If, in
the past, people tried to collaborate, recognize each other's work (often in the
absence of any higher level of recognition), now, Chu scolds, we need "strife"! To
wit: "We need a small number of very good monographs that we can really yell at
each other over. Can you think of a single significant debate in trans studies
today? Bickering is everywhere, but true disagreement, the kind that births theories, is rare. Why are we so nice to each other? I think a lot of us are itching for a
fight. 'On Liking Women' was a desperate attempt to be disagreed with. In that
regard, it's largely failed" (104).

I am happy to oblige. I do so with the witticism mouthed by Nikita
Khrushchev in the political satire *The Death of Stalin* (dir. Armando Iannucci,
2017) firmly in mind. Namely: "It's only comrades and friends that can yell at each
other like this." I think I can both answer the question as asked ("Can you think of
a single significant debate in trans studies today?") and—bonus!—offer some
deep disagreements in a somewhat elevated tone.

On the question of significant debates: there are so many I won't list them all, since to do so would contribute to Chu's sense of the tedium of the whole field. But even a quick survey of the last thirty years would reveal high-stakes disagreements about the categories of "the real" and "performativity" (played out in part between Jay Prosser [1998], Judith Butler [1993a], and myself [2005]). There have been lots of fights in queer and trans studies about a perceived trendiness of high theory that comes at the expense of the workaday and practical contributions made by ethnographers and others using empirical data (Vi Namaste weighed in on this several times, e.g., Namaste 2009). We all know of the endless debates about the category of "woman" between so-called radical feminists and trans women. Deep disagreements about race and class and the global adoption of the English-language term *transgender* for multiple modes of cross-identification have culminated in extraordinary scholarship by C. Riley Snorton (2017) on black histories of gender variability and by Martin Manalansan (2003) on cross-gender identification in non-Euro-American contexts. These have all been significant debates. These have not all preferred transgender people to transsexuals. These debates have evolved, twisted, turned, and returned, influencing some people and enraging others. The idea that the field does not encourage disagreements will come as a shock to many scholars who have sparred and parried, issued takedowns and retractions, and have learned from the process and shifted their positions. This happens in all fields, not only trans studies. This will happen in trans studies again. This will not be the end of trans studies, nor its beginning. It will just be part of the continued attempt to live in our differently difficult forms of embodiment and to make sense of the world from that perspective. Disagreements will continue to be part of the ongoing insistence that all gendered embodiment represents ongoing trouble.

So, enough said about whether there are any significant debates in trans studies today. How about the question of why we are so nice to each other? Well, I know personally that few people would accuse *moi* of being too nice. I have published blogs comparing queer studies to *Game of Thrones*, I have offered not very nice opinions on the turn away from "antinormativity," and I have contributed to the generalized and now caricatured critiques of 1970s feminism. I have had open critical debates with gay male theorists. I have named names. I have taken heat for it. I have survived. When people do not engage in shouting matches, of course, they are not simply "being nice"; they often are just trying to soldier on in a shared battle while avoiding the loud and unpleasant exchanges that have now come to dominate social media. And to do so, I believe, is not to draw hard lines between trans studies and queer studies but to recognize the shared spaces of study, practice, activism, and theory and to build on the work that has already been done. I, like many others, have always found myself on the capacious borders between queer and trans studies, and I see no reason to shore up that border or defend it or catcall across it. I have indeed, as Harsin Drager comments accurately in this article, argued for trans classifications that exceed the gender binary and blur the boundaries between trans and queer altogether.

Apparently, it is tedious to build on work that came before, or even to read it. What's better, more fun, is to just declare the field that you have just emerged into to be over, and then issue a series of takedowns. Chu majors in takedowns, so much so that one might quiver to see oneself cited by her. But, it turns out, the only thing worse than being cited by Chu is not being cited. And that is what happens over and over in her dialogue with Harsin Drager—entire groups of scholars are disappeared in an essay that insists that "most trans studies scholars are, in fact, just queer-studies scholars especially susceptible to fads" (Chu and Harsin Drager 2019: 105); "there is no object worse than a woman" (109); "trans studies remains a field in which two men can sit around and debate the merits of woman as a political category" (109); and "we are very bad at calling bullshit" (111).

Here we go then: I call bullshit. There are so many willful misreadings of trans studies, queer studies, feminism, and so on in this essay that I believe it quickly reaches a tipping point where one can confidently assert that it is "bullshit." And this is not necessarily a bad thing, in the sense that, using Harry Frankfurt's definition of the term, bullshit is both an unavoidable part of conversation and a rhetorical strategy that seeks to persuade without recourse to the truth. Bullshit I don't mind. It is more the target of the bullshit to which I object. Chu, indeed, has a problem with trans men and butches. Her deep antipathy to masculine people (although, oddly, rarely directed at straight men) puts the bull in bullshit, if you will allow the pun, and even if you won't. The bulldyke is the abject, pitiful object of so many Chu critiques that it is time to name this for what it is—transphobia.

Chu's essays, and indeed her book, *Females* (2019b), are all bullshit. And maybe because of this, her work is witty, funny, brilliant, and very pleasurable to read. Chu has no doubt honed the art of bullshit on Twitter and, indeed, might be among the very best of a new generation of Twitter intellectuals ("twitterllectuals"?): she is concise, arch, pointed, absurd and can convey much in 240 characters. Recent examples from her Twitter feed include "cute and also relatable how cats think everything is boobs"; "I may not be hot but at least I am hard to root for"; and, one of my faves, "a muppet Christmas Carol holds up. Michael Caine yelling at puppets. Cinema" (Chu 2019c, 2019e, 2020). Does a hilarious Twitter feed qualify someone to write a book? Well, yes, actually. *Females* is also full of compact zingers: "the female loves herself only because she hates herself" (26); "what makes gender *gender*—the substance of gender that is—is the fact that it expresses, in every case, the desire of another" (35); and "you do not get to consent to yourself" (38). This is bullshit of the finest order—persuasive, intuitively right on, and bearing no relation to actual bodies and experiences. My critique of Chu, indeed, is not an attempt to correct her, take her down, prove her wrong (although I may do any or all of these); it is more an attempt to engage her in the domain where she lives and breathes—conflict. Indeed, in a conversation with Thora Siemson (2019) published in the *Nation* and titled "Andrea Long Chu Is Ready for Criticism," Chu says, "As someone known a bit for writing scathing negative reviews of things, I think I would be impressed if someone did that to me. I don't think I would be angry. I would be angry at limp dismissal. To be taken down, I'm sure, would be an honor." I aim to oblige, and I take Chu at her very negative word.

Females seeks to persuade us that "everyone is female and everyone hates it," with *females* in this context being the name for the social processes by which bodies, subjects, and people take form only through the ebb and flow of discursive processes that come from without, rather than from within. "Everyone is female and everyone hates it" (1), in other words, means that no one is a clearly willful agent, and everyone chafes at such a predicament. But let's face it, this is old news. Lacanians have formed an entire cult around this notion. Indeed they, too, offered a figure for the "lack" we all face—woman! Sound familiar? It should.

Butler (1993b) called bullshit long ago on this fusing of lack and woman, asking in "The Lesbian Phallus" and other places why it would make sense to use the figure of the woman to represent lack, given that women are well trained in recognizing their own castration. Men, on the other hand, in a sad and impactful twist to this story, continue to believe that women lack but that they are in possession of knowledge, the phallus, power, wisdom, and other such desirables. Would it not make much more sense, Butler asked, to take the male body as the site of lack and ask us to recognize that lack where we believe we see fullness, wholeness, and plenitude? Since *Bodies That Matter* advanced these claims some twenty-five years ago, theorists, intellectuals, and grade schoolers have understood and acknowledged that everyone would like to believe in the myth of wholeness, but, ultimately, we have to face the truth about bodies. We are not all females, but we are all messy, incoherent, and fragmented, phallus or no phallus.

In a scathing and brilliant essay on Chu's book in the *Los Angeles Review of Books*, Kay Gabriel (2019) accuses Chu of not simply bullshit but also a "commitment to the bit," in which "the bit" is satire played straight, and which remains invested more in "attitude" than in the integrity of the argument, which is just a vehicle for "tone." After skillfully dissecting the category of "female" as Chu uses it as warmed-over Lacanian lack, Gabriel describes how Chu, for shock value, and on behalf of her bold universalism ("everyone is female"), subscribes to a second-wave feminist view of gender. Remember that second-wave feminism also relied on universals like "women-born-women" and accused trans women of trying to infiltrate women-only space. Chu actually turns for support to Catharine McKinnon and transphobic feminist Janice Raymond. Like MacKinnon, Chu understands females to be "objects," and like Janice Raymond she sees trans-sexuality as the possession of women by men and as "the product of the pathological assimilation of misogynist stereotypes." In Gabriel's (2019) words, Chu "happily throws trans women under the bus." But while Chu sees trans women as dupes of a gender system, her main antagonism is often directed at butches and trans men. Gabriel comments astutely, "*Females* regurgitates the anti-trans ethics of earlier decades—including the notorious second-wave tendency to refuse any acknowledgment of the subjectivity of trans men—blended together with its own particular political fatalism: transitioning is politically bad, Chu argues, and so is every other gendered disposition."

The figure of the drag queen in *Females* represents, much as she did for Butler in *Gender Trouble*, "the model for all gender" (Chu 2019b: 33). The trans-sexual assigned female at birth, however, represents a "commitment to being stereotyped." And as for trans men and butches, they play an odd role in the world according to Chu. Despite her idol and role model Valerie Solanas's own bulldyke appearance and persona, Chu barely mentions her masculinity. And, in the *TSQ* essay, butch theorists are Chu's main targets. And here lies the proverbial rub. If we are all female, then how can you accuse a queer theorist (Chu picks Karen Barad) of appropriating the experiences of something called "transsexuality"? And, if everyone is female, then why object to two men working in trans studies, Kai Green and Marquis Bey (also females in her world), sitting around debating "the merits of woman as a political category" (Chu and Harsin Drager 2019: 109)? And if everyone is female, how is it possible that butch or transmasculine queer theorists—Butler and Barad—have cannibalized trans studies? Chu writes at the outset of the essay, in an amendment of a famous quip by Stryker: "Trans studies is the twin that queer studies ate in the womb" (103). In other words, Chu's call for new ideas in trans studies comes out of a sense that queer studies has already covered the ground that trans studies comes to claim. But even as Chu acknowledges the contributions of queer studies to the study of gender, she also suggests that queer studies reaches an end point when it arrives at the figure of the transsexual: "The transsexual is the only thing that trans can describe that queer can't. The transsexual is not queer; this is the best thing about her" (107). The transsexual, we are asked to believe, and this hearkens back to the work of Prosser, is a stubbornly nonradical and nonresistant subject with desires for normative gender that simply do not fit into queer studies' political agenda. And the version of queer studies that has so completely misunderstood the transsexual, both Prosser and Chu claim, is that version authored by Butler.

Butler, of course, has long been a target from some quarters of trans studies, despite the fact that by any number of metrics Butler, a gender-nonconforming subject, can be considered trans and has, for the most part, done much of the heavy lifting that has made space for the kinds of fights and debates Chu wants to have. No surprise to find them dissed and dismissed in Chu's essay, but what about Barad, another gender-nonconforming subject who, Chu informs us, is a new materialist who enlists trans subjects to make arguments about materiality without "frankly . . . making a lick of sense" (111). Chu then goes on to line up two Barad essays on queer and trans materiality and then asks, "Well, which is it, Karen? Is matter queer or is matter trans? Both, of course, because for her, like for most people who claim to be working in trans studies, queer and trans are obviously synonyms. If I sound angry about this, good. I am" (112).

Angry? Angry that queer and trans are slip-sliding into each other? Now, after shoveling everyone into exactly one category, "females," and after arguing for a relation to gender and sexuality that is self-hating and self-demolishing, we need strict boundaries between men and women, queers and trans? Seeming to realize that the expression of anger in her "commitment to the bit" takes her away from the "tone" of ironic witticism and the genre of "trans satire," Chu quickly switches gears to ask her interlocuter, "But let's try to be nice trannies for a second. What work gives you cheer these days?" (112).

Not so fast. Let's linger for a moment on the oddity of Chu's fury with butches. See also her scathing review of Jill Soloway's memoir (Chu 2018b) (somewhat deserved), and her takedown of Masha Gessen (not at all deserved) and swipes at Hannah Gadsby on Twitter for being a TERF (not true).[1] They are odd not simply for their intensity, but in that the butch should be the central character of her one-act play called *Females*! Why? Because, here's a thought, if we are all females and we all hate it, then, we are all stone butches. Stone butches like Butler, like me, like Leslie Feinberg—hell, like Solanas—are female people who hate being female but do not believe that any amount of nipping or tucking, packing or binding will change the way femaleness hurts when you are in it but not of it. In taking Solanas as her Virgil, in talking about the experience of being female and hating it, Chu is on the well-worn terrain of trans masculinity, which she willfully mines for ideas and then quickly discounts. Stone butches are the definition of what Chu calls gender: namely, the expression of the "desires of another." As Butler explained decades ago, the courtly stone butch, in the process of tending to their partner, sacrifices themselves to her desires. In fact, most of what seems new in Chu is warmed-over Butler, even if written in a sharp and funny way. And this is not to say that queer studies already said everything that trans studies might want to claim, but that Butler's theory was already trans studies and that this separation of queer and trans just cannot hold! Chu's work, to be fair, is not claiming to be original or new, but, by not citing people, it seems to spring from an entirely independent mode of thinking when it is actually dependent on Solanas's satires, Butler's poststructuralist theories of material embodiment, Snorton's theories of Black gender formation, never mind Barad's wild theories of virtuality, Bey's (2019) theories of fugitivity, Cáel M. Keegan's (2018) account of *The Matrix* in *Trans Sensing*. None of these references come with citations in the text, and all are used only to bolster Chu's biting trans satire (see Butler 1993a, 1993b; and Snorton 2017).

Solanas's own satire, by the way, directed its most bullying, withering, castrating wit at bio-men. A man, for Solanas (2016: 36), was "a half-dead, unresponsive lump, incapable of giving or receiving pleasure or happiness; consequently, he is at best an utter bore, an inoffensive blob, since only those capable of absorption in others can be charming." Got it. This is misandry at its finest, not misogyny at all unless you have already cast men as "female." Solanas goes on: "To call a man an animal is to flatter him; he's a machine, a walking dildo. It's often said that men use women. Use them for what? Surely not pleasure" (37). Now this is funny! It is wicked humor at the expense of a group who have much to answer for and little to be worried about. Out of the intense atmosphere of 1960s feminism, and within a deep-seated critique of patriarchy, Solanas expresses the outrage that so many women felt about the blobs of white manhood who ruled without trying, benefitted without deserving, took without giving, and expected something for nothing. Solanas was describing a system of gender that naturalized power relations between men and women and admitted of no critique. She was busting a hole in that false "nature," blasting away at the category of manhood, and trying to take the whole system down. Solanas's target as far as Chu is concerned is not men but women, specifically Daddy's Girls who seek Daddy's approval and put other women down. But Chu is simply wrong here. Solanas may be angry at heterosexual women, but she wants to cut up heterosexual men!

Let's face it, to quote someone without mentioning them, if we are all female, then there are no queer studies, no trans studies, no feminism. No lines can be drawn, no territory defended. In fact, if we are all females, then there are no transsexuals, no queers, no men. In the future, may I suggest, we who are queer, or trans, or feminist might remain focused on a more conventional enemy: namely, the beneficiaries of hetero-patriarchal systems who, far from being females and hating it, are deeply invested in being males and loving it. If you think we are all female and we all hate it, you should look up the Jewish prayer where men thank God every day that they were not born female. You should then visit a gay bar where trans men are not particularly welcome, and ask if we are all female and we all hate it. You should go over the details of the various sex scandals engulfing men like Jeffrey Epstein, Bill Cosby, Harvey Weinstein, and others who love being male. You should take a look at Grindr where men advertise for real men, males, "no sissies, no fats, no Asians." And, of course, no females. Ever.

Trans studies is not over. It is well under way and has a long way to go. The next time *TSQ* appraises the field, let's hope we can say that we have moved beyond internal critique, that we have hammers and we have smashed the patriarchy, and that we are not all females and that we do not all hate it. Let's hope we can even imagine a future to be trans in. Let's hope we are capable of being nice trannies able to recognize that there was life before us and there will be life after us.

Jack Halberstam is professor of gender studies and English at Columbia University. Halberstam is the author of six books including, among others, *The Queer Art of Failure* (2011) and *Trans*: A Quick and Quirky Account of Gender Variance* (2018). *Places Journal* awarded Halberstam its Arcus/Places Prize in 2018 for innovative public scholarship on the relationship between gender, sexuality, and the built environment. Halberstam has a book coming out in 2020 titled *Wild Things: The Disorder of Desire* and is now finishing a second volume on wildness titled *The Wild Beyond: Art, Architecture, and Anarchy*.

Note

1.   Examples of her tweets about Gessen and Gadsby are as follows: on Gadsby's "terf energy," she writes, "is hannah gadsby a terf? not as far as we know. but the terf ENERGY is off the charts" (Chu 2019d) and then "australian accent, butch presentation, smug second-waver, claiming to talk about women but always addressing the men in the room... big sheila jeffreys energy" (Chu 2019a). In terms of Masha Gessen, Chu objected to a piece Gessen wrote in the *New Yorker* and proposed in response, "masha gessen wouldn't know a trans person if one lived in her mirror" (Chu 2018a).

References

Bell, Daniel. 1965. *The End of Ideology: On the Exhaustion of Political Ideas in the Fifties*. New York: Free Press.

Bey, Marquis. 2019. *Them Goon Rules: Fugitive Essays on Radical Black Feminism*. Tucson: University of Arizona Press.

Bloom, Allan. (1992) 2002. *The Closing of the American Mind: How Higher Education Has Failed Democracy and Impoverished the Souls of Today's Students*. New York: Simon and Schuster.

Butler, Judith. 1993a. "Gender Is Burning: Questions of Appropriation and Subversion." In *Bodies That Matter: On the Discursive Limits of Sex*, 81–98. New York: Routledge.

Butler, Judith. 1993b. "The Lesbian Phallus." In *Bodies That Matter: On the Discursive Limits of Sex*, 28–57. New York: Routledge.

Chu, Andrea Long (@andrealongchu). 2018a. "masha gessen wouldn't know a trans person if one lived in her mirror." Twitter, August 29, 3:26 p.m. twitter.com/andrealongchu/status /1034885094249558022.

Chu, Andrea Long. 2018b. "No One Wants It." *Affidavit*, November 5. www.affidavit.art/articles /no-one-wants-it.

Chu, Andrea Long (@andrealongchu). 2019a. "australian accent, butch presentation, smug second-waver, claiming to talk about women but always addressing the men in the room. . . big sheila jeffreys energy." Twitter, July 26, 10:40 a.m. twitter.com/andre alongchu/status/1154765793739120640.

Chu, Andrea Long. 2019b. *Females.* New York: Verso.

Chu, Andrea Long (@andrealongchu). 2019c. "I may not be hot but at least I'm hard to root for." Twitter, April 4, 1:22 p.m. twitter.com/andrealongchu/status/1113854259177693185.

Chu, Andrea Long (@andrealongchu). 2019d. "is hannah gadsby a terf? not as far as we know. but the terf ENERGY is off the charts" Twitter, July 26, 10:40 a.m. twitter.com/andrealongchu /status/1154763451807555584.

Chu, Andrea Long (@andrealongchu). 2019e. "a muppet Christmas Carol holds up. Michael Caine yelling at puppets. Cinema." Twitter, December 12, 6:47 p.m. twitter.com/andrealongchu /status/1205272933293273088.

Chu, Andrea Long (@andrealongchu). 2020. "cute and also relatable how cats think everything is boobs." Twitter, January 12, 12:49 a.m. twitter.com/andrealongchu/status/121623579770 5371648.

Chu, Andrea Long, and Emmett Harsin Drager. 2019. "After Trans Studies." *TSQ* 6, no. 1: 103–16.

Fukuyama, Francis. (1992) 2006. *The End of History and the Last Man.* New York: Free Press.

Gabriel, Kay. 2019. "The Limits of the Bit." *Los Angeles Review of Books,* November 25.

Halberstam, Jack. 2005. "Unlosing Brandon." In *In a Queer Time and Place: Transgender Bodies, Subcultural Lives,* 47–75. New York: New York University Press.

Keegan, Cáel M. 2018. *Lana and Lily Wachowski.* Champaign: University of Illinois Press.

Manalansan, Martin. 2003. *Global Divas: Filipino Gay Men in the Diaspora.* Durham, NC: Duke University Press.

Namaste, Viviane. 2009. "Undoing Theory: The Transgender Question and the Epistemic Violence of Anglo-American Feminist Theory." *Hypatia* 24, no. 3: 11–32.

Prosser, Jay. 1998. "Judith Butler, Queer Feminism, Transgender, and the Transubstantiation of Sex." In *Second Skins: The Body Narratives of Transsexuality,* 21–60. New York: Columbia University Press.

Sedgwick, Eve K. 2003. "Paranoid Reading, Reparative Reading." In *Touching, Feeling: Affect, Pedagogy, Performativity,* 121–51. Durham, NC: Duke University Press.

Siemson, Thora. 2019. "Andrea Long Chu Is Ready for Criticism." *Nation,* November 4. www .thenation.com/article/archive/andrea-long-chu-females-interview/.

Snorton, C. Riley. 2017. *Black on Both Sides: A Racial History of Trans Identity.* Minneapolis: University of Minnesota Press.

Solanas, Valerie. 2016. *The SCUM Manifesto.* New York: Verso.

Are Jokes Going to Cut It?

Concerning Andrea Long Chu's Females

JULES JOANNE GLEESON

Abstract Intersex theorist Jules Joanne Gleeson finds Andrea Long Chu's *Females: A Concern* an indispensable read for those interested in recent struggles around sex and the blossoming of theory that has followed in their wake. While *Females* makes no pretense at being a comprehensive contribution to gender theory, its brevity and wit seem sure to succeed in causing a stir.
Keywords Andrea Long Chu, sexual difference, comedy, provocation, feminization, SCUM

Andrea Long Chu's debut monograph, *Females* (2019a), is a provocative piece of popular theory that tries to pull the rug from under the public's view of sexual difference. Chu argues both breezily and unsparingly: being female is not to belong to one half of the population; it is, rather, a universal condition. To be female is to live out another person's desires. This is a dire fate, and one which none of us can escape. As she has it, "Everyone is female, and everyone hates it" (11).

Dealing with material ranging from Valerie Solonas's *SCUM Manifesto* to Chu's former addiction to hypnotic "Sissy porn," to a satirist who swallowed and butt-chugged pages of *Infinite Jest* to mock middle-brow men, the book is especially wide ranging. It's also a brief read—without its surprisingly meticulous footnotes, *Females* runs ninety-four pages long.

Females' fleeting length and engaging style have already earned it widespread attention, including several reviews from two prominent and accomplished trans theorists in public life, McKenzie Wark ("Commitment to the Bit," 2019) and Kaye Gabriel ("The Limits of the Bit," 2019).[1] Despite this, I treated the prospect of reviewing the book with some trepidation. Like many trans women I know, I was discomforted by how much ground Chu's breakout *N+1* essay "On Liking Women" (2018d) conceded to transphobic feminists. If there ever was correct timing for this lightweight approach, it was certainly not 2018. Since its

TSQ: Transgender Studies Quarterly * Volume 7, Number 3 * August 2020
DOI 10.1215/23289252-8552950 © 2020 Duke University Press

publication, so-called gender-critical feminists have frustrated reforms to Britain's Gender Recognition Act and have worked up ties to the Heritage Foundation's campaigns supporting President Donald Trump's federal moves against trans people. In this context, Chu's acceptance of all the primary arguments of transphobic feminists before replying "And so what?" seems too clever by half.

Inevitably, "On Liking Women" proved a hit through its titillation of primarily cisgender audiences.[2] There was clearly an appetite for an "iconoclastic" figure telling home truths about easily caricatured trans activists. Evidently, many of the essay's readers took a transgender thinker's reading the *SCUM Manifesto* forgivingly to be an unprecedented breakthrough.

But to those in the know, trans women attempting to salvage apparently phobic theorists in this way was nothing new. It's a typical enough progression for well-read debutants facing down (or postponing) the harsh prospect of transition to immerse themselves in either radical feminist literature or psychoanalysis. That Chu opted for both demonstrates a talent for multitasking, but little more.

The personal hostility theorists such as Jacques Lacan or Mary Daly evidenced toward actual trans women has never discouraged all of us from intensive engagement with their elaborate theoretical constructs.[3] This was in fact the sole project of several prolific writers in earlier 2010s trans theory, such as the now retired Lisa Millbank.[4] Even unflinchingly critical readings of radical feminists by trans theorists have often demanded our taking their most polemical writings considerably more seriously than wider audiences would ever be likely to.[5]

It's understandable that those trained to read our way through problems reliably wind up in this trap. Nor is this a straightforward case of grad student self-loathing or amateur exposure therapy. Radical feminism and old-school psychoanalysis both offer explanations of how sexual difference *really* works. The blunter, more forceful, and cruder that explanation, the more a siren's song is offered to those passing through nearly unbearable everyday conditions, toward an uncertain fate. A wrong answer can feel more satisfying than no answer at all. It's also in the nature of radical scholars (and even more so, academic burnouts) to prize puncturing liberal truisms above all else, perhaps even to the point of self-injury.

An adult transitioner sympathetically reading Sigmund Freud and Valerie Solanas being received as innovative suggested to me a widespread ignorance of trans theory's history. And more specifically, it suggested the cyclical processes and painful dissonances that the meeting of higher education and gender dysphoria reliably produces.

Worse still, Chu's engagement with Twitter (beloved by aspiring writers across the anglophone world) twinned this prodigious career success with a string of loosely aimed irritants. Bisexual women in relationships with men were mocked and compared to tourists.[6] Judith Butler's style (both on and off the page) was mocked. Chu took to task unspecified "queer fucks" who didn't believe trans women transitioned to be pretty. And in an especially scandalizing missive, the notion of unconditional love from one's parents was ruthlessly deconstructed.

At best, all this seemed like "punching sideways"— publicly baiting other queers into a predictable rise. More often it seemed like an already well-connected writer making a name for herself by precision trolling (all a little more Paglia than Solanas).

Females provides Chu's clearest attempt at a justification for these antics: her ethics consist solely of "commitment to a bit." A term drawn from comedy, *bit* describes the conceit of any joke. Whatever humor is drawn from this spectacle, Chu explains, any comic is required to take at least this part of their craft entirely seriously. It's striking that this appeal deploys the world of light entertainment to renew theory's ability to unsettle. And doubly so that the original context she mentions for offering this opinion was an academic conference (clearly a context Chu is doing her best to surpass). *Females* is an explicit defense of a broader trend within left-wing culture toward in-group humor, with memes, YouTube videos, and podcasts increasingly coming to serve both a pedagogic and a polemical role.

This merger of comedy and critique has become inarguably popular in recent years. But are we really likely to gain much by replacing previous attempts at liberatory politics with the mores and philosophy of the comedy circuit? Are there not dire costs to explicitly reducing political discussions to battles between artfully generated personae that the "clued in" alone are able to fully grasp? Besides mockery as an easy mark, what happens to those who miss the joke? Do the especially extensively educated not have some basic responsibility to lift as they climb?

In contrast to her dubious Twitter game, within the #MeToo moment against workplace sexual harassment and abuse, Chu has played an indispensable role, albeit within a niche. In several incendiary essays, she sought to hold to account queer women and nonbinary people who use their identities to help shield themselves from well-deserved criticism, after either abusing men or shielding abusers. These figures are cases in point for the limits of liberal feminism, having made the most of existing victories of the women's and LGBT movements before reneging on their values for the sake of egocentric advancement.

Most notable was Chu's (2018a) daring attack on the environment generated across New York University (NYU) theory circles by its director of German, Avital Ronell. After Ronell was accused by one of her PhD students of prolonged harassment (including repeated, unwanted sexual fondling) and exploitative workplace practices,[7] the critical theory establishment appeared to close ranks to secure her position. (Despite the controversy, Ronell resumed teaching after a short suspension.) Appallingly, these defenses included both appeals to Ronell's accomplished career (as if being a minor intellectual celebrity ever ensured good conduct) and claims that Ronell and her victim's shared queer identity made the affair beyond the remit of legitimate critique by outsiders (exactly the kind of communitarian appeal that queer theory originally aimed to deflate). The affair seemed to make explicit a long-standing concern: that there was one law for tenured critical theory professors and another for their employees.

Chu's piece was widely praised as the most incisive response to the Ronell scandal. The exposé drew on both her personal experiences at NYU and theoretical training to hold her senior colleague to account. Extending well beyond a mere trashing of Ronell herself, the essay was an indictment of "capital-t theory" scholars who had gone to bat for Ronell more generally: "A culture of critics in name only, where genuine criticism is undertaken at the risk of ostracism, marginalization, retribution—this is where abuses like Avital's grow like moss, or mold" (Chu 2018a).

Needless to say, in the strictly hierarchical context of academia (where an effusive reference can be career making, or alternatively . . .), this take-no-prisoners tack was unusually bold. Considerably more NYU academics circulated Chu's writings in semiprivate forums such as Facebook or email lists than joined her offensive openly.

Equally skilled, if lower stakes for Chu personally, was a review (2018c) mocking *Transparent* creator Jill Soloway's debut book, mixing levity with a unique degree of scrutiny. Chu unflinchingly reproduced Soloway's account of an apparent cover-up after being accused multiple times of sexually harassing trans women on her set. Soloway's inadvertent confession climaxed with a bafflingly self-incriminating *Godfather* reference.

Wisely, Chu does not use her first book to relitigate her leading role in this recent (and ongoing) conflict. Recent developments in feminist movements get passed over altogether, or receive only an oblique mention. While carving the title of the *SCUM Manifesto* into a piano key, a still closeted Chu remarked in a typical display of male self-loathing: "Me too."

Far from being a retread, *Females* seems to refuse being a feminist text at all. Like another of the year's more ambitious theoretical releases from Verso Books—Sophie Lewis's *Full Surrogacy Now* (2019)[8]—the book explicitly disavows being a piece of gender theory. For Chu, gender is secondary—simply the varied forms of coping with a universal condition of others living through us. To be either a woman or a man is to pick between the two most popular means of coping. When it comes to being female, women have only the advantage of being "select delegates" of this objectifying process.

Chu casts feminism as exactly resistance to being female.[9] In her typical immanent style, Chu suggests that antifeminist propaganda contains plenty of truth in it: realizing one is female is often followed immediately by attempting to struggle free of it. Once again, we are urged to reply to bigots with only "Yes, and so what?"

To bolster her case, Chu notes that her icon Solanas was equally disenchanted with and dismissive toward the feminist movement as she found it. (Official feminist organizations such as the National Organization for Women responded in kind, offering Solanas no support during her trial for shooting Andy Warhol.) This doubling down on Solanas is found throughout *Females*, and it is a feature shared most obviously with her breakout hit "On Liking Women." Chu treats Solanas like a devout professional theologian might treat the Gospels on Christ: while rarely letting her off the hook for her failings, she is obviously, unabashedly influenced by this playfully extremist niche of the second wave (on both an intellectual and ethical level). Although more squeamish readers might protest at this elevation of an attempted murderer, *Females* is both charming and honest in its account of the relationship between reader and thinker. Solanas appears as part flawed, all-too-of-her-time theorist and part personal savior.

But how deep an impression did *SCUM* really leave? While Solanas was an unabashed revolutionary who wrote only indictments of existing society and lucid visions of its destruction, *Females* seems to have an apolitical heart. If all experiences of domination render us female, then all politics resists that state (or tries to). In Chu's account, getting political is a process that follows on immediately from realizing that you're getting fucked. While for Solanas it was males who were truly the most craven, passive, and weak—and female liberation would simply entail getting wise to this and overpowering them—for Chu females are ontologically excluded from taking political action. Although not spelled out explicitly, it seems heavily implied that politics is the art of manning up. This view will certainly cement Chu's reputation as a provocateur and stylist. It seems less likely that *Females* provides insights to be further developed by either revolutionary theorists or liberatory movements.

* * *

Females is at its best when applying Chu's remarkable close reading skills to the ephemera of internet culture, which surely serves as the front line of gender struggles today.

Teasing out unlikely questions such as which set of political memes best respond to the classic 1999 sci-fi *The Matrix*, or how effectively feminist it is to shove pages of *Infinite Jest* up your ass, *Females* shines when it treats contemporary web happenings and microcelebrities. Figures such as YouTube beauty vlogger Gigi Gorgeous are of course widely known among the young and the very online, but they are much less likely to feature in social theory. In each case, for all her sharpness Chu does admirably well in grasping these characters and episodes on their own terms.

Chu's most skillful read examines the so-called manosphere—the area of the internet where men's rights activism merges uneasily with the misogynistic scamming of pick-up artistry. Deftly acknowledging the loathsomeness of these spaces, Chu perseveres to show how their motivation (and even their tactics) are informed by a thoroughgoing fixation with what it means to be female. Reading this passage, I was put in mind of an anonymous 8Chan contributor venting his fury with women claiming that they were oppressed. Women were so privileged by society they could easily have sex any time they so pleased, he explained. Whereas he was cursed to lifelong involuntary celibacy, any woman could have her needs met simply by walking out into the streets, spreading her legs, and waiting. These incendiary, anonymized displays of overt misogyny express a more fraught relation to the fantasy of being female than their authors would ever realize. It's impossible not to see these rants as shot through with a dose of sublimated longing for shared experience (and, more explicitly, envy). Or at least impossible for me and Chu.

★ ★ ★

Let's consider the context of *Females'* knowingly overblown theoretical contention: that each and every one of us has to face up to being female, as best we are able. That *females* describes not a group of people but a shared human plight. And that genders are merely refracted responses to only one sex.

This is certainly a striking and memorable argument. Chu's account of becoming female owes as much to horror films as to earlier gender theory: "The self is hollowed out, made into an incubator or some alien force. To be female is to let someone else do your desiring for you, at your own expense. This means that femaleness, while it hurts only sometimes, is always bad for you" (11).

While jarring, claims of this magnitude are not unprecedented in feminist theory. The universal female seems most like a reversal of womanhood as theorized by French lesbian thinker Monique Wittig. Since Simone de Beauvoir had shown that womanhood was the "other" to the assumed default setting of the male, Wittig (1985) argued that women were in fact not one gender. They were the *only* gender. To be male was to be accepted as typical or universal, whereas women were only such because of a "mark" of gender that defined their body as specific.

For Wittig, this followed through into her equally stark and memorable claim: that lesbians are not women. As they refused to define themselves through primary relationships with men, they were left without a place in the heterosexual order. Clearly for Wittig, this was a point of pride. This polemical claim came in the context of a swelling number of European women prepared to openly declare themselves lesbians—in many cases after they had married men and reared their children. Wittig's provocation attempted to underscore, rather than ameliorate, the cultural dissonance this historical development generated. Wittig urged the development of a liberatory consciousness among those facing down homophobia and incomprehension.

While Chu was motivated by an equivalent insurgence from twenty-first-century transfeminism, it's less clear what form of mobilization her redefinition promotes.

Clearly, *Females'* universalist argument also owes a great debt to psychoanalysis. But Chu is not one for exhaustive genealogical discussion tracing the lineage of her claims. Freud's varying remarks on penis envy are briefly raised and examined. But *Females* is impossible to pin down to any particular tradition of psychoanalytic theory (and is none the weaker for it).

The most disappointing move made by *Females* is that its new view of femaleness is declared to be an "ontological" position. Chu makes this plain from the book's purposefully absurdist introduction, which declares that the first people to land on the moon and every US president were all female, and, more cryptically still: "Sharks exclusively attack females."

But this typical humorist's flair aside, ontological arguments are perfectly typical among Americans attempting innovative social theory. Afro-pessimism as developed by Frank Wilderson and Jared Sexton asserts blackness as an ontological state (rather than an identity), and Lee Edelman's "Queer Nihilism" claimed that the ontological condition of queerness was nonparticipation in reproduction. This trend has now gotten thoroughly out of hand, with the term *ontology* increasingly seeming to signal nothing besides a "raising of the stakes," in which social struggles are treated as vying arms races.

Still worse for the broader traction of *Females* is that its grandiose approach seems to require a blithe bypassing of decades of intersectional political struggle.

The absence of black feminism in *Females* is too striking to go unmentioned. Generations of black feminist scholars have tackled questions concerning gender, embodiment, and universalism. None of these thinkers appear as explicit citations in *Females*.[10] And it's hard to see their presence as sublimated influences, either. While a short book can't be expected to respond to the entire history of thought, in light of Chu's universalizing ambitions, this is concerning.

Black feminists have taken many views of the racialized particularities of the female. Hortense Spillers's widely cited 1987 essay "Mama's Baby, Papa's Maybe: An American Grammar Book" considers the experience of US black slaves by dividing between the body (as a juridical term, including ability to represent oneself in court, or head a household) and the flesh (the itemizable components that slavery often reduced human beings to). In this respect, slaves were "female" in that they were reduced to salable body parts (from their teeth to their muscles), and of course to breeding stock, while being denied womanhood. To be a female chattel slave was exactly to be tasked with bearing and rearing the next generation of chattel slaves. This dispossession then played out across generations, inherited from mother to daughter. Spillers argues that this dual process of dispossession, and reduction of slaves to male/female flesh, was central to divisions within womanhood that define US gender relations. This historical view seems to leave little room for Chu's sweeping attempt at ontology.

In the book's weakest chapter, *Females* attempts to preemptively assuage these concerns, dealing at once with her icon Solanas's use of the slur *spade* and today's insurgent fascist movement, the alt-right. Unwisely, a sissy porn producer's attempts at antiracist memetic humor playing off the "BBC" pornographic trope are also cited.

Chu does an effective enough job at teasing out the racialized anxieties of the alt-right, which certainly do twin a horror toward effeminacy with a nativist panic. But an immanent examination of contemporary fascism cannot substitute for direct engagement with black thought. Any critical rearticulation of the so-called second wave worth the name will have to include consideration of the nonresponsiveness of many of its white participants to black feminism. Correcting this heritage would require full integration of contemporary theories of racialization, and movements in resistance to it. Reading this chapter, I instead had the unmistakable sense of a thinker fully aware of the lacuna her line has opened up, but with no idea of how to resolve it.

★　★　★

Females is least interesting when engaging with overly familiar cultural episodes from 1960s and 1970s counterculture. Stale standards from Andy Warhol to Yoko Ono are (re)introduced. By the end of this boomer's parade, it feels like something of a mercy that Mick Jagger hasn't made an appearance. While this material may serve to help make *Females* marketable across generations, there's a played-out air that seems at odds with *Females*' billing as the cutting edge of a "second wave" in trans thinking. Did the world truly need another recounting of the most familiar figures of the so-called New York School from a young theorist?

Clearly, the most important figure of the bunch for Chu is Solanas. As well as being referenced throughout, extracts from her rarely performed play *Up Your Ass* (1965) serve as the book's guiding thread, with suggestive quotes beginning each chapter.

But even here, ground isn't broken. Chu is hardly the first theorist to make detailed use of the *SCUM Manifesto* to inform her contemporary thought. Without recourse to psychoanalysis, it's hard to know what to make of the fact that the *SCUM Manifesto* was also extensively cited by Chu's theory establishment nemesis, Avital Ronell (2010). (Ronnell also wrote the introduction to the recent Verso Books edition of *Scum Manifesto*.) This all produces a certain sense that we're being resold as innovations "breakthroughs" that are more accurately described as New York City thinker traditionals.

* * *

Confessional writing is a fraught topic for trans people. Memoirs have been so strongly encouraged by cisgender audiences that, until recently, it was near mandatory for trans writers to account for themselves, often in considerable autobiographical detail. Before we could make any argument, we'd be expected by both publishers and public to recite a potted life story.[11] Frustration at the stifling limits of this expected form, and its fictional counterpart the "gender novel," has defined the revitalized state of transgender writing across the 2010s (Plett 2015). Chu is clearly widely read in trans lit and skillful in her integration of telling snippets of it-happened-to-me content. These terse passages don't bog down a book primarily dedicated to swingeing social theory and biting cultural criticism.

Chu pulls no punches when describing herself but notably directs all her satirical talents at the male persona she has long since abandoned. At least by Chu's account, her old self was an unlikable specimen—unfaithful, obnoxiously well read, radical feminist by outspoken conviction, yet by night helplessly addicted to hardcore pornography (leading to an eventual fascination with forced feminization) and prone to lecturing women on cultural misogyny. An overwrought student, Chu produced art consisting of overblown citation of clearly semidigested theoretical reference points. Whereas *Females* presents its reference points sparsely, this male art was a clutter of lengthy quotes and aimless name checks—including a centerpiece of a deconstructed piano with the titles of theoretical works carved into each key. Yet another theory bro, lost in Manhattan.

The unflinchingly derisory self-portrait is remarkable, given the pessimistic tone dominating Chu's writings on transition elsewhere. In a predictably widely shared *New York Times* op-ed entitled "My New Vagina Won't Make Me Happy" (2018b), she offered the following account:

> Like many of my trans friends, I've watched my dysphoria balloon since I began transition. I now feel very strongly about the length of my index fingers—enough that I will sometimes shyly unthread my hand from my girlfriend's as we walk

down the street. When she tells me I'm beautiful, I resent it. I've been outside. I know what beautiful looks like. Don't patronize me.

I was not suicidal before hormones. Now I often am.

To read this *New York Times* piece, one might think that this whole process had been something of an ordeal—self-immiseration in pursuit of an impossible desire. Transition was cast in bleak terms, to advance the argument that taking a bad decision on her own terms was Chu's inalienable right. But in *Females* the fleeting, reversed bildungsroman narrative points in an altogether more hopeful direction. Representing herself as a pathetic male is simply the setup to introducing her more recent practice, as an exercise in contrasts. Having now made her name as a trans theorist, an art space invited her to offer a series of "provocations" (a task to which she was by any measurement uniquely well suited). Soon after her sex-reassignment surgery (SRS), in a homage to Yoko Ono's *Cut Piece* (1965) garishly entitled *Cunt Piece*, Chu tasked a volunteering audience member to use a remote control to activate a vibrator stationed against her newly formed vagina.

The resulting developmental progression is blatant, if rapidly disposed of: having been set to become yet another self-dramatizing but ultimately failed artist, able to succeed in little besides attracting more lovers than "he" could ethically negotiate, Chu instead ends the narrative in full acceptance of her female state. Coming to peace with her femaleness (as we must) led directly to artistic success, including a platform to put her own twist on the classics, and perhaps enjoy a little public pleasure.

A tension opens up between the thesis of the book and Chu's account of her personal breakthrough. The juxtaposition of her bygone male self carving into a piano and her current act requesting her post-SRS genitals to be stimulated at the discretion of a willing participant seems like an obvious doubling of her shift from attempted male to an equally symbolically and anatomically reordered state. But through going "male-to-female," her career as a performer or thinker (those most arrogant of trades, which impose musings and wit onto the world) was transformed nearly unrecognizably, and for the better. Submission to the inevitable seems to look an awful lot like becoming a star.

By this account at least, sometimes it pays to be female.

Jules Joanne Gleeson is a Londoner living in Vienna. She is an intersex historian, communist theorist, and Byzantinist. She is coeditor of the anthology *Transgender Marxism* (2020). Jules cofounded the Leftovers discussion group and the New Critical Approaches to the Byzantine World Network. She's writing a book on sex and indeterminacy.

Notes

1. As their titles suggest, both of these pieces take up the question of Chu's deployment of comedy conventions. Wark's description of Chu's style as parodic is clearly intended as generous. But this reading seems to foreclose grappling with the exact ambiguity that *Females'* refusal of sincerity opens. Gabriel explicitly introduces the history of thought that *Females* generally elides, an approach I broadly share in this essay. However, I am less inclined to read Chu's efforts as primarily responsive to Lacanian psychoanalytic theory, or as extending its understanding of castration. A fair amount of the implications for committed Lacanians seem to be read into this brief book, on the basis of Gabriel's (formidable) theoretical expertise. As will become clear, I fully share this second review's skepticism concerning the reliable salience of comedy for either insightful scholarship or emancipatory thinking. (While performing stand-up, I've consistently noticed audiences seem to enjoy being misled, teased, and disoriented—at least as much as they do being led toward the righteous path.)

2. Through no personal fault of Chu—this is simply a precondition for popularity that extends beyond the typical upper limit of social media circles or features in purpose-built publishing outlets such as Topside Press or Vetch Poetry. While post–Tipping Point we may be much more widely understood, we ourselves are not (yet) the masses.

3. Mary Daly's comments on trans women as Frankenstein's monsters and necrophiles seem too widely discussed to merit exploration. Interest in Lacan among trans people has revived since the publication of Patricia Gherovici's *Transgender Psychoanalysis: A Lacanian Perspective on Sexual Difference* (2017), which argued a revisionist case for Lacan as distinct from subsequent generations of Lacanians in his clinical practice. Lacan's personal attitudes, however, seem plainly displayed by an exchange quoted in Felippe Figueiredo Lattanzio and Paulo de Carvalho Ribeiro's "Transsexuality, Psychosis, and Originary Femininity: Between Psychoanalysis and Feminist Theory" (2017). While practicing at the Sainte-Anne Hospital Center in 1976, Lacan interviewed a female transsexual, Michel H., and expressed a crude skepticism toward transition as real:

    JACQUES LACAN: You must know that one cannot transform a man into a woman.
    MICHEL H.: It can be done.
    JACQUES LACAN: How? A woman has a uterus, for example.
    MICHEL H.: Regarding organs, yes. But I'd rather sacrifice my life, not have children, have nothing, but be a woman.
    JACQUES LACAN: No, not even emasculation will make you a woman. (331–32)

    Lacan's reduction of the potential for physical transition to the removal of the male gonads seems especially remarkable. It is noted by the translators that this encounter is "a confrontation that contradicts his own theory of clinical handling of psychosis" (77). It also seems oblivious to relevant endocrinological breakthroughs in exogenous sex hormone treatments that were (then as now) transforming gender relations along multiple fronts. Striking similarities seem obvious between Lacan's own explicitly expressed attitudes here and the worst of contemporary Lacanian clinical practical and cultural theory.

4. Like many transfeminists of her era, the probably pseudonymous Millbank's works were published almost exclusively online (radtransfem.wordpress.com/). As with Chu's approach to Solanas, Millbank's trans theorization was peppered with extrapolation from figures such as Mary Daly and Janice Raymond (including development of terms found in texts that elsewhere expressed open hostility toward trans people, such as Daly's "necrophilia").

5.   This fate of offering judicious parsing to obvious trolling seems to especially often befall trans theorists navigating the inhospitable climate of professional philosophy faculties. For an early and especially skilled example of sincere responsiveness to provocation, see Hale 1996. It's possible to read this review as another example.

6.   Bold, given that Chu's years identified as a lesbian could have been counted on one hand at the time.

7.   The formal accusation is available here: blog.simplejustice.us/wp-content/uploads/2018 /08/FINAL-Complaint-Reitman-v.-Ronell-and-NYU.pdf.

8.   A review by Kate Doyle Griffiths and Gus Breslauer (2019) teases out this hesitation around gender and more.

9.   A piece bluntly titled "The Impossibility of Feminism" (2019) also published this year sees Chu elaborate on *Females'* tacit rejection of feminist politics. This essay argues that it is impossible to make another feel what we want them to, rendering feminist politics fundamentally unviable. This begs the question of whether commanding all women's feelings was what any significant number of feminists intended to do, in the first place. Jo Freeman's classic essays notwithstanding, it seems curious that such a movement would ever have used the consciousness-raising circle as its key organizational form, rather than some more efficiently and obviously hierarchical structure. Once again, the absence of black and Marxist traditions of feminism in this (otherwise in-depth) account is jarring. Neither tradition has ever accepted the "M/F" split Chu explores as the innermost core of the social. As a result, Marxism and black feminism theoretically overlaps substantively more than is often realized, as explored in Ashley Bohrer's new book, *Marxism and Intersectionality: Race, Gender, Class, and Sexuality under Contemporary Capitalism* (2019). In this light, a truer title for Chu would have been "The Distinctive Limits of Radical Feminism" (I will admit this is less punchy).

10.   The work of one black gender historian, C. Riley Snorton, does feature. However, as Kaye Gabriel has noted, enlisting Snorton to support *Females'* argument seems to confuse the biological categorization explored by this vein of historical scholarship (which traces a racialization process that was particularizing by its very nature), and the broader sweep of "ontology" that Chu's redefinition centers.

11.   The worm might have turned here: I was surprised this year when a left-wing publisher urged me to excise a section of autobiographical material from a collection I was editing.

References

Bohrer, Ashley. 2019. *Marxism and Intersectionality: Race, Gender, Class, and Sexuality under Contemporary Capitalism*. Bielefeld, Germany: Transcript.

Chu, Andrea Long. 2018a. "I Worked with Avital Ronell. I Believe Her Accuser." *Chronicle of Higher Education*, August 30. www.chronicle.com/article/I-Worked-With-Avital-Ronell -I/244415.

Chu, Andrea Long. 2018b. "My New Vagina Won't Make Me Happy." *New York Times*, November 24. www.nytimes.com/2018/11/24/opinion/sunday/vaginoplasty-transgender-medicine.html.

Chu, Andrea Long. 2018c. "No One Wants It." *Affidavit*, November 5. www.affidavit.art/articles /no-one-wants-it.

Chu, Andrea Long. 2018d. "On Liking Women." *n+1*, no. 30. nplusonemag.com/issue-30/essays /on-liking-women/.

Chu, Andrea Long. 2019a. *Females*. New York: Verso.

Chu, Andrea Long. 2019b. "The Impossibility of Feminism." *differences* 30, no. 1: 63–81.

Edelman, Lee. 2004. *No Future: Queer Theory and the Death Drive.* Durham, NC: Duke University Press.

Gabriel, Kaye. 2019. "The Limits of the Bit." *Los Angeles Review of Books*, November 25.

Gherovici, Patricia. 2017. *Transgender Psychoanalysis: A Lacanian Perspective on Sexual Difference.* Abingdon, UK: Routledge.

Griffiths, Kate Doyle, and Gus Breslauer. 2019. "Every Surrogate Can Govern: Beyond the Family with Sophie Lewis' 'Full Surrogacy Now.'" *Regeneration*, June 18. regenerationmag.org /every-surrogate-can-govern-beyond-the-family-with-sophie-lewis-full-surrogacy-now.

Hale, Jacob. 1996. "Are Lesbians Women?" *Hypatia* 11, no. 2: 94–121.

Lattanzio, Figueiredo Felippe, and Paulo de Carvalho Ribeiro. 2017. "Transsexuality, Psychosis, and Originary Femininity: Between Psychoanalysis and Feminist Theory." *Psicologia USP* 28, no. 1: 72–82. www.scielo.br/pdf/pusp/v28n1/en_1678-5177-pusp-28-01-00072.pdf.

Lewis, Sophie. 2019. *Full Surrogacy Now: Feminism against Family.* London: Verso.

Ono, Yoko. 1965. *Cut Piece*, performed at Carnegie Hall. www.youtube.com/watch?v=lYJ3d Pwa2tI.

Plett, Casey. 2015. "Rise of the Gender Novel." *Walrus*, March 18. Updated April 10, 2020. the walrus.ca/rise-of-the-gender-novel/.

Ronell, Avital. 2010. "Media Technology and Society." YouTube video, 45:54 min. www.youtube .com/watch?v=VvV3n9-orLo.

Sexton, Jared, 2012. "Ante-Anti-Blackness: Afterthoughts." *Lateral*, no. 1. csalateral.org/issue/1 /ante-anti-blackness-afterthoughts-sexton/.

Sexton, Jared, 2016. "Afro-Pessimism: The Unclear Word." *Rhizomes: Cultural Studies in Emerging Knowledge*, no. 29. www.rhizomes.net/issue29/pdf/sexton.pdf.

Solanas, Valeria. 1965. *Up Your Ass.* solanasupyourass.wordpress.com

Spillers, Hortense J. 1987. "Mama's Baby, Papa's Maybe: An American Grammar Book." *Diacritics* 17, no. 2: 64–81.

Wark, McKenzie. 2019. "Commitment to the Bit." *Public Seminar* (blog), September 3. publicseminar.org/essays/commitment-to-the-bit/.

Wilderson, Frank. *Red, White, and Black: Cinema and the Structure of U.S. Antagonisms.* Durham, NC: Duke University Press.

Wittig, Monique. 1985. "The Mark of Gender." *Feminist Issues* 5, no. 2: 3–12.

A New Vagina Didn't Make Her Sad (It Didn't Have To)

RIKI WILCHINS

Abstract Andrea Long Chu's *New York Times* article, "My New Vagina Won't Make Me Happy (And It Shouldn't Have To)," marks a shift in trans discourse, raising issues about the challenges of surgical outcomes and being a post-op transgender woman with a candor that has heretofore been rare publicly. Yet it devotes little attention to the actual experience of being transgender. Similarly, much of gender theory succeeds at cycles of better and more accurate deconstruction, without mobilizing this to explore what it's like to be transgender. This article calls for renewed academic attention to the phenomenology of transgender—on issues like psychology, sexuality, and embodiment.
Keywords transgender, embodiment, phenomenology, sexuality, cisnormativity

As others have noted, Andrea Long Chu's *New York Times* article, "My New Vagina Won't Make Me Happy (and It Shouldn't Have To)," marks a shift in trans discourse. It does so by raising issues related to being a post-op transgender woman that I've been eager to see explored in more depth for some time.

Chu (2018)—a self-described "sad trans girl"—performs the overdue and salutary task of edging beyond the description of gender-confirmation surgery (GCS) as the "magic gender pill" that will "make it all better," declaring instead that "there are no good outcomes in transition . . . only people, begging to be taken seriously."

Public admissions like this used to be as rare as they were inadvisable. Attesting to anything less than the total efficacy of GCS risked providing trans-exclusionary radical feminists (TERFs) and right-wing bigots fresh ammunition for attacking trans medical care. Chu's essay holds out the hope that, decades now into the transgender rights movement, we might at last begin publicly admitting the true complexity of gender transition and its varied outcomes. Yet I find myself also wishing she had devoted more attention to the actual experience of being transgender.

TSQ: Transgender Studies Quarterly ∗ Volume 7, Number 3 ∗ August 2020 **345**
DOI 10.1215/23289252-8552964 © 2020 Duke University Press

I have similar concerns with the growing body of trans and queer theory that demonstrates how the gender system denies trans people of visibility, voice, and agency. While I've written several books on this myself, I worry that such writing may become locked into better and more precise deconstruction of the cisgender world's apparently infinite grotesquerie of oppressions.

In both cases, we are perfecting talking back at the cisgender world at a very high level, when I would like to see us devote some of this considerable expertise to explicating the experiential side of transgender. Doing so might highlight some issues that trans experience is uniquely positioned to address.

For instance, when Chu speaks of being swamped by the same regret I've certainly felt—watching a girlhood forever out of reach played out on other women's bodies and in other women's lives—I find my ears pricking up. She takes such experiences, including her own (unexplained) suicidality, as givens; but they could also be springboards for more detailed exploration of trans phenomenology. Suicidality, depression, and other symptoms often connected to posttraumatic stress disorder (PTSD) seems especially common among transgender people, but I've seen few studies of the rates of trans PTSD or how such suicidal depression is experienced by us.

When Chu writes of feeling increasing shame about the size of her hands, or her growing resentment at her girlfriend seeing her as beautiful, I find myself curious that she attributes such experiences to her ballooning dysphoria rather than the accelerating deployment of cisnormative bodily norms that often don't "fit" trans bodies.

I find myself wondering if Chu doesn't wonder about how the perception of one's hands as too large or one's face or body as unlovely is accomplished. If this was brought on by transitioning, then how does this happen? Perhaps more to the point is what she leaves unsaid: Too large compared to what? Unlovely compared to whom? Are there ways to experience transgender embodiment that are untethered from and unmediated by narrow cisnormative gender ideals?

The fact that Chu seems to take her own negative aesthetic perception of her body for granted is even more interesting because she then notes that her girlfriend does not share her perception and in fact finds her lovely—thus demonstrating that a competing and positive understanding of the aesthetics of her transitioning body is not only possible but immediately at hand.

Yet Chu dismisses her girlfriend's positive experience of her trans body as *pandering*. I would love to see this explored further. As transgender women's bodies change, what is the process by which we learn to reinterpret them? And what prompts us to reject positive aesthetic experiences of our bodies in favor of ones that cause us shame, depression, and pain?

When Chu writes, "Until the day I die, my body will regard the vagina as a wound," I find myself wondering, will her mind also regard it as a wound? Will she struggle to perceive of herself as having a vagina? How will either of these affect her sense of herself as a sexual being or her experience of intimacy?

Whatever the answer, I find myself wondering how such experiences of gendered embodiment are possible. Despite the stale right-wing canard that trans women are really self-hating gay men, getting surgery is not about having sex. For most trans people, in my experience, it's more directly tied to issues of bodily integrity and identity.

But it's not entirely *not* about sex, either. And the silence about this is an interesting one. Forty years ago—breaking the silence about butch/femme sex—Amber Hollibaugh and Cherrie Moraga wrote "What We're Rolling around in Bed With" ([1979/80] 2000). Perhaps it is time to devote more attention to what trans people are rolling around in bed with: how we experience our sexuality before and during whatever medical interventions we undergo. How do we integrate new physical borders and organs only recently under construction into a coherent sense of embodiment or into what we do (or can do or want to do) in bed?

I believe that transgender discourse may be uniquely positioned to address these issues about embodiment and phenomenology. These issues raise questions that a cisnormative discourse probably cannot pose because the experiences of embodiment that give rise to them are largely inaccessible to it.

Yet while there are literally hundreds of books on transgender and queer theory, there are perhaps only a handful specifically focused on such questions of transgender experience and embodiment, and I can think of none devoted to the experience of transgender sexuality.

If, as Simone de Beauvoir (1973: 301) famously noted, "the body is a situation," it is because embodiment itself is a situation—and transgendered embodiment perhaps most of all.

Of course, deeper and more public attention to such issues of embodiment, sexuality, and the inner experience of being trans is not without risks. We are still vulnerable to political attacks. But I believe they are risks worth taking and may even be ultimately inevitable if transgender studies is to more fully address the full ambit of transgender phenomenology. In any case, I believe they are risks that our struggles and sacrifices and the work of writers like Chu more than entitle us to take.

Riki Wilchins is the author of a half dozen books on gender theory and transgender politics. Her newest book is *Gender Norms and Intersectionality: Connecting Race, Class, and Gender* (2019).

References

Beauvoir, Simone de. 1973. *The Second Sex*. Translated by E. M. Parshley. New York: Vintage, 1973.

Chu, Andrea Long. 2018. "My New Vagina Won't Make Me Happy." *New York Times*, November 24. www.nytimes.com/2018/11/24/opinion/sunday/vaginoplasty-transgender-medicine.html.

Hollibaugh, Amber L., and Cherrie Moraga. (1979/80) 2000. "What We're Rolling around in Bed With." In *My Dangerous Desires: A Queer Girl Dreaming Her Way Home*, by Amber L. Hollibaugh, 62–84. Durham, NC: Duke University Press.

Against Queer Theory

CÁEL M. KEEGAN

Abstract The author explores how current disciplinary conditions force trans studies against queer theory: Because queer theory is the institutional context through which trans studies is invited into the university, it is also the containing ideological architecture against which trans studies must articulate itself. Trans studies is therefore pressed "against" queer theory as a discursive surface in a manner that limits it from being able to exit this disciplinary scenario.
Keywords queer theory, transgender studies, discipline, disciplinarity

> a·gainst
> /əˈgenst/
> *Preposition*
> 3. in or into physical contact with (something), so as to be supported by or collide with it: she stood with her back against the door.
> —*New Oxford American Dictionary*

Bear with me: trans studies is against queer theory. Or, to express this another way, queer theory is the disciplinary surface against which trans studies must constantly narrate itself, the field against which trans studies finds itself pressed in a stipulated intimacy. Queer theory is both the door through which trans studies enters and the room in which it is institutionalized. If we abandon linear periodization as the model by which to order our relations, then we are not yet "after trans studies" (Chu and Harsin Drager 2019) but are now (and still) against the conditions of perceptibility that queer theory enforces. We cannot yet say that queer theory recognizes trans studies as a discrete field, except perhaps as a stimulating friction generated around queer theory's most universally accepted claims, or a trailing set of concerns worked through in a slightly different register. Although trans studies has long understood that "queer" needs "trans" to tell its foundational stories about gender (Prosser 1998: 21), queer theory continues to

TSQ: Transgender Studies Quarterly ∗ Volume 7, Number 3 ∗ August 2020   **349**
DOI 10.1215/23289252-8552978   © 2020 Duke University Press

pretend that trans studies has only just arrived. Any pretense that trans somehow follows queer, that we have moved from "queer to transgender" (Weigman 2012: 22), thus requires us to join queer theory in willfully ignoring a long-present and coconstituting counterforce.

This is a situation trans people know well: the problem of the impossible phenomenon, the haunting sensation, the phantom object, the missing limb. To be here and yet-not, made absent by the way your name lives in others' mouths. Oh, how this paradox follows us everywhere we drag ourselves!

Two short tales about being against.

1. It is 2017, and I am interviewing for a position at Large Southern Research University. The job is for a queer-specific position inside a feminist research collective. Everything seems to be going well until, when asked about my activist work on transgender issues, I mention that it is vitally important that trans people be allowed to narrate ourselves—that we be recognized as "speaking subjects." A committee member who is a postmodern queer literary scholar immediately expresses doubt that this could be important, since subjectivity and authorship are structuralist conceits. I do not get the job offer.

2. It is 2019, and I am giving a talk at Large Midwestern Research University. I am presenting a piece that discusses the similarities and differences of queer versus trans theories (Keegan 2020), using Susan Stryker's (2004) figure of the "evil twin" to illustrate how these are supplemental rather than opposing discourses. I am careful to note that the two fields constitute a "critical relation" (Halley 2006: 272) in which the first principles of each discourse enliven the other's claims, producing an enriching and yet confounding paradox that perhaps best expresses the actual structure of gender. As I finish the talk, a faculty attendee raises their hand and notes that this piece is "controversial" because it "sets up a binary between queer and trans."

These encounters illuminate at the granular level how trans studies—while nominally accepted as an existing field—is not yet generally understood or treated as one in institutional practice. In these two instances, it is not that trans studies is excluded per se, but that it is welcomed to perform only in alignment with specific, preexisting scripts: in both stories, trans studies scholarship is expected to uphold values central to queer theory (deconstruction and anti-normativity) and present itself as if it is an affirmative subfield, or at least a congruent body of thought. In the first example, my interlocutor does not appear familiar with how transgender studies departs from queer theory's deconstructive mode to place high value on constative self-knowledge, or how this value developed as a political response to the specific medical narratology of trans-gender (i.e., transsexual) life. In the second example, the talk attendee appears to be already so acculturated to queer studies methods that even though I am careful to present a nonbinary model of differentiation, they perceive me as constructing a binary—and therefore intellectually suspect—formation. In both examples, my interlocutors expect to hear something familiar because they presume trans studies to be "like" (rather than against) queer theory. When I trouble that assumption, trouble of a disciplinary kind can follow: to the extent that I insist on trans-specific knowledges or methods that depart from the more familiar conceits of queer theory, I risk being rendered unhirable, unintelligible—a "bad fit."

In the two instances I recount, we can see how the universalizing trend in queer theory, in which any form of perceived nonnormativity must be elevated and collected into "queer," has had disciplining effects for trans studies—which must struggle against them to appear as anything except a similar set of moves. If queer studies expects trans studies to not cause trouble, this can force trans into a feedback loop in which it is pressed to become more and more indistinguishable from queer, thus further obscuring its own methods and claims. We might look around and notice that we can't notice trans studies as a distinct field, never realizing that this is a structural effect of how the more privileged discourse of queer theory disciplines—by including and citing trans only in ways that affirm its own investments (Keegan 2018). The implicit normativities of queer theory as an institutionalized discourse require trans studies to give an account of itself that renders it either (1) indistinguishable from queer or (2) as a "bad object" and therefore a source of trouble. Trans thus becomes a sort of usefully disposable guest: one who can provisionally broaden the applicability of queer studies' claims but still be disinvited from the room whenever it starts to tell a bad story. The result is an impossible yet paradoxically real situation. To name these conditions and ask for others—to resist them even as we refuse to leave the room (because where would we go, honey?) means to be against.

While I have written elsewhere about the unexpected benefits of trans studies being only partially welcomed into the academy (Keegan 2018), there is nonetheless an affective and intellectual cost to living and laboring against these fricative conditions of presence/absence. Writing that trans studies is "against queer theory" is therefore meant to provoke a set of institutionally unutterable questions, such as:

1. When queer studies scholars peer-review trans studies work, is it with the knowledge of trans studies' specific methods, aims, or vocabularies?

2. Are the multiple established monograph series and journals that are invested in queer theory capable of soliciting and publishing trans studies scholarship on its own terms?

3. Are the multiple academic press editors who are well versed in queer theory also familiar with trans studies?

4. Can graduate students interested in trans studies attend multiple programs where they are able to study with and be mentored by experts in trans studies, rather than queer theory?

5. Do graduate programs understand the differences between queer theory and trans studies?

6. Are graduate programs investing in and hiring experts to teach trans studies outside the framework of queer theory?

7. Are scholars who practice trans studies as a discrete field being hired into elite research universities?

8. Are there robust discussions taking place about the ethics of queer studies scholars engaging in trans studies work or teaching trans studies?

9. Are there transgender studies programs or departments that do not have to operate through the context of queer theory?

10. Are transgender studies scholars working at universities that support them to create programs or courses in trans studies, rather than appending trans studies content to queer studies programs or courses?

11. Are transgender studies scholars working at universities that sufficiently support new knowledge production in their field, rather than expecting them to publish in established queer studies journals?

12. Are there regular conferences in trans studies?

13. Is trans studies work recognized as legitimate by conference programming committees?

14. Can trans studies scholars regularly speak to one another without having to be placed in the intervening disciplinary context of queer theory?

If we cannot say yes to most of these questions, then trans studies must remain in the position of against. For trans studies, these conditions are how one can be invited and disinvited at the same time: trans people are highly familiar with the loaded game of recognition, how passing as a discrete gender is both expected by others and yet shamed as a failed exercise, required by others to been seen as human and yet simultaneously treated as a naïve performance. How is the phenomenological position of trans studies in the academy uncannily similar to these forced paradoxes of appearance and disappearance? One thing we might want from trans studies now is further conversation about how to be up against the impossible project of recognition on these terms: how to live and make work inside these abrasive conditions, how to remain willing to engage in the service of "a new hope" (Snorton 2009: 88)—even when it feels like our back is against the door.

Cáel M. Keegan is associate professor of women, gender, and sexuality studies at Grand Valley State University and cochair of the Queer and Trans Caucus of the Society for Cinema and Media Studies. He is the author of *Lana and Lilly Wachowski: Sensing Transgender* (2018) and coeditor with Laura Horak and Eliza Steinbock of "Cinematic Bodies," a special issue of *Somatechnics* (2018).

References

Chu, Andrea Long, and Emmet Harsin Drager. 2019. "After Trans Studies." *TSQ* 6, no. 1: 103–16.

Halley, Janet. 2006. *Split Decisions: How and Why to Take a Break from Feminism*. Princeton, NJ: Princeton University Press.

Keegan, Cáel M. 2018. "Getting Disciplined: What's Trans* about Queer Studies Now?" *Journal of Homosexuality* 67, no. 3. doi.org/10.1080/00918369.2018.1530885.

Keegan, Cáel M. 2020. "Transgender Studies; or, How to Do Things with Trans*." In *The Cambridge Companion to Queer Studies*, edited by Siobhan B. Somerville, 66–78. Cambridge: Cambridge University Press.

Prosser, Jay. 1998. *Second Skins: The Body Narratives of Transsexuality*. New York: Columbia University Press.

Snorton, C. Riley. 2009. "'A New Hope': The Psychic Life of Passing." *Hypatia* 24, no. 23: 77–92.

Stryker, Susan. 2004. "Transgender Studies: Queer Theory's Evil Twin." *GLQ* 10, no. 2: 212–15.

Weigman, Robyn. 2012. *Object Lessons*. Durham, NC: Duke University Press.

Institutionalizing Trans* Studies at the University of Arizona

SUSAN STRYKER

Abstract This article reports on the successes and challenges of institutionalizing trans* studies at the University of Arizona. It describes the Transgender Studies Faculty Cluster Hire Initiative of 2013–18, efforts to establish a curricular program of some sort in trans studies, barriers to achieving some of the the initiative's early goals, and future prospects for the field's institutionalization at the University of Arizona and elsewhere.
Keywords transgender studies, institutionalization, field formation, women's and gender studies

August 30, 2013, the day I hit "send" on the following announcement, was one of the most satisfying days of my working life:

Transgender Studies Faculty Cluster Hire at University of Arizona

The University of Arizona is pleased to announce a cluster hire of 4 tenure-track faculty positions in transgender studies over the next two years. Two positions are being offered this year in the College of Social and Behavioral Sciences (SBS), with a start date of fall 2014. Two positions to be based elsewhere in the university will be advertised next year, with a start date of fall 2015. This cluster hire is one element of the University of Arizona's unprecedented investment in the field of transgender studies. Other elements include support for a new peer-reviewed journal, *TSQ: Transgender Studies Quarterly*, which will be published by Duke University Press starting in 2014, with the editorial office housed at the University of Arizona's Institute for LGBT Studies; a new interdisciplinary Center for Critical Studies of the Body; and an anticipated graduate degree program in transgender studies.

Transgender Studies concerns itself with the variability and contingency of gender, sexuality, identity, and embodiment across time, space, languages, and cultures. It pays particular attention to the sociopolitical, legal, and economic consequences of noncompliance with gender norms; to the histories and social

TSQ: Transgender Studies Quarterly ★ Volume 7, Number 3 ★ August 2020
DOI 10.1215/23289252-8552992 © 2020 Duke University Press

organization of minoritized transgender lives and communities; to forms of cultural production that represent or express gender variance; to the medicalization of identity and the depathologization of bodily difference; and to the emergence of novel forms of embodied subjectivity within contemporary techno-cultural environments. Because we seek to hire the most innovative scholars in this rapidly evolving field, we are open to considering any area of specialization, research agenda, and inter/disciplinary training compatible with faculty service in the College of Social and Behavioral Sciences.

We invite applications for two assistant professor positions, one of which will be based in the Department of Gender and Women's Studies, and the other of which will be based in another suitable department within SBS (see sbs.arizona.edu). In addition to possessing requisite expertise in transgender studies, applicants must be qualified to teach core courses in their home department, and ideally will fulfill strategic priorities set by SBS in the following areas, broadly defined: health, the environment, technology, and global impact/regional roots. Our goal is to hire interdisciplinary scholars who can contribute to a new program in transgender studies while also meeting the needs of their home department.

I knew even then that faculty job searches were difficult and often fail; that the candidates who successfully navigate the hiring process do so on the basis of matching some institutional priority as much as, or more than, on the basis of their scholarship and pedagogy; and that the promotion, tenuring, and retention over the long haul of any faculty actually hired was far from guaranteed. Program building is hard work. Still, my sense was that in the very act of hitting "send" to announce this hiring and field-building initiative to the world, the nebulous undertaking called "transgender studies," which had been "arriving" for more than two decades, had arrived once again, in a whole new way, in the seemingly unlikely location of Arizona. That sense proved largely correct. Over the past half-decade, perhaps in response to the announcement of its arrival at the University of Arizona, jobs in transgender studies subsequently began to arrive in an accelerating number of other places. Whatever might happen at Arizona, that in itself has been success enough.

How It All Went Down

Between joining the precariat with my PhD in 1992 and being appointed with tenure as associate professor of gender studies at Indiana University in 2009, I earned my money largely outside the academy, working as a sales clerk, cab driver, telemarketer, pro-dom, door-to-door canvasser for a rape crisis center, freelance writer, researcher, nonprofit sector employee, public speaker, post-doc, filmmaker, dabbler in the arts, adjunct instructor, and visiting scholar, all of which

eventually cohered into a teachable body of text and film that constituted a
marketable "brand" for me that made me legible to the academy. Over these same
years, I had done the largely uncompensated labor of writing academic articles
that did not contribute to the tenure and promotion file I didn't have, prowling
professional meetings to help network an ever-growing number of trans and
trans-friendly scholars who all had better jobs than me, finding parasitical ways to
organize conferences and symposia at institutions that hadn't hired me, and
coediting anthologies and special issues of journals on trans studies to help seed a
core literature for a field that didn't quite exist. But by doing the intellectual work
along with the work of building a network of friends, colleagues, mentors,
mentees, and coconspirators who helped open the academic employment door
from the inside, I eventually landed a job-job.

Wanting to do my part to help cultivate a field in which I and others in the
same precarious boat could be hired was self-serving and altruistic in equal
measure. It's low-hanging fruit to critique the institutionalization of minority
forms of expert knowledge production within the interdisciplines as merely
contributing to the university's profitable management of difference, in service to
state and capital. For those of us who do the work, or want to, we also know that
the kinds of labor we perform, intellectual and otherwise, in and around the
university, can be part of liberatory, abolitionist, and transformational social
justice practice, and not just a paycheck job—particularly when steady academic
jobs with tenure are vanishingly rare. Who does the knowledge work, for whom
and with whom, under what conditions and for which purposes, both "upstairs"
and in the undercommons, is precisely where the struggle lies. I'd managed to
make a life for myself and do work that found an audience outside the academy,
but it was the prospect of working from the inside to open new possibilities for
trans scholars and scholarship within the university that enticed me into the
professoriat. I have no qualms whatsoever about undertaking the overarching
project of working to change the conditions of knowledge production regarding
trans issues, in ways that can contribute to more livable lives for people marginalized by their gender identities and expression, whether that's through
teaching, researching, publishing, editing, training, hiring, or organizing. There
are many ways to work toward the world we want to live in, and doing field-
building work has been one of mine for most of my adult life.

Changes in departmental leadership at Indiana University's Gender Studies department early in my time there made the kind of work I understood
myself to have been hired to do infeasible. I was pleased when another opportunity presented itself at the University of Arizona (UA), where I was recruited in
2011 as director of the Institute for LGBT Studies—a free-standing, university-
wide unit reporting to the vice president for research, with a mission to facilitate

interdisciplinary research collaboration among faculty and students. I was hired full-time as associate professor in gender and women's studies and given a 50 percent reduction in my other responsibilities to serve as the institute director for five years, 2011–16. I was hired with the understanding that, while I would have responsibilities at the institute for all the letters in the LGBTQ rainbow alphabet, I intended to give special attention to the relatively underserved *T*, which would also constitute the principal area of my own research and teaching. That the trans community in Tucson had organized a grassroots campaign on my behalf while I was interviewing for the job, packing the room for my talks and writing letters in support for my hiring, gave me an additional sense of responsibility for following through on those commitments.

Paisley Currah and I had been laying the groundwork for launching *TSQ* ever since 2009, and when Duke ultimately agreed in 2013 to publish the journal, UA provided generous financial support to help launch it as part of its earlier commitment to the agenda they had hired me to pursue—including support for a graduate student assistant, Abraham Weil, to serve as managing editor. Later that same year, Aren Aizura and I coedited *The Transgender Studies Reader 2*. The field seem poised for a new burst of growth, and UA was entirely supportive. In the midst of this quickening activity, however, I was invited to apply for another job at a more prestigious university. Although I was actually quite content with my work at UA, the other job would offer some intangible quality-of-life benefits that were simply too good not to consider. I applied; I was short-listed, and my campus visit went well. Although members of the search committee assured me off the record that the job had my name on it, I suspected that the committee chair was actually stacking the process to favor one of their own colleagues. Rather than risk losing out and forfeiting either the job itself or its offer as a potential bargaining chip for other uses, I decided to pursue preemptive retention at UA. I figured the worst that could happen would be to get neither the prospective job nor a retention offer, leaving me in a position that was already enabling me to march steadily toward some major career goals. And the best that could happen . . . ?

I asked for a brief meeting with UA's provost, who by sheer coincidence was the former associate vice president for research who had hired me to run the institute two years earlier, to whom I had reported for a year before his promotion to provost, and with whom I had a good personal rapport. He suspected why I wanted to talk and gave me fifteen minutes at 7:45 the following morning. He told me to make my pitch quickly. I said I was being courted by a university capable of offering me a salary, level of prestige, and quality of life he couldn't compete with, but I wanted to know if he was open to a creative opportunity to retain me. He asked what that might be. I said that at the other university, despite all its upsides, I'd be just another associate professor working on my next book and trying to go up for full; if I had an opportunity to do something at UA that would better serve my aspirations, why would I go anywhere else? He said, "What do you want?" I said, "To establish a program in transgender studies." He said, "I'll give you four faculty lines." Just like that.

We haggled for a few minutes about some additional bells and whistles and strategized about when, where, and how to place the lines, before he schooled me in my talking points for navigating this newly hatched initiative through the shoals of a neoliberal public university, in what was still at that time an unequivocally conservative state. Because this was the first such program in the world, it was the best such program in the world, and being first and best at something drives brand and profile and therefore market share of an untapped resource called "transgender studies"; it would help "change the narrative" in an expansive way about what was possible in Arizona and at UA; it would be good for recruiting and retaining diverse faculty and graduate students; and it opened up new external funding opportunities, notably those created by Obamacare for addressing disparities in LGBT health care. There would still be endless rounds of wordsmithing, internal approvals, and sign-offs that went all the way to the president, who on the provost's recommendation shepherded the initiative past the hostile attention of conservative members of the board of regents, but by 8:00 of the morning I made my quick pitch, the UA transgender studies cluster hire was pretty much a thing.

The faculty lines were not, as I was instructed to say, "commitments of new resources" for faculty hiring but rather a "reallocation of existing resources" drawn from the fund set aside for strategic hires, which would allow UA to better exploit a recently identified preexisting body of research expertise among its current faculty. That is, Francisco Galarte and I were already tenured and tenure-track faculty within Gender and Women's Studies, and the Institute for LGBT Studies was already slated to host the editorial office of *TSQ*. Departments were not being promised full new lines but rather incrementally decreasing bridge funding, in which the Office of the Provost paid 100 percent of salary the first year, 75 percent the next, 50 percent the third, and 25 percent the fourth, with the department needing to carry the full cost of the line after that. This meant that the trans studies positions needed to align with a given department's strategic hiring plan, with ongoing salary costs eventually being covered by retirements, resignations, increased enrollments, endowment funding, or some other source. This in turn meant that there were strong candidates for departments that had no interest in a trans hire, as well as departments that were interested in particular candidates but couldn't fund the line, besides the departments that were both interested and able. To be a true university-wide cluster hire, the lines would need to be distributed to at least three different colleges; as noted in the job announcement, the decision was taken to offer the first two lines in the College of Social and Behavioral Sciences (SBS), with one being dedicated to Gender and Women's Studies (GWS), and the other being available to another SBS department. The Institute for LGBT Studies, where the initiative was to be administratively housed, served as the hub for the entire process. Two search committees were constituted—one SBS-wide, the other GWS-specific. I chaired both; Francisco Galarte served on both, along with trans graduate students and queer faculty and faculty of color from throughout SBS.

We received roughly two hundred applications. Fewer than twenty were from trans women—a stark testament to the disproportionate barriers and challenges that transfeminine people face at every step along the educational pipeline. The SBS-wide committee vetted the applicant pool for those who met the minimum criteria (PhD in hand by start date, in a field within SBS, with a research agenda commensurable with tenure-track employment at an R1 university) and also actually did work in trans studies. That left us with one hundred viable potential candidates, only one of whom was a trans woman. We then divided up those candidates based on their training and specialization, and forwarded those lists to all department heads in the college, including GWS, to see if they were interested in any of the candidates. At the end of the departmental sorting process, there were twelve strong "long short-list" candidates sought by five departments for the two positions. The college-wide committee, in coordination with the GWS committee, then narrowed that list to the top seven candidates invited for on-campus interviews, based in part on our assessment of their relative strengths as trans studies scholars, and in part on the relative strengths and advantages of the departments that sought them for the purpose of building an intracampus trans studies program.

Departments initially interested in two candidates (who have since been hired and tenured at other comparable universities) declined to pursue their candidacies further after their campus visits. Another candidate had a more competitive offer and withdrew from consideration (and is now also tenured at that institution). The four remaining candidates were extremely competitive for the two positions available. Although we had announced only the two lines in SBS, I worked with the deans of other colleges to place the other two candidates elsewhere as target-of-opportunity hires, to try to complete the cluster hire in one fell swoop. We ultimately managed to place three lines in the first round, with the fourth declining our offer to take a position elsewhere. The successful candidates were Eric Plemons in Anthropology, Max Strassfeld in Religious Studies, and Eva Hayward in Gender and Women's Studies. By 2014, UA had a total of five tenured or tenure-track faculty members in trans studies, including Francisco Galarte and me.

The next round of hiring did not go smoothly. Although there had been candidates of color on the short list to whom offers were made, none of those who ultimately accepted the positions were people of color; in light of this, the initiative faculty sought to pursue the targeted hiring of a particular trans-of-color scholar deemed to be a good fit with the other faculty but who wound up taking another job elsewhere. We next sought to place the remaining line in a medical or health field, with no success, and similarly struck out with Fine Arts and Law. The College of Education expressed interest, and the line was eventually awarded to them, resulting in the hire of Z Nicolazzo in 2018. In the intervening years, unrelated to the trans studies cluster hire, the Norton School of Family and Consumer Sciences in the College of Agriculture and Life Sciences had hired Russell Toomey as assistant professor in Family Studies and Human Development, and he was folded into the initiative. We lobbied for Tucson poet laureate TC Tolbert, who taught as an adjunct at UA, to be hired tenure-track in the English Department, but we were unsuccessful. Still, at the end of a four-year process, UA had seven tenured or tenure-track trans faculty working in trans studies, in four different colleges. The Institute for LGBT Studies hosted the editorial office of *TSQ* and coordinated the trans studies initiative in addition to its other activities. We secured a six-figure grant from an outside source to support individual faculty research projects, began attracting graduate students and postdocs to our respective departments, placed a new trans studies undergraduate course on the books, hosted a large international transgender studies conference and several smaller symposia, entertained visitors from other institutions eager to emulate our success, and bandied about ideas for launching a curriculum-based credential, minor, or degree program of some sort. It felt that trans studies had indeed arrived in a new way—not only at Arizona but as a field.

What's Happened Since

In practice, it has proven very difficult to advance the elements originally announced in the trans studies faculty cluster hire beyond this promising beginning. The first casualty was the proposed "Center for Critical Studies of the Body" (CCSB), to be administered as a subsidiary unit of the Institute for LGBT Studies. It was proposed based on conversations I had with an administrator who had an interest in creating a hub for disability studies, trauma studies, and feminist science and technology studies, in addition to trans studies, and who thought the name might provide a bit of camouflage against transphobic or otherwise hostile opponents. We used it as a place to host the mailing list of the preexisting Somatechnics Research Network, which I had helped organize in the early 2000s, and as a point of contact for "Open Embodiments," the biennial international somatechnics conference we organized in Tucson in 2015. But the administrator moved on to other strategies for pursuing their interests, the Somatechnics Research Network found a new administrative home, and it turned out the trans studies initiative didn't particularly need cover, so the "CCSB" quietly withered away.

Arizona is a demographically shifting state that has become far more politically heterogeneous than it was in the early 2010s, but it is still a poor state with an entrenched conservative power structure that does not particularly value or invest in higher education, which makes for a very unstable state university. There has been constant churn at the highest levels of the UA administration: in a little less than a decade, I've worked under three presidents and one acting president, and three provosts and two acting provosts, and I've seen a steady parade of senior vice presidents play musical chairs with their ever-shuffling portfolios of expanding and contracting administrative domains. Three years into being institute director, I had more time in my position than anybody to whom I reported or who reported to me, from the president down to the part-time office assistant. My academic department has had eight heads or acting heads over the past ten years. With that level of turnover, it's difficult to carry out multiyear planning. With the state providing only about 15 percent of UA's budget, high-level administrators speak openly about the land-grant university being "a historically public institution" that needs to pursue its mission through whatever tuition the market will bear, lucrative high-end real estate developments geared toward providing posh apartments for well-heeled student-consumers, corporate partnerships, private philanthropy, technology and patent transfers, and federal funding—all while tightening its belt with regard to salaries, services, and benefits for students and employees in ways that don't necessarily inspire faculty loyalty, trust, security, or satisfaction.

Most significantly, the State of Arizona health plan does not cover transition-related health-care benefits for trans employees or the trans dependents of other employees. (Students are covered statewide under a different health plan through which transition-related care is provided, but access has proven difficult in practice.) This has posed a serious recruitment barrier and retention challenge that the university has failed to address effectively. With remarkably few exceptions, and despite professed good intentions, high-level administrators who otherwise have been supportive of the hiring and field-building initiative have tended to pass the buck and say that it's a problem with the state and therefore above their pay grade. This is true, but they have also been unwilling to pursue solutions such as buying a supplemental policy (as was the case when the state did not cover domestic or same-sex marriage partners), or establishing a set-aside fund through which the university could reimburse otherwise uncovered transition-related health-care costs for trans people on the state plan. After years of kicking the can down the road, the university eventually suggested that a trans employee simply sue for health care. This had the benefit for them, in a politically conservative state, of potentially being compelled to do something that would have cost the university political capital had it voluntarily offered some trans-affirming solution. Russell Toomey ultimately obliged, and as of this writing is the plaintiff in a suit against the State of Arizona, the Arizona Board of Regents, and the University of Arizona.

It has likewise proven challenging to coordinate a curricular program of any sort with so few administrative resources, across so many institutional silos. Should it be at the graduate or undergraduate level, or both? Should it admit new students for a stand-alone certificate or degree, or concentrate on developing a minor aimed at students already admitted to some major or graduate program? Should it have a core curriculum, or be entirely free form? What is "trans studies" anyway, and how do we teach it? Given that the Institute for LGBT Studies is not an instructional unit, any such program would need to be based in a department, or as an interdisciplinary program in the Graduate College—but which one? Faculty in the non-degree-granting departments would need to be cross-appointed as faculty in the degree-granting one, new courses created and cross-listed, and teaching schedules coordinated across departments and colleges. All of which is utterly possible in theory but virtually impossible in actual practice without administrative support staff or course releases for faculty administrators. Further support of that sort has not been forthcoming from the university, after the initial investment in the hiring initiative.

It is also the case that the trans studies faculty members who were hired, while certainly collegial with one another, do not all see eye to eye, have competing agendas and different visions for their careers, and experience a wide range of conflicting demands on their time. There are divisions between people in quantitative and behavioral studies and those in cultural studies, those in social sciences rather than humanities. There are disagreements about whether trans studies is about studying trans people or whether it's about looking at the world through a trans lens. There are people who just want to be left alone to do their own research, and people who have enthusiastically jumped into positions of responsibility in their home departments that have nothing to do with trans studies. There are people who want to build a curricular program, and people who don't. All of these routine sorts of challenges in building an interdisciplinary program are capable of being solved but currently require faculty to solve them on their own time, in ways that may not count as recognized university service activities.

The most dispiriting challenges have to do with direct and indirect forms of interpersonal, ideological, and institutional transphobia, sometimes coupled with racism. For instance, a trans faculty member experienced anonymous death threats from a student or students in a large lecture class, resulting in the class being reassigned to another instructor (while leaving in place trans and gender-nonconforming graduate teaching assistants who led the discussion sections). A trans faculty member was physically assaulted at an off-campus social event by the friend of another faculty member, without consequence. A trans faculty member who felt sexually harassed was told to take it as a compliment regarding their passability. Pronomial misgenderings, even after years of opportunity to practice addressing people as they ask to be addressed, are inexcusably frequent—including in a department head's solicitation of an external reviewer for a trans professor's tenure and promotion file. This has been a problem, too, for the grad students who have come to work with us, and for the undergrads in our classes, particularly if they are nonbinary or gender nonconforming and use gender-neutral pronouns. It should be stressed that, overall, the respective departments that have hired a majority of the trans faculty have been enthusiastically supportive of them. There are no out-and-out trans-exclusionary radical feminists or "gender-critical" feminists to contend with, no explicitly fundamentalist or ethno-nationalist bigots in our day-to-day working lives, no bathroom wars, and no great difficulty changing names and gender markers in administrative systems. Nevertheless, all of the trans faculty have experienced ambient, unevenly distributed, microaggressive forms of transphobia, even in ostensibly collegial relationships. These acts seem rooted in unconscious motives that are not recognized, acknowledged, or understood as such by people who do them, and are thus nearly impossible to address in a rational, problem-solving way.

The deepest problems with institutionalizing trans studies at Arizona are harbored within the Department of Gender and Women's Studies (GWS), where three of us have had our faculty appointments. While I've encountered a few departments of women's, gender, and sexuality studies that are truly supportive of trans scholars and scholarship, a cynical quip circulates among many of us who work in trans studies within them that such programs often constitute "structural violence against trans people." It is easy for us to be positioned as a threat to the political unity of "woman," as "queer theory's evil twin," as embodying a neoliberal identity politics, as white and therefore racist, as a distraction from "real issues," as poststructuralism pushed to the point of absurdity, as trigger-warning-happy snowflakes, or as bad objects who incite the wrong kinds of desire. We are positioned as the problems who become bigger problems when we talk about our problems. All of this is par for the course in the workaday world of the trans studies academic, but GWS at UA has a deeper dysfunction, given the particular ways that vocal and powerful minority factions within the department's faculty have construed feminism, queer theory, leftist politics, and race and mapped these ideological positions onto particular personalities and interpersonal dynamics. A department that has prided itself on its radicalism, theoretical acumen, attention to intersections of race/gender/sexuality, and specialization in borderlands feminisms and migration studies literally flung itself apart, to a significant degree, over its inability to deal with having the greatest concentration of trans faculty in a single department in all of academe. We simply could not be accommodated. It's not possible at this time to air everything that has happened with regard to trans studies, trans faculty, and trans students in the GWS Department, given that doing so could have legal consequences, as well as negative practical ramifications for those with ongoing employment or study at the university. Suffice it to say that what has transpired there motivated all of us in the department to leave.

After Trans Studies at Arizona

Despite the symbolic value of announcing the institutionalization of trans studies at UA, the initiative actually amounts to far less in practice than most imagine it to be from the outside. It is not nothing, and is perhaps as much as it can be, right now, given the institutional climate and the particular personalities involved. Eric, Russ, Eva, Francisco, and Z have all been tenured and promoted, and Max, who needed to pause his tenure clock, is on track for going up soon. I have been promoted to full. Russ has stepped back from active involvement in the Transgender Studies Research Cluster (TSRC) because of new professional responsibilities and a change in research focus, while continuing to pursue what could prove to be a landmark legal case for transgender employment rights and healthcare access nationwide.

While the prospect of a curricular program in trans studies is not on the near-term horizon, trans studies classes are being offered in various departments and programs, at both the graduate and undergraduate levels. There are clusters of doctoral students working on trans studies dissertations with individual faculty members. Given the dysfunction in the GWS Department and the continuing affiliation there of faculty who have in the past acted with perceived hostility toward trans faculty and students, we do not recommend the department for students working in this area. Eva Hayward was seeking to move her line to another department when the COVID-19 crisis temporarily halted that plan, Francisco Galarte has taken a job at the University of New Mexico, and I have retired. The mess in GWS is a serious blow to the trans studies initiative, but one that the department, and the university, seem unwilling or unable to address.

The Institute for LGBT Studies still provides administrative and fiscal support for the TSRC, but the editorial office of *TSQ* has moved with coeditor Francisco Galarte to New Mexico. The TSRC, now co-led by Eric Plemons and Z

Nicolazzo, convenes a regular reading group and semesterly social gatherings for faculty and grad students, and it has had some success in winning internal university grants for program activities; collaborations on major external grants are in the pipeline. The first of what is hoped to be an annual trans studies symposium was held in Fall 2019, and there's a plan to launch an endowment campaign to fund an annual lecture. I currently expect to be hired back as an emerita professor at a fraction of my current full-time equivalency to continue contributing to the TSRC from outside GWS, without having any additional responsibilities, while working—once again, though far from precariously—in a series of short-term visiting gigs at various institutions over the next several years, which is exactly what I want.

My sense, after nearly a decade of work institutionalizing trans studies at UA, after more than a quarter century of effort in the broader field, is that perhaps the idea of a traditional academic program, certainly one concentrated to a significant degree in a women's, gender, or sexuality studies department at a large research university, is not actually viable for transgender studies right now, given the cross-currents and headwinds of identity politics, the instability of the higher education sector as a whole, the larger sociopolitical, economic, and ecological circumstances in which we live, and the reality of structural transphobia. Better, perhaps, would be a more distributed model, with scholars and students dispersed across any number of institutions or beyond them all together, working in any number of programs and disciplines or outside them all, finding opportunities to come together periodically, here and there, in tightly knotted groups or more expansive groupings, for more intensive bursts of conversation and collaboration, deeper levels of study and training, denser networking, and heightened interactions between peers, mentors, students, artists, activists, and friends. That is, better perhaps the field as it has actually come to exist in the past half decade, within which trans studies at Arizona is just one node among many, rather than being imagined as a "flagship program" or the "epicenter" of the field. The gathering of energies that planted trans studies at Arizona will give it a persistent presence in that place, even as that energy dissipates in a flow toward and circulation between new locations, along emergent paths. It's all good.

There are still a couple of things I think the field of trans studies could use, that I would like to see accomplished before I actually retire, or at least before I die: the creation of an international transgender studies association that holds regular annual or biannual meetings, with which *TSQ* might become affiliated, and the establishment of a summer program or institute for intensive study, at the faculty and graduate level, perhaps as part of a low-residency degree or certification program in trans studies. I see these as small pieces of infrastructure that can provide a resource for keeping trans people alive, for using transness to learn and teach how we might better decenter human privilege in our cohabitation with the nonhuman world, extract all of our bodies from the coloniality of gender, untether ourselves from the racializing biopolitical assemblages that fasten on the flesh of us all in different ways, and heal from the wounded attachments to identity categories through which we live but that can thwart our collective work, in this moment of political, economic, and ecological crisis that demands our undivided attention. I would be delighted if somebody else decided to take the lead in working on those two infrastructural projects. Meanwhile I have a plan, to which I will turn my attention in the years ahead. So get busy, if you are so inclined, and stay tuned.

Susan Stryker, executive editor of *TSQ*, is professor emerita of gender and women's studies at the University of Arizona and Barbara Lee Distinguished Professor of Women's Leadership at Mills College.

Indigenist Origins

Institutionalizing Indigenous Queer and Trans Studies in Australia

MADI DAY

Abstract Indigenous queer and trans studies will be available as part of the Indigenous Studies major in the Bachelor of Arts program at Macquarie University beginning February 2020. Institutionalization of Indigenous queer and trans studies occurs in a context in which education and institutionalization have been tools of settler colonialism used against Aboriginal and Torres Strait Islander people. This article considers Aboriginal and Torres Strait Islander engagement with institutions in the discipline of Indigenous studies, and what this means for Indigenous queer and trans studies as it emerges in a tradition of Indigenist and decolonial thought.
Keywords Indigenous studies, queer studies, trans studies

In February 2020, Indigenous queer and trans studies became available as part of the Indigenous studies major in the Bachelor of Arts program at Macquarie University. The Department of Indigenous Studies offers three incremental classes that explore Indigenous queer and trans identities and activism as transformative of the social, cultural, and political landscapes of Australia and beyond. These units prioritize Indigenous queer and trans worldviews that challenge, enrich, and recalibrate students' understandings of community, culture, gender, sexuality, the body, and desire. Graduates of these classes will be proficient in critical engagement with historical and contemporary forms of settler colonialism, and the function of colonial conventions of sex/gender. This is the first offering of its kind in Australia. Institutionalization of Indigenous queer and trans studies occurs in a context in which education and institutionalization have been tools of settler colonialism used against Aboriginal and Torres Strait Islander people. In this piece, I consider Aboriginal and Torres Strait Islander engagement with institutions in the discipline of Indigenous studies, and what this means for Indigenous queer and trans studies as it emerges in a tradition of Indigenist and decolonial thought.

TSQ: Transgender Studies Quarterly * Volume 7, Number 3 * August 2020   **367**
DOI 10.1215/23289252-8553006   © 2020 Duke University Press

Here I implement the terms *Aboriginal* and *Torres Strait Islander people* to refer to the first peoples of the continent and surrounding bodies of land understood in a settler colonial context as Australia. I implement the term *Indigenous* to describe academic fields and engagements that may involve Indigenous people more broadly. I also use *Indigenous queer and trans people* to refer to communities in Australia who occupy identities that are both Indigenous and outside settler colonial understandings of sexuality and gender. While I recognize that *queer* and *trans* are different and separate terms in a Western context, such a divide is not always distinct among Aboriginal and Torres Strait Islander people. Terms like *Sistergirl* and *Brotherboy* are in use broadly to refer to transgender women and men, but they can also be used to refer to people of varying genders and sexualities because of their relational nature (Sullivan and Day 2019). I have omitted discussion of precolonial understandings of gender and sexuality from this piece, as well as conversations around intercommunity discrimination among Aboriginal and Torres Strait Islander people. I am limiting discussion of these issues for non-Indigenous audiences, given that they can and do use them against us (Clark 2014). While I recognize Indigenous queer and trans studies as a global discipline, I see its emergence in Australia as both distinctive and connected to global developments. While Native American and Two-Spirit scholars have contributed greatly to Indigenous queer and trans studies in Australia, it is important to recognize our contexts as socially, culturally, and politically separate and different. This article reflects my early optimism as a coconspirer with Andrew Farrell and Bronwyn Carlson in the institutionalization of Indigenous queer and trans studies at Macquarie University. My hopefulness stems from its founding in Indigenous studies as a discipline, and from a legacy of resistance and transformation lead by Aboriginal and Torres Strait Islander academics.

Indigenist Origins and Becoming Official

The histories of institutionalization and settler colonialism in Australia run parallel, particularly in relation to education. Aboriginal resistance to settler modes of education occurred as early as 1790, when Bennelong, a Wangal man whom historians consider the first Aboriginal person to arbitrate colonial and Aboriginal relations in Australia, escaped from Governor Arthur Phillip and his men after they kidnapped him with intent to educate him in European ways of life (Heiss and McCormack 2002). This was the beginning of not only a complex relationship between Bennelong and Phillip but also a tradition of settlers holding Aboriginal people against their will for the purpose of education. The first Aboriginal education institution opened on Dharug country in Parramatta, New South Wales, in 1815. Governor Lachlan Macquarie and missionary William Shelley removed Dharug children from their families to educate them as either domestic servants or manual laborers according to their sex (Brook and Kohen 1991)—which in itself demonstrates how settler colonial education has functioned to assimilate Aboriginal people into European ways of life, including rigid systems of sex/gender.

Institutionalization, to Aboriginal and Torres Strait Islander people, is complex in the sense that we have been educated and enculturated into a settler colonial system through the abduction and incarceration of our ancestors by religious and government institutions, and we have fought tirelessly to fully participate and incorporate our own knowledges into educational projects. Aboriginal and Torres Strait Islander cultures have always highly valued education. This is evident in our continued practices of traditional knowledge transfer as well as our dedication to full access to educational opportunities. However, due to violent settler colonial policies and actions, many Aboriginal and Torres Strait Islander people came to fear educational institutions as sites of abuse, racism, and child removal (Burridge and Chodkiewicz 2012). Our engagement with educational institutions is thus tainted by these histories. And yet, so many of us embrace them as a means of intellectual sovereignty, and of social and economic mobility (Rigney 2001).

Indigenous studies as a discipline is concerned with Indigenous engagement with higher-education institutions because, for Indigenous academics, investment in our communities and our futures bolsters our participation in this interdisciplinary field (Nakata 2006: 266). Indigenous studies differs from other academic disciplines in the sense that our work is informed and regulated by community benefit and interest. In Australia, the *Guidelines for Ethical Research in Australian Indigenous Studies* (AIATSIS 2011) produced by the Australian Institute of Aboriginal and Torres Strait Islander Studies (colloquially known as the AIATSIS guidelines) regulate how research is to be conducted with and for Aboriginal and Torres Strait Islander communities. While the discipline remains fraught owing to histories of how institutions and researchers have mistreated Indigenous peoples (Moreton-Robinson and Walter 2009), and while tensions between Indigenous and settler academics in the field remain high (Whittaker 2019), there is general acceptance of the principles outlined in the guidelines. These principles set an expectation that institutional outcomes of research in the discipline must be toward Indigenous self-determination and futures, and must benefit Aboriginal and Torres Strait Islander people.

It seems appropriate then, that in Australia, Indigenous queer and trans studies emerged in the field of Indigenous studies rather than the other way around. Indigenous queer and trans academics have been actively researching and writing within Indigenous studies for the past decade, reflecting the field's interdisciplinary nature through their varied focuses on politics, law, performance, visual arts, curatorial studies, geography, health, and media. In this way, Indigenous queer and trans studies began in an Aboriginal and Torres Strait Islander context long before 2020, through the work of Sandy O'Sullivan (2015), Maddee Clark (2015), Corrinne Tayce Sullivan (2018), Allison Whittaker (2016), and Andrew Farrell

(2016), to name a few. The formal institutionalization of Indigenous queer and trans studies occurs within a rich tradition of queer and trans Indigenist thought. This is an important distinction in relation to queer and trans research, in which information produced by settlers about Indigenous peoples is appropriated to validate settler projects and identities of similar character to those explored below.

Trans studies is in the early stages of institutionalization in Australia. Transgender theory, primarily from the United States, is gradually entering gender, sociology, and cultural studies curriculum. We are yet to see trans-specific units or departments. Since 2014, we have seen growth in trans-inclusive research in areas related to health and well-being (Department of Health and Human Services 2014), resulting in increased attention to Sistergirls, Brotherboys, and other Indigenous queer and transgender people as a vulnerable group (Western Australia Department of Health 2019). We appear in this research as victims of discrimination, as existing at the margins of the margins and subject to intersecting oppressions. For instance, "Aboriginal LGBTI people may experience inequalities in health and wellbeing outcomes as a consequence of determinants such as discrimination and marginalisation from within their own people, LGBTI populations and from non-Aboriginal people" (12). Simultaneously, such publications recognize the lack of data and research as key findings of their studies (15). Little information emerges other than acknowledgment that we do exist and we are, in fact, oppressed. So far, we have seen queer and trans health research extend the narrative of "a mismanaged or disadvantaged Indigenous public" (Whittaker 2019) in need of colonial interrogation and management.

Trans studies has consistently recognized rigid categorization and regulation of gender as Eurocentric and therefore distinctly colonial in relevant settings: "A rigid gender binary was instituted as part of the violence of colonialism; this binary was an attempt to eradicate more open gender possibilities" (Haefele-Thomas 2019: 241). However, this claim too often occurs in service of a narrative of timelessness in relation to trans identities. The quote above is from chapter 7 of *Introduction to Transgender Studies*, titled "Global Gender Diversity throughout the Ages: We Have Always Been with You" (240). While the chapter offers a critical and detailed account of the impacts of forced colonial gender binaries on Indigenous people, implying that transness has always existed can perpetuate a sense of trans settler exceptionalism, as if having a trans identity somehow exempts members of the settler society from practices of colonialism and cultural imperialism. Such a claim can be understood as a move toward settler nativism, or settler innocence: that is, as "an attempt to deflect a settler identity, while continuing to enjoy settler privilege and occupying stolen land" (Tuck and Yang 2012: 11). Claims such as these sustain skepticism around advancements in trans studies moving potentially toward white ends (Ellison et al. 2017). Precolonial gender diversity among Indigenous people does not validate the existence of trans settlers because, in the context of settler colonialism, settlers are not legitimately present on stolen Indigenous lands. In Australia, the United States, and any other lands occupied through ongoing land theft and genocide, settlers are present because of atrocities committed against Indigenous peoples. Indigenous queer and trans studies necessarily critiques and corrects settler colonial narratives that exclude or appropriate our stories and identities.

As Susan Stryker notes in her preface to Ardel Haefele-Thomas's *Introduction to Transgender Studies*, imagining oneself as part of a global transness requires a very complex and politically nuanced sense of "we" (Haefele-Thomas 2019: xxvii). The same is true for Aboriginal and Torres Strait Islander people. We are immeasurably diverse. Indigenous queer and trans people identify ourselves collectively and relationally according to experiences of colonialism, legacies of resistance, and connection to place (Farrell 2020). As the terms *Sistergirl* and *Brotherboy* imply, our worldviews are kincentric. That is to say, we understand our identities in relation to the people and places to which we are connected and accountable (Dudgeon and Bray 2019). This worldview informs our approach to research and institutions. Aboriginal and Torres Strait Islander academics have worked hard to incorporate our ontologies and epistemologies into institutional research practices, producing significant reform and foundations to build on in Indigenous studies and other disciplines (Martin and Mirraboopa 2003; Rigney 2006). These foundations make it possible to build Indigenous queer and trans studies as a field of interdisciplinary focus from a "particular and interested position" (Nakata 2007: 12). This Indigenist and decolonial tradition situates its practitioners as knowers and critics, settlers and their institutions as our subjects, and our communities as beneficiaries of our work.

Our commitment to other Aboriginal and Torres Strait Islander people and communities, in combination with our historically informed distrust of educational institutions, situates us in a unique way within them. We are, of course, under no illusions that settler colonial institutions are not exactly that. Indigenous queer and trans studies has been formally institutionalized on Dharug land at a university named after Governor Lachlan Macquarie, the man who decimated Dharug communities through massacres and removal of children for education with gendered and assimilationist ends (Brook and Kohen 1991). It emerges in a context of cultural resurgence and resistance in which high-ranking academic staff at Macquarie such as Bronwyn Carlson (Van Extel 2017) and Leanne Holt are leading public truth telling about Macquarie's legacy and working to contest the university's name in solidarity and collaboration with the Dharug community. Carlson (2019), the head of the Department of Indigenous Studies at Macquarie University, has also stated publicly that she has no loyalty to institutions—only to Aboriginal and Torres Strait Islander people. She is one of many Aboriginal and Torres Strait Islander academics continuing a tradition in Indigenous studies of working for Indigenous communities from within settler colonial institutions.

Indigenous queer and trans studies institutionalizes as a separate yet related discipline to Indigenous studies, building on the legacies of Aboriginal and Torres Strait Islander academics as well as a separate and related field vis-à-vis trans and queer research emanating from within settler colonial society. These origins are significant, for while Indigenous queer and trans studies connects to trans studies at intersections, the history of Aboriginal and Torres Strait Islander engagement with education institutions has defined our approach to research and our expectations of disciplines. There is much to be gained from global and cross-disciplinary collaborations between trans peoples. Certainly, we have our complications and differences, but it seems that many of us can agree that the rigid rules of gender and sexuality we have inherited are markedly settler colonial, and that we are ready for transformation. It is in this moment of recognition and resistance that Indigenous queer and trans studies becomes both relevant and official.

Madi Day is a research associate and higher degree research student in the Department of Indigenous Studies at Macquarie University. Their research focuses on the relationship between settler colonialism and heterosexuality in an Australian context, and Indigenous queer and trans strategies of resistance.

References

AIATSIS (Australian Institute of Aboriginal and Torres Strait Islander Studies). 2011. *Guidelines for Ethical Research in Australian Indigenous Studies.* Canberra: AIATSIS.

Brook, Jack, and James L. Kohen. 1991. *The Parramatta Native Institution and the Black Town: A History.* Vol. 15. Kensington: New South Wales University Press.

Burridge, Nina, and Andrew Chodkiewicz. 2012. "An Historical Overview of Aboriginal Education Policies in the Australian Context." In *Indigenous Education: A Learning Journey for Teachers, Schools, and Communities,* edited by Nina Burridge, Frances Whalan, and Karen Vaughan, 9–21. Rotterdam: Sense.

Carlson, Bronwyn. 2019. "Love and Hate at the Cultural Interface." Paper presented at the conference "Digital Intimacies 5.0: Structures, Cultures, Power," Monash University, Melbourne, December 10.

Clark, Maddee. 2014. "Against Authenticity CAL-Connections: Queer Indigenous Identities." *Overland*, no. 215: 30–36.

Clark, Maddee. 2015. "Indigenous Subjectivity in Australia: Are We Queer?" *Journal of Global Indigeneity* 1, no. 1. ro.uow.edu.au/jgi/vol1/iss1/7/.

Department of Health and Human Services. 2014. *Transgender and Gender Diverse Health and Wellbeing.* www2.health.vic.gov.au/about/publications/researchandreports/Transgender-and-gender-diverse-health-and-wellbeing.

Dudgeon, Pat, and Abigail Bray. 2019. "Indigenous Relationality: Women, Kinship, and the Law." *Genealogy* 3, no. 2: 23–34.

Ellison, Treva, Kai M. Green, Matt Richardson, and C. Riley Snorton. 2017. "We Got Issues: Toward a Black Trans*/Studies." *TSQ* 4, no. 2: 162–69.

Farrell, Andrew. 2016. "Lipstick Clapsticks: A Yarn and a Kiki with an Aboriginal Drag Queen." *AlterNative: An International Journal of Indigenous Peoples* 12, no. 5: 574–85.

Farrell, Andrew. 2020. "Identity and Place." *Archer*, no. 13. archermagazine.com.au/2020/01/archer-magazine-issue-13-the-first-nations-issue/.

Haefele-Thomas, Ardel. 2019. *Introduction to Transgender Studies*. New York: Columbia University Press.

Heiss, Anita, and Terri McCormack. 2002. "Bennelong." *Barani: Sydney's Aboriginal History*. www.sydneybarani.com.au/sites/bennelong/.

Martin, Karen, and Booran Mirraboopa. 2003. "Ways of Knowing, Being, and Doing: A Theoretical Framework and Methods for Indigenous and Indigenist Re-search." *Journal of Australian Studies* 27, no. 76: 203–14.

Moreton-Robinson, Aileen, and Maggie Walter. 2009. "Indigenous Methodologies in Social Research." In *Social Research Methods*, edited by Maggie Walter, 1–18. South Melbourne: Oxford University Press.

Nakata, Martin. 2006. "Australian Indigenous Studies: A Question of Discipline." *Australian Journal of Anthropology* 17, no. 3: 265–75.

Nakata, Martin. 2007. "The Cultural Interface." *Australian Journal of Indigenous Education* 36, no. S1: 7–14.

O'Sullivan, Sandy. 2015. "Queering Ideas of Indigeneity: Response in Repose: Challenging, Engaging, and Ignoring Centralising Ontologies, Responsibilities, Deflections, and Erasures." *Journal of Global Indigeneity* 1, no. 1. ro.uow.edu.au/jgi/vol1/iss1/5/.

Rigney, Lester-Irabinna. 2001. "A First Perspective of Indigenous Australian Participation in Science: Framing Indigenous Research towards Indigenous Australian Intellectual Sovereignty." Canberra: National Centre for Indigenous Studies, Australian National University. ncis.anu.edu.au/_lib/doc/LI_Rigney_First_perspective.pdf.

Rigney, Lester-Irabinna. 2006. "Indigenist Research and Aboriginal Australia." In *Indigenous People's Wisdom and Power: Affirming Our Knowledge through Narrative*, edited by Julian E. Kunnie and Nomalungelo I. Goduka, 32–50. Aldershot, UK: Ashgate.

Sullivan, Corrinne Tayce. 2018. "Majesty in the City: Experiences of an Aboriginal Transgender Sex Worker in Sydney, Australia." *Gender, Place, and Culture* 25, no. 12: 1681–1702.

Sullivan, Corrinne Tayce, and Madi Day. 2019. "Indigenous Transmasculine Australians and Sex Work." *Emotion, Space, and Society* 32, art. 100591. www.sciencedirect.com/science/article/abs/pii/S1755458619300271.

Tuck, Eve, and K. Wayne Yang. 2012. "Decolonization Is Not a Metaphor." *Decolonization: Indigeneity, Education, and Society* 1, no. 1. jps.library.utoronto.ca/index.php/des/article/view/18630.

Van Extel, C. 2017. "Most Indigenous People Will Call for Statues to Be Removed." *RN Breakfast*, August 29. Sydney: Australian Broadcasting Corporation.

Western Australia Department of Health. 2019. *Western Australian Lesbian, Gay, Bisexual, Transgender, Intersex (LGBTI) Health Strategy 2019–2024*. Perth: Health Networks, Western Australian Department of Health.

Whittaker, Alison. 2016. *Lemons in the Chicken Wire*. Broome, WA: Magabala.

Whittaker, Alison. 2019. "Not My Problem: On *The Colonial Fantasy*." *Sydney Review of Books*, November 8. sydneyreviewofbooks.com/maddison-colonial-fantasy/.

On the Intersection of Somatechnics and Transgender Studies

CAITLIN JANZEN, HOLLY RANDELL-MOON,
IRIS VAN DER TUIN, and MELISSE VROEGINDEWEIJ

Abstract The relationship between transgender studies and somatechnics has been generative. In this reflection on the intersection between somatechnics and transgender studies, the editorial collective of the *Somatechnics* journal provides a brief outline of what has been accomplished in the latter through an engagement with the former. This reflection is not intended to be an exhaustive review of trans*-somatechnics relations. Instead, here we highlight topics and modes of study that are indicative of critical interest in trans* matters at this time and how these matters intersect with our related areas of research. We outline how the somatechnical understanding of transgender as relational and constitutively realized through particular kinds of sociopolitical contexts explains the critical purchase of somatechnical investigations to trans* matters. We also cover somatechnics and transgender studies' engagements with technologies of mobility, race, and coloniality as well as media. We suggest that work in the journal on somatechnics and transgender studies constitutes a trans-substantial dialogue that trans*-identified scholars make specific via their contributions to social sciences and the humanities.

Keywords somatechnics, transgender studies, race, coloniality, flows, bodies, technologies

In this reflection on the intersection between somatechnics and transgender studies, the editorial collective of the *Somatechnics* journal provides a brief outline of what has been accomplished in the latter through an engagement with the former. That is, what kinds of transgender studies have been made possible through a somatechnics approach to bodies and technologies? This reflection is not intended to be an exhaustive review of trans*-somatechnics relations (for that we encourage readers to peruse the journal at length!). Instead, here we highlight topics and modes of study that are indicative of critical interest in trans* matters at this time and how these matters intersect with our related areas of research. In his seminal book, *Black on Both Sides*, C. Riley Snorton (2017: 2) theorizes "trans" as "more about a movement with no clear origin and no point of arrival," which intersects with "blackness" as signifying "an enveloping environment and

TSQ: Transgender Studies Quarterly ★ Volume 7, Number 3 ★ August 2020 **374**
DOI 10.1215/23289252-8553020 © 2020 Duke University Press

condition of possibility." As a collective comprising cis-gender, queer, white scholars, the authors benefit from social categorizations that enable mobility across critical, political, and geographical terrain. Some of us write from Indigenous Country as a result of the transportation of economies, peoples, and racial ideologies across oceans and lands, which have enabled contemporaneous positions of white settler privilege. We are conscious of the possibilities and limitations enabled by our engagement with transgender studies. Our comments here build on the important contributions trans* scholars, activists, and artists have made to the pages of *Somatechnics*, and we hope that our somatechnics work offers a space for trans* voices, experiences, and theories, particularly for Indigenous and trans* peoples of color.

The relationship between transgender studies and somatechnics has been generative. Informed by an understanding of the body (soma) and technology (technics) as constitutively interdependent (see Sullivan 2014), *Somatechnics* publishes work in a variety of disciplines that examines the body-technology nexus. Somatechnics as a methodology and theory has been purposefully left to construction by its different applications. That is, there are no founders or foundations for somatechnics as such. Scholars, activists, and educators participating in the Somatechnics Research Network and themed symposia were encouraged to define the concept through the productive relations of their work in a move that we would now, with Karen Barad's 2007 *Meeting the Universe Halfway: Quantum Physics and the Entanglement of Matter and Meaning*, call an onto-epistemological move of knowing-in-being. *Somatechnics* in some sense codifies the term and by way of publishing and marketing exigencies offers a definition in the journal blurb. In practice, somatechnics research is improvised by critical attention to queer, feminist, and critical race matters and applied to explicate how bodies are technologized and become the site for politics, performance, philosophy, media, design, sport, medicine, law, education, and environment, among other assemblages. For the purposes of this reflective piece, Nikki Sullivan (2014: 188) offers a useful definition of *somatechnics* as investigating how the body is "continuously engendered in relation to others and to a world." Iris van der Tuin and Holly Randell-Moon (2019) explored this engendering further in a recent editorial on the somatechnics of social categorizations in which the socially informed methods of identifying and differentiating bodies can be usefully understood as somatechnical. Sullivan (2014: 188) continues their definition of the term by suggesting:

> The categories of being that are integral to our (un)becoming-with, and the orientation(s) that shape them, are somatechnological (rather than simply natural or cultural, internal or external to us, enabling or oppressive). For example,

transgender, like forms of bodily being commonly presumed *not* to be techno-
logically produced, is a heterogeneous somatechnological construct that comes to
matter in contextually specific ways and in relation to other discursive formations.

This somatechnical understanding of transgender as relational and constitutively
realized through particular kinds of sociopolitical contexts explains the critical
purchase of somatechnical investigations to trans* matters. Notable trans* special
issue themes have featured in the journal, including "Trans Temporalities"
(Fisher, Katri, and Phillips 2017) and "Cinematic/Trans*/Bodies" (Keegan, Horak,
and Steinbock 2018a), along with significant individual articles (Bremer 2013;
Sundén 2015; Weaver 2013). These self-identified "trans" topics do not account for
the diversity of approaches to bodies, gender, embodiment, technology, and
representations that fall within the purview of transgender studies. Aside from the
intentional work of defining (or purposely not defining) the parameters of both
the journal and somatechnics as a methodology and theory by, for example,
planning special issues to intervene in emerging interdisciplinary conversations
and areas of theorization, the selection of books to be reviewed forms another
mode of engagement for an academic journal. A survey of the book review editor's
mailbox over the past few years provides insight into how authors and publishers
position *Somatechnics* in terms of scope, as well as (inter- or trans)disciplinarily
and politically. Our book review editor, Caitlin Janzen, has been very fortunate to
receive a wide range of new books on trans* theory and identity published over
the past few years. In fact, it is evident based both on the books we receive from
publishers and the reviewers we have been privileged to feature, that *Somatechnics*
is increasingly considered a venue for trans* theorization. This is in part due to
our lineage as a research network founded in 2005 at Macquarie University in
Sydney, Australia, and based at the Institute for LGBT Studies at the University of
Arizona in the United States during the 2010s, and partially due to those past
issues mentioned above. In any event, it is a designation that we nourish by
providing a space of engagement for the ideas and propositions put forward in
these new developments in trans* theory.

These engagements are at least two-way discussions. In the strongest
reviews, not only are the arguments of the book authors' brought forward, but the
reviewers (trans*-identified writers and theorists themselves) write back to the
authors in a trans-substantial dialogue, pushing the arguments beyond their
original problematics (both in context and communities) and insisting on an
even deeper intersectional analysis that is responsive to anticolonial, antiracist,
and critical dis/ability movements. For example, in a review of Aren Z. Aizura's
Mobile Subjects: Transnational Imaginaries of Gender Reassignment (2018), Nael
Bhanji (2020) reiterates the author's analysis of destination gender-reassignment

surgery as a form of "biomedical tourism" (Aizura), writing, "Mobility is not a universal right but a neoliberal fantasy that has material effects. Delimited by the differential positioning of bodies, and constrained by the realities of capitalism, the allure of transsexual reinvention is always already haunted by the specter of racialized otherness." Similarly, in the same issue of *Somatechnics* C. L. Quinan (2020) reviews Toby Beauchamp's (2019) *Going Stealth: Transgender Politics and U.S. Surveillance Practices.* Again, the ethical implications of homonormative and transnormative politics and desires arise, this time in the strategies of transgender advocacy groups. Quinan (2020) highlights Beauchamp's analysis of how the inability of "some mainstream transgender rights organizations . . . to address how the policing of gender is intertwined with that of racial difference" results in "strategies and approaches that actually reconsolidate US nationalism and allow for increased policing of those who fall outside normative categories." As Beauchamp's analysis illustrates, the surveillance technologies exacted on and resisted by gender-nonconforming bodies have been perfected through centuries of practice on colonized, racialized, and disabled bodies (on this, see Simone Browne's [2015] pivotal *Dark Matters: On the Surveillance of Blackness*).

While the above books and reviews point to the enduring life and death necessity of theorizing the trans* body as it is made visible through inscriptions of gender, race, class, and dis/ability, there is a contemporaneous indication that the body is just the beginning in the future of transgender theory. In *Going Stealth* as well as in Cáel M. Keegan's (2018) *Lana and Lilly Wachowski: Sensing Transgender*, which was reviewed in *Somatechnics* by Atalia Israeli-Nevo (2019), trans* is extended beyond the corporeal to do more than identity work. In both books, trans* is skillfully employed as an analytic. In Keegan's reading of the Wachowski sisters' filmography, trans* is innovatively expanded into an immersive aesthetic experience. Thus Keegan (2018: 6) "evolv[es] the cinematic sensorium in the same manner that trans* disrupts, rearranges and evolves discrete genders and sexes." As his reviewer, Israeli-Nevo (2019: 414), identifies, however, "throughout the book it seems that it can also be the other way around; through his reading, one can start to engage in the notion of cinema as a technology of trans*. Keegan's sensorial reading invites us to feel differently the trans* body." Hence trans* technologies, trans* epistemologies, trans* aesthetics, and trans* analytics are at once sutured to, borne out of, and enacted on bodies (some more than others), and yet they are not confined to the corporeal.

The increasingly "anticolonial turn" in the book reviews is illustrative of a critical inquiry into the racialized assemblages that inform transgender studies but also the critical purchase of somatechnics for understanding the racialized constitution of bodies. The first issue of *Somatechnics*, entitled "Combat Breathing: State Violence and the Body in Question," suggests that Frantz Fanon's critical corpus encapsulates how "the indissociable relation between technologies and bodies is always bought into uncompromising focus" (Perera and Pugliese 2011: 1–2). As the editors Suvendrini Perera and Joseph Pugliese note, "To be on the receiving end of state violence is always to be reduced to a body in question" (2). Returning to Snorton's account of the movement of trans* into blackness, the somatechnics of race and whiteness demarcate the racializing assemblages and function of coloniality in biopolitically producing bodies for state violence. At the same time, somatechnics' understanding of bodies as performed and lived in movement can also illustrate the experiential modes of refusal to these forms of violence and outline how bodies and communities have always existed outside biopolitical state vectors. In a later editorial for *Somatechnics*, Randell-Moon (2019) discusses how Jasbir K. Puar's *The Right to Maim* (2017) offers somatechnical insights into the intersectional capacitation and debilitation of bodies which are tied to racialized biopolitics. In her discussion of the relationship between trans* bodies and the right to maim, Puar (2017: 56) distinguishes between trans becoming and becoming trans in the following way: "Trans becoming masquerades as a teleological movement, as if one could actually become trans" in a "linear telos, as a prognosis that becomes the body's contemporary diagnosis and domesticates the trans body into the regulatory norms of permanence." Becoming trans* highlights the "impossibility of linearity, permanence, and end points" (56). As with her previous work on homonationalism (2007), Puar asks queer scholars and activists to consider what is at stake in the incorporation of queer and trans* rights into state recognition and who is able to embody "progress" as a signifier of state benevolence. In the settler colonial context from which Randell-Moon writes as a "beneficiary" of state violence, and which recently "celebrated" marriage equality, what does it mean to have identity recognition yoked to a state that continues the failure to recognize Indigenous sovereignties? During the Australian Marriage Law Postal Survey, the Sistergirls of the Tiwi Islands and other Indigenous trans* and queer peoples contested the terms of state equality by pointing out how the transmission of the survey was in English and the presumption of a home address for receiving it posited a particular kind of Australian subject as a respondent to state address (Noyes 2017). This activism highlights how Indigenous and First Nations sovereignties, relations, and identities remain paramount and critical to livability as trans*. The strand of somatechnics work focused on coloniality and critical race studies may prove helpful for disclosing how transgender studies and subjects emerge from specific geographical and historical locations that are "the product of a largely . . . settler culture" (Aizura et al. 2014: 308).

And yet it must be acknowledged that there is also a version of somatechnics that focuses on questions of gender and sexuality, including in intersections with transgender studies, that leaves somatechnics racially unmarked with an assumed whiteness. The journal has so far published only one article by a self-identified Indigenous author, and, despite the provocation of the first issue, investigations of Indigenous-specific matters remain marginal in the journal. As the current editorial collective, we have addressed the white focus of somatechnics by diversifying the editorial board to include more scholars of color and Indigenous scholars. We are committed to producing multifaceted and rich discussions that both consider race as a primary technology that engenders the body through its enactments of difference, and consider how technology is always already equipped with both racializing and imperialist functions. We look forward to analyses that imagine possibilities for recoding and harnessing technology for the aims of resistance and resurgence.

What is transmitted through a somatechnics lens delimits particular areas of focus and draws attention to modes of communication and representation. In their editorial introduction for "Cinematic/Trans*/Bodies," Cáel M. Keegan, Laura Horak, and Eliza Steinbock (2018b: 1) offer that cinema engenders bodies that "touch each other, constitute each other." In outlining cinematic relations as trans*, the editors, as we understand it, are suggesting that trans* as somatechnics forms assemblages that (however temporarily) orient bodies to screen. Such work is productive for understanding media technologies and their flows. In Randell-Moon's field of research in media and communications, terms such as *convergence*, *seriality*, and *transmedia*, for instance, constitute an accepted form of grammar, but their theoretical genealogy as linked to cultural notions of biological variation, incorporation, and divergence could be further unpacked. Accounts of transmedia rarely probe the genealogies and orientations of what "trans" means in terms of media being sent "across" systems and formats. As Susan Stryker, Paisley Currah, and Lisa Jean Moore (2008: 11) argue, there are many different ways of conceiving "trans," each with political implications for how this substrate engenders relations. They suggest that "trans-" "marks the difference between the implied nominalism of 'trans' and the explicit relationality of 'trans-,' which remains open-ended and resists premature foreclosure by attachment to any single suffix" (11). How might trans- methodologies then account for the relationships engendered by the trans-ing process of spreading media across spaces and the cultivation of particular media audiences therein? (see also Chen and Olivares 2014).

Our mentioning of a "trans-substantial dialogue" above captures on many levels what transgender studies brings to the humanities and social sciences in the widest sense possible, and to somatechnics research specifically, and what it is that trans*-identified scholars make specific via their contributions to special issues, journal articles, and conversational (critical and creative) book reviews. The study and theorization of the body-technology-world relationship in trans- (including trans*) keys can help deepen our scholarly understanding of transmedia but also other phenomena such as transgenerational, transnational, and even transdisciplinary flows. Indeed, how might trans- methodologies account for the relationships engendered by the trans-ing process of disseminating technics, subjects, or discourses across spaces and through time, and the cultivation of particular classified technologies, bodies, or identities therein? Somatechnics and transgender studies are about the dialoguing across human-human, human-nonhuman, natural-cultural divides that are internal or external to us, and that may be enabling or oppressive, in various milieus and environments. Such dialogue seeks to radically upset the long-treasured dichotomies of organic and technological, then and now, us and them, by occupying a space of imbrication, entanglement, and mutuality.

Van der Tuin has written previously about trans-substantial dialoguing across identitarian domains, a form of dialoguing that we, as an editorial collective, engage in both among ourselves and in our work with authors and reviewers. In *Generational Feminism: New Materialist Introduction to a Generative Approach*, van der Tuin (2015) reflected on reading and affectively relating to Stryker's 1994 article "My Words to Victor Frankenstein above the Village of Chamounix: Performing Transgender Rage," a relating that was based on trans-substantial dialogue. Stryker's critical engagement powerfully transmits the point about the need to horizontalize somatechnically produced inequalities. Notably at a crucial point in the original text, the creature learns to position itself in relation to stories of European imperial and colonial discovery, weeping "over the hapless fate of" the "original inhabitants" of what are now known as the Americas (Shelley 1993: 92). These elements of self-subjectification reiterate how settler colonial logics underprop somatechnical constitutions of the self and relations with others. Van der Tuin wrote about Stryker's text as addressing the performativity of boundary-work, as acting as a reminder of where lines are drawn and how Stryker and her readers are all implicated in such boundary-work. Echoing Sullivan's somatechnological enablement and oppression, we learn and reflect on the fact that "boundary-work closes down as it opens up. In fact, even in its oppressive nature, a closing-down is never final" (van der Tuin 2015: 7). Readers of "My Words" are affected by Stryker's style, her courage, and the engagement with her own body, the emergent bodies of those who identify as trans*, the body politic, and Mary Shelley's novel *Frankenstein; or, The Modern Prometheus*. Previously, van der Tuin testified that this affection got her going, that it is part of a "generative force that infuses the feminist archive" (7–8) by way of what she would call, with her *Somatechnics* colleagues, a "trans-substantial dialogue."

Caitlin Janzen is a PhD candidate in sociology at York University. Her current work brings together feminist theory, psychoanalysis, and cultural studies to explore the aesthetics and ethics of aggression in the feminine. Caitlin has published in *Hypatia, Psychoanalysis, Culture and Society*, and *Continuum: Journal of Media and Cultural Studies*.

Holly Randell-Moon is senior lecturer in the School of Indigenous Australian Studies, Charles Sturt University, Australia. Her publications on popular culture, biopower, and gender and sexuality have appeared in the edited book collection *Television Aesthetics and Style* (2013) as well as the journals *Feminist Media Studies, Social Semiotics*, and *Refractory*. Along with Ryan Tippet, she is the editor of *Security, Race, Biopower: Essays on Technology and Corporeality* (2016). She is coeditor of the journal *Somatechnics*.

Iris van der Tuin is professor in theory of cultural inquiry at Utrecht University. Trained as a feminist epistemologist and working as an interdisciplinarian, Iris works at the intersection of philosophies of science and the humanities (including science and technology studies), cultural theory, and cultural inquiry.

Melisse Vroegindeweij is an interdisciplinary scholar specializing in gender and postcolonial studies. She is a student in the research master program Media, Art, and Performance Studies at Utrecht University, and her current research interests are climate racism, greenwashing, and responsible storytelling.

Acknowledgments

We would like to acknowledge the sovereignty of the Wiradjuri peoples on whose land Charles Sturt University Dubbo campus is located and pay respects to elders past, present, and . . . emerging! We would also like to acknowledge that Toronto is situated on the traditional land of the Huron-Wendat, the Seneca, and the Mississaugas of the Credit River. This unceded meeting place is still home to many Indigenous people from across Turtle Island and is the subject of the Dish with One Spoon Wampum Belt Covenant, an agreement between the Iroquois Confederacy and Confederacy of the Ojibwe and allied nations to peaceably share and care for the resources around the Great Lakes.

References

Aizura, Aren Z. 2018. *Mobile Subjects: Transnational Imaginaries of Gender Reassignment.* Durham, NC: Duke University Press.

Aizura, Aren Z., Trystan Cotton, Carsten Balzer/Carla LaGata, Marcia Ochoa, and Salvador Vidal-Oritz. 2014. "Introduction." *TSQ* 1, no. 3: 308–19.

Barad, Karen. 2007. *Meeting the Universe Halfway: Quantum Physics and the Entanglement of Matter and Meaning.* Durham, NC: Duke University Press.

Beauchamp, Toby. 2019. *Going Stealth: Transgender Politics and U.S. Surveillance Practices.* Durham, NC: Duke University Press.

Bhanji, Nael. 2020. Review of *Mobile Subjects: Transnational Imaginaries of Gender Reassignment*, by Aren Z. Aizura. *Somatechnics* 10, no. 1: 142–44.

Bremer, Signe. 2013. "Penis as Risk: A Queer Phenomenology of Two Swedish Transgender Women's Narratives on Gender Correction." *Somatechnics* 3, no. 2: 329–50.

Browne, Simone. 2015. *Dark Matters: On the Surveillance of Blackness*. Durham, NC: Duke University Press.

Chen, Jian, and Lisette Olivares. 2014. "Transmedia." *TSQ* 1, nos. 1–2: 245–48.

Fisher, Simon D. Elin, Ido H. Katri, and Rasheedah Phillips, eds. 2017. "Trans Temporalities." Special issue, *Somatechnics* 7, no. 1.

Israeli-Nevo, Atalia. 2019. Review of *Lana and Lily Wachowski*, by Cáel M. Keegan. *Somatechnics* 9, nos. 2–3: 411–16.

Keegan, Cáel. 2018. *Lana and Lilly Wachowski: Sensing Transgender*. Urbana: University of Illinois Press.

Keegan, Cáel M., Laura Horak, and Eliza Steinbock, eds. 2018a. "Cinematic/Trans*/Bodies." Special issue, *Somatechnics* 8, no. 1.

Keegan, Cáel M., Laura Horak, and Eliza Steinbock. 2018b. "Cinematic/Trans*/Bodies Now (and Then, and to Come)." *Somatechnics* 8, no. 1: 1–13.

Noyes, Jenny. 2017. "'We Want to Be Heard': NT Sistergirls Say Plebiscite Ignores Them." *Sydney Morning Herald*, August 17. www.smh.com.au/lifestyle/we-want-to-be-heard-nt-sistergirls -say-plebiscite-ignores-them-20170816-gxxgkz.html.

Perera, Suvendrini, and Joseph Pugliese. 2011. "Introduction: Combat Breathing: State Violence and the Body in Question." *Somatechnics* 1, no. 1: 1–14.

Puar, Jasbir K. 2007. *Terrorist Assemblages: Homonationalism in Queer Times*. Durham, NC: Duke University Press.

Puar, Jasbir K. 2017. *The Right to Maim: Debility, Capacity, Disability*. Durham, NC: Duke University Press.

Quinan, C. L. 2020. Review of *Going Stealth: Transgender Politics and U.S. Surveillance Practices*, by Toby Beauchamp. *Somatechnics* 10, no. 1: 137–42.

Randell-Moon, Holly. 2019. Editorial. *Somatechnics* 9, no. 1: v–ix.

Shelley, Mary. 1993. *Frankenstein; or, The Modern Prometheus*. Hertfordshire, UK: Wordsworth Classics.

Snorton, C. Riley. 2017. *Black on Both Sides: A Radical History of Trans Identity*. Minneapolis: University of Minnesota Press.

Stryker, Susan. 1994. "My Words to Victor Frankenstein above the Village of Chamounix: Performing Transgender Rage." *GLQ* 1, no. 3: 237–54.

Stryker, Susan, Paisley Currah, and Lisa Jean Moore. 2008. "Introduction: Trans-, Trans, or Transgender?" *WSQ* 36, nos. 3–4: 11–22.

Sullivan, Nikki. 2014. "Somatechnics." *TSQ* 1, nos. 1–2: 187–90.

Sundén, Jenny. 2015. "Temporalities of Transition: Trans- Temporal Femininity in a Human Musical Automaton." *Somatechnics* 5, no. 2: 197–216.

van der Tuin, Iris. 2015. *Generational Feminism: New Materialist Introduction to a Generative Approach*. Lanham, MD: Rowman and Littlefield.

van der Tuin, Iris, and Holly Randell-Moon. 2019. "Editorial: The Somatechnics of Social Categorizations." *Somatechnics* 9, nos. 2–3: v–xi.

Weaver, Harlan. 2013. "Monster Trans: Diffracting Affect, Reading Rage." *Somatechnics* 3, no. 2: 287–306.

Egg Theory's Early Style

GRACE LAVERY

Abstract This essay contemplates an enduring form of reasoning it titles "egg theory": the type of reasoning that trans people use, prior to transition, to prove transition's impossibility or fruit-lessness. It follows this reasoning in a critical and ironic framing in the work of the novelist and critic Sybil Lamb and then, in a less ironic mode, through some essays of Eve Sedgwick and, more broadly, the tranche of queer theory that her work continues to inspire. Egg theory's hostility to the logic of transition inheres in queer theory's own insistence on universality and virtuality as key aspects of queer politics. The essay concludes by considering, through Freud's "Schreber Case" and Dali's "Metamorphosis of Narcissus," alternatives to egg theory for approaching the condition of the egg before it hatches, the trans person before transition.

Keywords egg theory, Eve Sedgwick, Sybil Lamb

If every refusal is, finally, a loyalty to some other bond in the present or past, refusal is simultaneously preservation as well. The mask thus conceals the loss, but preserves (and negates) this loss through its concealment. The mask has a double function which is the double function of melancholy. The mask is taken on through the process of incorporation which is a way of inscribing and then wearing a melancholic identification in and on the body; in effect, it is the sig-nification of the body in the mold of the Other who has been refused.
—Judith Butler, "Prohibition, Psychoanalysis, and the Heterosexual Matrix"

What the neurotic shrinks back from is not castration, but from turning his castration into what the Other lacks. He shrinks back from turning his castration into something positive, namely, the guarantee of the function of the Other, this Other that steals away in the indeterminate echo of significations, this Other in which the subject no longer sees himself except as fate, but fate that has no end, fate that gets lost in the ocean of histories.
—Jacques Lacan, *Anxiety: The Seminar of Jacques Lacan, Book X*

TSQ: Transgender Studies Quarterly ∗ Volume 7, Number 3 ∗ August 2020 **383**
DOI 10.1215/23289252-8553034 © 2020 Duke University Press

never ever tr*nsition

One only becomes an egg in retrospect, when one has hatched, and the chick has emerged. So I remember being told, in the very early part of my transition, that I had been, until now, an egg, and—as powerfully rooted in a belief in latency as I found myself—I resented it deeply, this unlovely shadow of an unchosen object that, therefore, I had always (not yet) been. Thirty-four years of one's life, one hopes, are more than mere latency—and less, too—and I recoiled from the notion that I was in a shell, "a shell of a man," as the cliché goes. D. A. Miller begins his monograph *Bringing Out Roland Barthes* (1992: 3) with a fantasy of having been close to the man himself: "Twenty years ago in Paris, long before I, how you say, *knew myself*, a fellow student told me he had seen Roland Barthes late one evening at the Saint Germain Drugstore."[1] I never met Roland Barthes or Barbara Johnson, but, if I had, it would have been in boy drag. Was I, even then, tucked into a shell, insincere or stupid or both? *Mais non*, of course not. Still, to be called an egg is not to be insulted: by the time one is called one, it must be understood that one is *not* one, or not one any longer. An egg is displaced in time, "retconned" back into one's own being; a protocol for a new, and newly incommensurable, sense-making procedure. Just because one cannot say "I am an egg," then, without falling afoul of the liar's paradox, does not mean that there aren't eggs—any more than the same problematic proves that there are no liars. (Eggs are not liars, again by definition.) Just because one cannot point to a text as an egg text, therefore, does not mean that there are none as such. It simply means that "egg" is a heuristic that necessitates deployment of the judgment of the interpreter, that any such deployments reflect the observer's judgment as much as they depict the egg.

But: eggs have theories. Chiefly, the egg's theory is that they (he, she, ze, etc.) cannot transition. Not, generally, *must* not—though doubtless beneath the sacerdotal cassocks of a few "gender critical" ministers one can catch a glimpse of chalazae.[2] Egg theory is not generally ethical, but technical. One simply cannot. Which among us, given the chance, would not? But of course it is not so simple; indeed, the categories at issue are endlessly complicated, existing on different ontological orders (sex and gender, for example), and battened by chaotic forces so powerful and incoherent (desire, say, or sexuality, or "socialization") that to attempt something like a sex change would not so much be malicious as it would be gauche.

The second step of egg theory is its abstraction, via a curious and ambivalent universalism, into a set of general observations about a system in which the desire is found aerosolized into a fine spray. Here is egg theory at its purest, a medium of thought form and desire, a desire with no object and with, perhaps, not even a subject to speak of; here, at last, is the compensatory hallucination of a system of delight and foreclosure. We may have different names for this system—we may call it "affect," we may call it "queer," we may call it "aesthetic"; there are plenty of other names—all that is required is its ontology be both virtual and plastic. And it must assure us that transition is both impossible and inevitable, without exposing the dialectical negative of that contradictory image to too much light.

The punk trans poet and novelist Sybil Lamb (n.d.) lays out the logic of egg theory in a broken, split manifesto titled "You Best Never Ever Tr*nsition, Tr*nny." It begins:

> DETRANSITION !!! if you are one of the 1:12000 people born with GID, if your assigned gender is not your gendxer ID, if you are a fag who thinks dressing like a woman will get you more boyfriends, then you are crazy. your head is all fucked up and you are a social pariah. NEVER EVER TRANSITION. becoming a tr@nny these days means comiting yourself to years of being a gender mutant on the fringes of society. alientaion and discriination and violence are your only possible rewards. best case scenario you can get a job in porn. she-male yum dot com pays $500 for a 2 hour photo shoot. all tr*nnys get to do for the rest of their life is attend support groups and write volues of tr@nny essays. do you really want to spend the rest of your life as a trans intellectual ?? i mean sometimes i get invited to do a workshop at a tr*nny conference but its been a while since that happened and people know i talk alot of nasty hatefull dhit and swear too much. and i never got a free train ticket or motel room outta doing a tr4nny conference.

It hits like a blizzard. Lamb's irony is of that relentless, manic kind that cannot finally be forced to line up on one side or the other of its apparent meaning: it is both a bitter pastiche of egg ideology and its no less bitter reinstantiation. It begins with scarcity: only "1:12000" are "born with GID," and access to transition depends on, even in the virtual domain of desire, a kind of mathematical accreditation—unless I can say with confidence that I am one of this number (and who could), then I count myself out. The irony begins to separate into yolk and albumen in the following sentences, however, with the alienation of the "tr*nny" being, also, a ticket to a more romantic being, "fucked up" and "a gender mutant." A little more sexy. Yet the irony does not settle into mere parallelism. Rather, a second pairing takes precedence over "pariah"/"mutant," which opposes the two jobs that a "tr*nny" is qualified to discharge: porn ("best case scenario") and being a "trans intellectual," which pays less well and seems, perhaps, to require one to moderate one's language. Another specifically trans dyke dimension of this reasoning, another clue that this is egg theory, cast back in time from a hatched present, rather than simply propaganda: under the conditions of patriarchy, to be a woman is to desire not to be, so the transsexual desire oscillates around a gravitational center that can never be inhabited until the abolition of patriarchy in general.

Lamb (n.d.) continues:

> BROTHERS AND SISTERS ! TR*NSEXUALITY IS FUCKING HORRIBLE ! never ever transition. I mean first off do you really identify as the other gender ?? do you even act more like or kinna physically resemble the other gender ?? such qualifications are highly subjective and arbitrary. If your a tr*nny or junior tr*nny cadet then you should know by now that gender, at least in the modern western understanding is actually about 8 factors including a lot of socialization and other peoples perceptions. Once again we are living in the eye of the hurricane of the 20th century western world. Now is a great time to be a dyke or fag. Or if your not that way you can be a Nelly boy or a Rosy the Riveter tough lady. Or if you really want to, what with all the punks and weirdos around there's people with face tattoos and 20 rings in their face working at the coffee shop. So it shouldn't be to big a deal for you to cut your tits off or get some installed or whatever. Similar like sexuality is biological and its near impossible to sufficiently brainwash someone out of being a queer. And penguins and dogs are queer so that's cool. Butch women and nelly boys is also just part of how society is way over genderpated and needs to stop telling kids which toys are appropriate. So to be perfectly clear and make complete sense : gays and lessies and bull daggers and swishy fops: all natural normal members of society. Tr*nsexuality is some kind of government plot to sell penises and 'ginas !!!

Switching into another register, the egg speaks to us as a pedant ("actually about 8 factors"), even a mansplainer ("highly subjective and arbitrary")—that is, as a kind of professorial authority. An authority that positions trans people against other queers—"all natural normal members of society"—whose thriving depends on the exclusion of the "tr*nny," a figure scapegoated for the fact that "society is way over genderpated" and somehow responsible for the gendering of toys. The sheer incommensurability of the various registers deployed against the would-be transitioner, whose character Lamb revises through turns (romantic outsider, cheap fuck, tiresome intellectual, inattentive student) must culminate in a conspiratorial unity—and so it does, with the "government plot" that alone can explain the phenomenon of transsexual desire. Egg theory contends with a distinctive kind of paranoia, not without its love for the "gender mutant," but which must contend at some point with the friction between the life of the "tr*nny" and that of the queer others whose transness has been sublimated into a more nuanced, sophisticated orientation toward gender. Like Leslie Feinberg, whose *Stone Butch Blues* Lamb (n.d.) positions as a futurological egg theory, the post-detransition text that completes the cycle of foreclosure: "Or remember Les, the stone butch blues guy ?? He's my fucking hero cuz stone butch was all about how freaking scary and upsetting tr*nnsexual life is and after forcing himself through 20 years of loneliness and workplace discrimination he called bullshit and ripped his beard out with tweezers and proclaimed him self *neither yet both*." The reduction of the text to a violently detransitioned body: pushing back in Leslie Feinberg.

As Lamb's reference to Feinberg implies, queer theory is, in certain of its guises, indistinguishable from egg theory—not because the two habits of thought are the same but because egg theory is drawn to queer theory's engagement with a sexuality athwart identity, an account of sexuality that derives from something more, less, or other than identity. And perhaps one can say something more direct, even, than that. Among the blueprints of queer theory—the foremothers— one finds some egg theory: several figures within queer theory either wrote, at the time, about a transsexual desire that they kept at arm's length (most famously Eve Kosofsky Sedgwick), or made late-career pitches to trans identity claims. Since describing the latter would entail dreaming a dream as dreamy as Miller's reverie of the Saint Germain Drugstore (though major queer theorists are interviewed enough that it isn't hard to google what I'm gossiping about), I will restrict myself to the case just mentioned, with the proviso that I am not attempting to do justice to Sedgwick's complex and nuanced account of queerness or sexuality, and simply to ask a question about the egg-theoretical style as it is explored in a body of work whose importance to antiessentialist practices of queer criticism can be followed quite easily.

Egg theory gets in at the root; it seems always to be felt as the historical-dialectical antecedent of any position. It can be grown, for example, in this kind of soil, from *Epistemology of the Closet*: "Axiom 1: People are different from each other" (Sedgwick 1990: 22). This is a statement that has been formulated not to provoke an argument or to clarify a difference, but to accomplish two quite contrary rhetorical goals. On the one hand, the statement seeks to ground and to found a discipline in difference, and therefore to establish incommensurability, division, discrimination, and distinction as its characterizing techniques. On the other hand, Sedgwick boils down this new discipline, which we have come to call "queer theory," into an unobjectionable, even quite staggeringly bland, position. By virtue of being unexceptionable, the position is thereby also universalist: the axiom, if it is true at all—and how, of course, could it not be—it follows that it must be true for every "each other" that one could conceptualize. People may be different from each other, but everyone is differenced in the same way. In the sentence that follows, "it is astonishing how few respectable conceptual tools we have for dealing with this self-evident fact" (22), Sedgwick seems to evoke the first axiomatic of the United States Declaration of Independence, if not in a citational form then at least in a tonal shift into mock epic—as well as, in this case, a politics of the "respectable." (Respectable according to whom?) The rhetorical bind is similar too: we may hold these truths to be self-evident, but to the degree that we are required to hold them, they are not self-evident but require evidencing and instantiation. Likewise, though perhaps it is a "self-evident fact" that "people are different from each other," that fact nonetheless requires the ancillary labor of "dealing with." Yet why anything so grandiose as "conceptual tools" are necessitated by a statement as bland as "people are different from each other" remains, at the very least, an open question.

queer oviparity

Perhaps an answer is supplied in "White Glasses," a short paper of Sedgwick's delivered at the City University of New York (CUNY) Center for Lesbian and Gay Studies in 1991, the year after the publication of *Epistemology of the Closet*, and collected in *Tendencies* (1993). It comprises a lyrical reflection on Sedgwick's friendship with the queer poet and intellectual Michael Lynch. It is a text whose egg theory seems designed to provoke trans readers to bifurcated rage and sympathy, much like Lamb's. "One of the first things I felt when I was facing the diagnosis of breast cancer was, 'Shit, now I guess I must really be a woman'" (262), Sedgwick writes, marking a shift into cancer memoir with one of the genre's characteristic discursive modes—gallows humor. The gallows humor in question, moreover, is one that conditions the speaker not merely to mourn the fantasy of bodily integrity that cancer threatens—in fact, it is explicitly not bodily totality that is under siege, since Sedgwick explicitly rebuts the notion that breast cancer could be "the secret whose sharing defines women as such" (262). Rather, the joke is that cancer has forced Sedgwick into a position where she has to reject a political alignment (that of "women as such") that has, within her community, attempted to force a competition for resources between research on breast cancer and research on AIDS. "As though AIDS were *not* a disease of women, of lesbians!" (262) as Sedgwick exclaims. That disgraceful attempt to draw a line between two different kinds of disease determines, for Sedgwick, a difference not between men and women but between queer men and "that-thing-that-is-not-man, that is not the male labeled queer, that thing not vulnerable through poverty or racism, through injection, through an insertive or hot and rubbed-raw sexuality to the bad luck of viral transition" (262–63).

(Do you know, when I started taking synthetic progesterone in the summer of 2018, my expectation is that it would do precisely nothing for me? Trans people I knew—the cultists!—had insisted that the "titty skittles" would make my breasts grow. But my prescribing doctor could not confirm that with me. The only clue was that I had to sign a form indemnifying the clinic in the case that I developed breast cancer. But why would I be at increased risk of breast cancer? Only because the progesterone would make my breasts grow: the doctor couldn't confirm it, but the actuarial staff said differently My tits *have* grown, for whatever that's worth. Not enough.)

In the paragraph of most direct interest to the trans reading of Sedgwick, we acquire a discipline of identity:

> Now, I know I don't "look much like" Michael Lynch, even in my white glasses. Nobody knows more fully, more fatalistically than a fat woman how unbridgeable the gap is between the self we see and the self as whom we are seen; no one, perhaps, has more practice at straining and straining to span the binocular view between; and no-one can appreciate more fervently the act of magical faith by which it may be possible, at last, to assert and believe, against every social possibility, that the self we see can be made visible as if through our own eyes to the people who see us. The stubborn magical defiance I have learned (I *sometimes* feel I have succeeded in learning) in forging a habitable identity as a fat woman is also what has enabled the series of uncanny effects around these white glasses; uncanny effects that have been so formative of my—shall I call it my identification? Dare I, after this half-decade, call it with a fat *woman*'s defiance, my identity?—as a gay man? (256)

Like Lamb's, Sedgwick's disclosure here comes from a setting-into-the-past of an identity that can be claimed, overtly, because it has been earned over time—"after this half-decade." Yet if there is irony in the remainder of "White Glasses," there is here a rather different affect, and one that—unlike irony—can name itself safely: "stubborn magical defiance." Though the sentence in which something is defied without being named is complex for more reasons that that, and for reasons more submerged than the characteristic rhetorical pyrotechnics (em dashes) with which Sedgwick interrupts the articulation of an identity claim. Where, after all, does the sudden surge of defensiveness come from? Has someone been telling Sedgwick that she shouldn't identify as a gay man? If so—and here is where the ironic bifurcation of interest in "White Glasses" reveals itself as egg theory—then the dominating voice against whom Sedgwick articulates her defiance is not the voice of (let us risk being embarrassed and call it) the patriarchy; rather, the voice that must be forced back is the voice of the tr*nny herself, for whom only an elect cadre can be allowed to make such identifications. Sedgwick's rage is not directed at anyone who might, indeed, impede the expression of gay male identity, but at those who are perceived as already having made the crossing.

If we contrast, for example, these reflections on identifying as a gay man with AIDS and those of Lou Sullivan, Sedgwick's contemporary and a gay trans man who had died of AIDS two months and seven days before Sedgwick delivered "White Glasses" at CUNY (Sullivan passed on March 2, 1991), we can notice some similarities and some differences. Consider this letter from Sullivan to Judy Van Maasdam, of the Gender Dysphoria Program in Palo Alto, dated May 21, 1987.

> Dear Judy,
>
> I'm writing to let you know what's happening with me:
>
> Have finally completed my genitoplasty via Michael Brownstein. It was a long haul, as I had trouble keeping the left testicular implant, and it had to be reinserted two additional times before it "took." But I'm all there now.
>
> Don't know if you've heard it from Paul Walker, but this past New Year's Eve I was diagnosed with pneumocystis pneumonia AIDS. Brownstein was good enough to finish my surgery despite the risk.
>
> So, Judy, even though your Program did not believe I could live as a gay man, it looks like I'm going to die like one.
>
> Yours in liberation,
> Louis G. Sullivan

By this point, the egg has fully hatched—hatched athwart the grave. The enormous moral seriousness of the letter does not deter Sullivan, any more than it deters Sedgwick, from deploying a little genre craft: in this case, a sharp escalation in seriousness from the difficult but still broadly comical tale of repeated ball insertion into a disclosure of AIDS status that can be asserted, explicitly, with pride, a pride that overwhelms the vacillation of egg futurity ("I could [not] live as a gay man") with the finitude of trans certainty ("I'm going to die like one").

Do Sedgwick and Sullivan have anything to say to each other? Perhaps the question is rather, what is the futurity of egg theory? How do we understand the choices that transsexual orientation (a word I am using here distinct from, but not in contradiction to, *identity*, from Sedgwick, or *desire*—a term I have used elsewhere) can enable or tolerate? I will say, for my part, that an identification that remains psychic or notional, as Sedgwick's does, is not merely the theory of an egg voice that prevented me from seeking transsexual health care for a couple of decades, and still admonishes me for having done so; it is also, and more consequentially, the voice that harasses trans people for the force of our identifications in the name and voice of queer theory. For example, Christopher Reed constructed his 2018 antitrans manifesto out of axioms, "a format that pays homage to Eve Sedgwick," and explicitly of the post-1980s moment, which he associates with a kind of anti-"essentialist" queer liquidity, a pleasing slipperiness that allows one to aestheticize and thus incorporate difference without it departing from the ambit of "play."[3]

Others—Aren Aizura (2018), Blu Buchanan (2018), and Ellen Samuels (2018) especially—have assessed the irony of a text that speaks for "English professors" in laying down the law of queerness for the youngsters, while declaring, with a rather irradiated sense of irony, that while "the feeling of asserting authority can be very seductive," nonetheless "that doesn't make it right" (Reed 2018: sec. 7) My point here, in this assessment of queer trans-antagonism, is merely that Reed's reading of Sedgwick in "Axiomatic" is, basically, right; or at least, it is in the same spirit as Sedgwick's reading of Sedgwick in "White Glasses." Egg theory suffuses the entire disciplinary scene that Reed has convened. Like Lamb's egg, Reed blames trans people for the authoritarian patrolling of gender—for Lamb, in the canny reference to "toys"; for Reed, in the fourth axiom: "People feel real pain because of artificial social expectations. One response is to help people meet those expectations. Another is to dismantle the expectations." The first of these, Reed apparently thinks, is the accommodationist trans position; the latter position is that of queer theory, which is revolutionary. Yet the affect that Sedgwick has committed to, and I suppose in the end it's not so different to Reed's own, is that of the "stubborn magical defiance," an asymptotic and repetitive performance of foreclosed femininity, the femininity of the difficult woman, that can always be relied on to supply a compensatory pleasure to the subject that fails to transform itself into the object of its own desire.

Which is, how you say, *fine*. The force worth resisting is not outright hostility to transition among queer scholars, which, after all, trans people have no chance of defeating on any existing institutional grounds, but the holding of trans thought to the implicit standards of egg theory. Sedgwick's thought, of course, is multivalent and supple, juicy if one likes juicy, and really good at rubbing on various surfaces and exposing various textures. Nonetheless the continued appeal of Sedgwickian paradigms of criticism seems, to this former egg at least, strangely looped into the temporal rhythms of egg theory. I was reading a supposedly trans-friendly review of Andrea Lawlor's book *Paul Takes the Form of a Mortal Girl* the other day, which ends with the following:

> Despite the fact that the question of bodily or sensate commensurability is staged across the putative chasm of what we call "sexual difference," however, Lawlor refuses to let bodily sex provide or remain any sort of stable explanatory frame for experience, precisely because of Paul's ability to change his body. Indeed, while Sedgwick's "people are different from each other" does point to the endless collection of differences, both large and small, that gather under the auspices of most identity descriptors (but especially gender and sexuality), her deceptively simple little maxim also quietly suggests that, from the start, people are simultaneously always different from themselves.

> In this sense, Lawlor's novel is both about trans experience and a vision of trans experience that is not yet, but could be, and nowhere is this more clear than in our encounter with Paul. His body's special capacity for change physically stages the limitless potential for a self not curbed by the stabilizing energies of identity—a potential that exists on psychic, social, physical, and cultural levels for all of us. (LaFleur 2019)

What is this citation of Sedgwick doing? Clearly articulating a universalism of some kind, in line with the "violent universal bang" that Lawlor's titular character experiences in her first lesbian orgasm. But of what kind? A universalism predicated on the infinite divisibility of self into ever more complex and contradictory fragments, an "endless collection of differences." This is not, obviously, an attempt to police the bodies of trans people—although it is, perhaps, a refusal to assess the grounds on which trans people's experience is already constituted by a policed body. By failing to register that the condition of the body as a "stable explanatory frame" is precisely the fact on which dysphoria depends, the reviewer generates an account of embodiment that entirely elides even the possibility of transition, let alone the lived reality of trans people. This "vision of trans experience that is not yet, but could be" is a vision of "trans experience" as microdosing, as commodified, low-risk, performance enhancement. It is a diet of purest egg. To put that another way: since what is being salvaged from Sedgwick, by Lawlor's reviewer as well as by Reed, is an idea of conspicuous, bland superfluity, one is prevented from disagreeing. Yes, people are different from each other. This reviewer did not, of course, go so far as to agree with Reed (2018) that "a stable gender identity may be like an iPhone X: a lot of people tell you need one—but maybe you don't," but the argument is substantially the same, and formally very similar. To define trans as "a self not curbed by the stabilizing energies of identity"—I suspect the difference between that position and Reed's is reducible to a difference of tone. But the tone entails a complex little twist: by reducing the difference between "trans" and "queer" to nothing, and tucking the former term neatly into the latter, this writer is able to diffuse the tension between the two constituencies by entirely eradicating the distinctiveness of one of them. A difference that, under the sign of egg theory, can only be felt as anxiety.

scrambled

Anxiety is nonadaptive, as everyone learns; the anticipation of suffering does not produce the prophylactic effect that we pin our hopes on. What Sigmund Freud ([1926] 1958: 53) calls "the affect of anxiety" he enmeshes within the complex of feelings, fears, and desires around castration—and therefore around transsexual ideation—an association that, from "Inhibitions, Symptoms, and Anxiety"

([1926] 1958) onward he treats as an affect that precedes and catalyzes repression. Which is to say that anxiety is structural and reproduces itself irrespective of conditions. For those whose bodies are subject to repressive biopolicing, not merely anxiety but that-which-anxiety-anticipates is reinstantiated as bodily threat; the regime of biopolitics thus becomes, for racial capitalism, a regime of terror. What Freud means by "castration" is somewhat different from what trans people signal with the term *transition*, at least insofar as Freud's conception produces recoil ("anxiety") in the (male) subject who experiences it, and trans women only produce recoil in those around us. Nonetheless, the problematic of castration anxiety depends on the anticipated loss of an ego ideal, and therefore it looks different once one has relinquished the ego ideal. To use the term *transition* in this context indicates an accession to Freud's reality principle—the surrender of a fantasy of phallic wholeness that enforced the paranoid-schizoid reproduction of the policed presentation of self.

Freud, ultimate egg theorist, was positioned on the precipice of a castration he couldn't even immanentize as theory, and never as practice without delegating the body to the authority responsible for taxonomizing and containing those marshaled under the diagnosis of schizophrenia. Nowhere is this problematic clearer than in the case of Schreber, who "believed that he had a mission to redeem the world and to restore it to its lost state of bliss, [which] he could only bring about if he were first transformed from a man into a woman" (Freud 1958: 16). Freud, as is well known, attributed the desire to become a woman to "the appearance in [Schreber] of a feminine (that is, a passive homosexual) wishful phantasy, which took as its object the figure of his doctor" (47). Critiques of that position ground the metapsychological accounts of castration of both Giles Deleuze and Félix Guattari, and Jacques Lacan, yet in both cases what is found most troubling in Freud's text is his reduction of Schreber's cosmologically scaled ambition to the scale of the Oedipal family. Neither objects that to attribute transsexual desire to thwarted homosexuality abolishes the former while ontologizing the latter. Freud's commentary on Schreber's *Memoirs*, as it goes, does leave some room for a transsexual ontology, although it is sequestered within an ambiguous modal verb:

> The most essential part of [Schreber's] mission is that it must be preceded by his *transformation into a woman*. It is not to be supposed that he *wishes* to be transformed into a woman; it is rather a question of a "must" based upon the Order of Things, which there is no possibility of his evading, much as he would personally prefer to remain in his own honorable and masculine station in life. But neither he nor the rest of mankind can regain the life beyond except by his being transformed into a woman (a process which may occupy many years or even decades) by means of divine miracles.

One can sense, from the tenor of Freud's observation, that he would rather take transsexual desire off the diagnostic table because mere desire—manifest content—would fail to account for the principle of libidinal necessity that Schreber has articulated. Transsexual desire, then, is in fact nondesire; the delusional fantasy derives from the occlusion of homosexual desire. (Freud will not, therefore, line up on these grounds with those who reduce trans orientation to the workings of desire, because "desire" is an epiphenomenal condition: explication depends, in "The Schreber Case," on a firm grappling with the structures that preexist and govern desire.)

What one cannot fail to sense, however, is the looming identification that Freud feels with Schreber, which makes itself known in a modular syntax that places Freud before, after, inside, and athwart Schreber. A list of the modal verbs in this short section of prose: (1) "it *must* be preceded," a free indirect formulation that suspends the subject/object relation the sentence had initially erected (Freud does not say "he wanted/needed it to be preceded"); (2) "it *is not* to be supposed," presumably by a third party, the reader/supposer, whose scene of supposing is detached from, and incompatible with, the scene in which Schreber's mission *must* be preceded; (3) "a 'must' based upon the Order of Things," in which Freud pulls the necessity initially attributed to Schreber, back within the scene of his own text, in the form of a citation that one cannot confidently ascribe either to Freud or to Schreber; (4) "a process which may occupy many years," a framing which, given the difficulty governing the citational position of *must*, we are variously prohibited from confidently assigning either to Freud or Schreber. Let us underline this more fully: after introducing Schreber through a conspicuous attempt to take his megalomania seriously, or at least to appear serious and sympathetic while taking Schreber's megalomania, Freud now introduces in parentheses a claim that, perhaps, could be taken to indicate that Schreber's delusion was not that he could be transformed into a woman, but that he could be so transformed quickly. Does Freud really believe that, given enough time, Schreber could have achieved his singular goal of transforming himself into a woman? I don't think the prose will allow us to rule it out.

Sedgwick's (1991) essay "How to Bring Your Kids up Gay" performs a related sleight of hand around the figures of effeminate boy and the gay man. The affective and political climate Sedgwick names is "a culture's desire that gay people *not be*" (26), and the problem she names is the emerging gay-affirming psychotherapies of the late 1980s that separated gender expression from sexual identity. This separation, Sedgwick argues, "is how it happens that the *de*pathologization of an atypical sexual object-choice can be yoked to the *new* pathologization of an atypical gender identification" (21). This "pathologization" is, of course, the basis of a diagnosis of what we now call gender dysphoria that, while roundly criticized by trans activists calling for demedicalization, provides the basis for self-determination for trans people. Sedgwick, quite clearly, understands the medicalized subject of such a pathologization as a "proto-gay" child (22), and the child's medicalization within what we might as well call the apparatus of trans health care is problematic not, in the end, because it requires the recitation of a medical script as a condition of transition (as Dean Spade [2006] shows), but because the mechanism removes embryonic gay men from the pipeline into gay adulthood, and that homosexuality, in the process of its depathologization, has thus been heterosexualized. The unspoken premise, then, is that any and all effeminate boys will grow up to be gay men unless they are medically directed to become trans women with male object-choices. The argument then sets up, with a strategy that one could only call paranoid, an apparent conflict of interests between gay and trans people that evaporates the moment one observes that not all effeminate boys grow up to be gay men, nor do all masculine girls grow up to become lesbians.

I suppose some remark on "cancel culture" is necessary, since us vicious trans bitches are so frequently convicted of having performed in that grotesquerie—often, rather strangely, by those who in other diners order most enthusiastically from the critique-only menu. As though criticism were the same as censorship. But to say something reductive: I am not trying to cancel Sedgwick. I would look—anyone would look—utterly ridiculous if I attempted to do such a thing to a critic of such profound and continentally broad sophistication. My arguments here have been (1) that the construction of queer universalism in a certain thread of queer theory has been predicated on the impossibilization of transition, which I have called "egg theory"; (2) that egg theory has been explicitly deployed in trans-antagonistic contexts; and (3) that it has also begun to shape certain elements of trans discourse itself, as though we were rushing to prove the impossibility of our own existence. That Sedgwick's case for foundationalist gayness incorporates both the arguments and the premises avowed by Stock and the other gender criticals would likely unnerve everyone except for Reed. But the point can hardly be made urgently enough, in a context in which the same genocidal animus Sedgwick correctly attributed to 1980s America is now being directed against trans people—by a political and cultural establishment that threatens, routinely, to prevent us from accessing medicine, restrooms, rape crisis centers, and so forth—that the practical manifestation of egg theory would be the removal of health care provision for trans children. Not, as Jules Gill-Peterson (2018) has argued, that "protect trans kids" is an altogether adequate method for historicizing desires trans people feel in the present, or a sophisticated enough ethic by which to assess the applicability of a rubric for creating and sustaining life for trans people, across ages and generations. As Gill-Peterson suggests, the drive to protect may also be a drive to "propertize," and the very idea of the egg, as I began by saying, seems to imply a claim to know others better than they know themselves—a claim that, however functionally indispensable to queer and trans relations, can hardly be generalized or scaled. As she puts it, "Trans-affirmative voices struggle to find a way to protect trans children that does not imagine them as deserving of protection because they are, finally the *property* of adults, not people with the right to gender self-determination" (ii). The same is surely true of pretransition adults. Eggs become chicks, chicks become hens, hens lay on top of eggs. The whole question of how to bring your kids up trans, of how to bring yourself up trans, instantiates the problematic of oviparous reproduction, which is to say the temporal formulation of dialectics as such: "Which came first, the chicken or the egg?" Is the ruse of trans latency one in which the past reveals itself as latent content only in light of the symbolic images that it appears to have hatched? The grievance incurred by such a trauma (that of hatching) would then entail the loss of a being that could never have been, that never was, much like the temporal doubling that occurs when the cognitive subject occasioned reignites herself and experiences, long after the first, a second puberty. Given which, it is not surprising that transition rarely works perfectly; the more remarkable fact is that it works at all. That we do, indeed, submit our bodies to programs of radical transcription, such that what is remodeled is not merely the ornamental or plastic accidents of the enfleshed soul but its definitive essence.

(I write now as a hen, which is to say as a person who not only assumes the right to read and interpret egg theory but, more pressingly, as someone to whom self-avowed eggs—closeted trans women—have shared stories, fears, desires. There are many ways to prep an egg. One of the strangest of all is that of the masculine-presenting people who, on learning that I was not always a woman but have chosen to be one, respond wistfully, "oh, I have always wanted to do that," as though I were talking about taking a trip to Iceland or beginning a comprehensive physical detox. I do not always believe that they are telling me the truth. There are others, many others, perhaps some in every room of people I have ever addressed, whose relation to egg theory is one of absolute, disassociated foreclosure: who cannot transition, and can only barely stop the drive to do so from pulling their ribs out of their flesh.)

Salvador Dalí's *Metamorphosis of Narcissus*, painted in 1937, presents a set of strange and incompatible mirrorings. On the left, Narcissus, with a walnut for a head, leans heavily down onto his own knee; his obscured gaze, we assume, is planted like his shin and wrist in the pool, love and shame interbled. His torso is a yellowed marble, and though we see his "reflection" as less a reflection and more an extension of his body, we do see imprinted next to him in the lake the virtual replication of the cave behind him: as Dalí writes, "With the loss of his divinity the whole high plateau pours itself out" (quoted in Etherington-Smith 1993: 222) Narcissus is not doubled in the virtual space of the lake, but in the virtual space of the painting, nudged into the right-hand side of the visual field. What is the difference between the two like figures? Dalí wrote a poem to accompany the painting, which distinguishes these two figures from the "heterosexual group" in the background between them, but he does not name them. We cannot tell if these two figures, who share a geometric form, also share consciousness, or some other kind of nonspatial continuity, but we can tell that there is a formal congruity, and that while the left pulls energy downward toward the lake, plunging languorously, the right is almost a plinth, gripping or balancing an egg, out of which grows a flower. Dalí's image reminds us that the metamorphosis of Narcissus is not merely a mutation of plastic matter but a transition, in the full sense, from one form of object into another. Here, indeed, there are two such mediations: the nudge, whose spatialization endows the composition with its unusual geometrical arrangement, and then, as though recapitulating that theme through a miniature thematic fragment, the emergence from the egg of, not a chicken but—a flower. Unlike Freud's Schreber, Narcissus transforms out of a surplus of desire, rather than its obliviation. For this reason, and others, it is surely a transsexual Narcissus, and not a homosexual one, that Dalí has in mind as the other of the "heterosexual group," when he ends his poem with the egg: "When that head slits when that head splits when that head bursts, it will be the flower, / the new narcissus."

Grace Lavery is associate professor of English at the University of California, Berkeley, and the author of *Quaint, Exquisite: Victorian Literature and the Idea of Japan* (2019). Her essays have appeared in *Critical Inquiry, ELH, Novel, Modernism/Modernity,* and *differences.*

Acknowledgment
With thanks to Isaac Fellman, Nat Hurley, Alex Marraccini, and Susan Stryker for their comments on these thoughts as they emerged.

Notes

1. The pleated temporality of this line is the centerpiece of Barbara Johnson's (2002) essay "Bringing Out D. A. Miller," an important appraisal, in the aftermath of the first wave of queer theory, of the queerness evinced by and through Miller's signature mode of critical analysis.

2. I deploy the absurd term *gender critical* here to refer to that group of antitrans activists, academics, and journalists, including Kathleen Stock, Germaine Greer, Sophie Allen, Jane Clare Jones, Holly Lawford Smith, Mary Long, Rebecca Reilly-Cooper, and Graham Linehan. By using this term, I am avoiding the more value-neutral *TERF,* an acronym for "trans-exclusionary radical feminist," partly on the grounds that *exclusion* is not the best word for the hostile actions of members of this group—the forced inclusion of trans men within the category "adult human female," for example, is as objectionable as the repeated physical molestation and relentless vilification of trans women. But I also partly do so because the term *gender critical,* which on its own distinguishes Stock et al. from

precisely nobody, is conspicuously stupid enough that I think it is worth letting the group defend. For a concise digest of the position of the group, see Stock et al. 2019.

3.   Reed's "Axiomatic" has, fortunately, been removed from the Penn State University English Department website that was hosting it, and it is difficult to find. I have a private copy in my own personal archive, and I'm sure one can find it by searching Reddit—I'm not going to, though.

References

Aizura, Aren. 2018. "Kill Your Dads: On Reed and Castiglia's Response to Grace Lavery." *Medium*, December 13. medium.com/@aren.aizura/kill-your-dads-on-reed-and-castiglias-response -to-grace-lavery-28857b636a2c.

Buchanan, Blu. 2018. "A Burning White Ga(y)ze: On 'Free Speech' and White Gay Men." *Los Angeles Review of Books* (blog), December 19. blog.lareviewofbooks.org/essays/burning -white-gayze-free-speech-white-gay-men/.

Etherington-Smith, Meredith. 1993 *The Persistence of Memory: A Biography of Dalí*. New York: Random House.

Freud, Sigmund. 1958. "Psycho-Analytic Notes on an Autobiographical Account of a Case of Paranoia (Dementia Paranoides)." In *The Standard Edition of the Complete Psychological Works of Sigmund Freud*, vol. 12, edited by James Strachey, Alix Strachey, and Alan Tyson, 3–84. London: Hogarth.

Freud, Sigmund. (1926) 1958. "Inhibitions, Symptoms, and Anxiety." In *The Standard Edition of the Complete Psychological Works of Sigmund Freud*, vol. 20, edited by James Strachey, Alix Strachey, and Alan Tyson, 75–176. London: Hogarth.

Gill-Peterson, Jules. 2018. *Histories of the Transgender Child*. Minneapolis: University of Minnesota Press.

Johnson, Barbara. 2002. "Bringing Out D. A. Miller." *Narrative* 10, no. 1: 3–8.

LaFleur, Greta. 2019. "A Fairy's Tale." *Public Books*, July 10. www.publicbooks.org/a-fairys-tale/.

Lamb, Sybil. n.d. "You Best Never Ever Tr*nsition, Tr*nny." Tranny Punk. www.trannypunk.com /TSPX/detransition.html (accessed January 15, 2020).

Miller, D. A. 1992. *Bringing Out Roland Barthes*. Berkeley: University of California Press.

Reed, Christopher. 2018. "Axiomatic." Originally published on personal webpage. Available from author's personal archive.

Samuels, Ellen. 2018. "Remember Who the Real Enemy Is: In Support of Trans Existence." *Medium*, December 12. medium.com/@ellensamuels/remember-who-the-real-enemy-is -in-support-of-trans-existence-4bed6d489a27.

Sedgwick, Eve Kosofsky. 1990. *Epistemology of the Closet*. Berkeley: University of California Press.

Sedgwick, Eve Kosofsky. 1991. "How to Bring Your Kids up Gay." *Social Text*, no. 29: 18–27.

Sedgwick, Eve Kosofsky. 1993. "White Glasses." In *Tendencies*, 252–66. Durham, NC: Duke University Press.

Spade, Dean. 2006. "Mutilating Gender." In *The Transgender Studies Reader*, edited by Susan Stryker and Stephen Whittle, 315–32. New York: Routledge.

Stock, Kathleen, Sophie Allen, Jane Clare Jones, Holly Lawford-Smith, Mary Leng, and Rebecca Reilly-Cooper. 2019. "Doing Better in Arguments about Sex, Gender, and Trans Rights." *Medium*, May 23. medium.com/@kathleenstock/doing-better-in-arguments-about-sex -and-gender-3bec3fc4bdb6.

Sullivan, Lou. 1987. Letter to Judy Van Maasdam, May 21, 1987, box 2, folder 45, Louis Graydon Sullivan Papers (1991-07), the Gay, Lesbian, Bisexual, Transgender Historical Society, San Francisco.

Cisgender Commonsense and Philosophy's Transgender Trouble

ROBIN DEMBROFF

Abstract Analytic philosophy has transgender trouble. In this article, the author explores potential explanations for this trouble, focusing on the notion of "cisgender commonsense" and its place in philosophical methodology.

Keywords philosophy, analytic philosophy, feminist philosophy, philosophy of gender

> I just want to know the ordinary view [of gender].
> —Unnamed philosophy professor

Analytic philosophy has transgender trouble.[1] Many readers are likely aware of the controversy surrounding Rebecca Tuvel's 2017 paper, "In Defense of Transracialism." But the Tuvel imbroglio is the tip of the iceberg. Those interested in further details can read Talia Bettcher's (2018) "When Tables Speak" or Samantha Hancox-Li's (2019) "Why Has Transphobia Gone Mainstream in Philosophy?" (see also Flaherty 2019). Both outline a disturbing and increasing pattern of antitrans rhetoric being uttered, endorsed, or excused by analytic philosophers. They could also read Gayle Salamon's (2009) "Justification and Queer Method; or, Leaving Philosophy" or Naomi Scheman's (1997) "Queering the Center by Centering the Queer" to situate this antitrans sentiment in the context of philosophy's historical prejudice against queerness. Or they could read Kristie Dotson's (2012) "How Is This Paper Philosophy?" to better understand philosophy's generally chilling environment for persons that Doston calls "diverse practitioners."

I'm daunted by the task of diagnosing analytic philosophers' seemingly incurable tendency to at best ignore transgender issues and, more recently, barge into them swinging. I've watched transgender graduate students leave philosophy

TSQ: Transgender Studies Quarterly ∗ Volume 7, Number 3 ∗ August 2020   **399**
DOI 10.1215/23289252-8553048   © 2020 Duke University Press

rather than cope with coming out in it. I've had my research mansplained to me by philosophers who hadn't read a single piece of gender theory. I've been asked in Q&A why gender is a philosophical topic. I've been informed that I was passed up for a job because I am transgender. As a graduate student, a senior faculty member told me to my face that he would not use my pronouns because they are "ungrammatical." More generally, I'm constantly aware of philosophers who take to social media and blogs to forcefully opine about trans people from a place of complete ignorance. Using dog whistles and misinformation in addition to philosophical tools, these philosophers spend their time and talents on creating more sophisticated versions of dominant gender ideology. They then wield this ideology nearly exclusively against trans persons. Maybe worse, I've heard colleagues—many, well meaning—rise to the defense of this behavior in the name of "academic freedom."

The situation in philosophy is, to be blunt, a massive, complex, and thorny transgender trashfire. This trashfire manifests most explicitly in the context of social media, blogs, interpersonal interactions, and the occasional journal publication, and it has serious repercussions. (To name one, a number of high-profile court briefings opposing trans rights in both the United States and the United Kingdom cite blog posts by philosophers such as Kathleen Stock and Alex Byrne as evidence that trans persons are dangerous and deluded.)[2] I hope to show that it also manifests in the very methods and views that are considered philosophically legitimate, and how they are related to philosophy's long-standing troubles with race, class, disability, and gender more broadly.

While reflecting on philosophy's transgender trashfire, I found myself repeatedly coming back to a particular memory. Near the end of my first semester of graduate school, I brought a draft of my metaphysics term paper to my professor's office hours. I was writing on the philosophy of time but had run up against a problem with my argument. After explaining this problem, I assured my professor that I would read more of the relevant literature to make progress on a solution. Eight years later, I still clearly remember what happened next. My professor leaned forward and pushed the draft back to me. "Don't read," he said. "Go think!" I hold a lot of affection for that professor. But reflecting on these four words—Don't read: go think—helped me make headway on the question, why does analytic philosophy have transgender trouble?

First, I should admit that I am a pluralist by philosophical disposition. More often than not, I think that philosophical questions have multiple legitimate answers. In my own work, this means that I defend polysemy about gender terms and context-specific pluralism about gender categories. With respect to the metaphilosophical question of why philosophy has transgender trouble, I'm again disposed to pluralism: there are many legitimate answers. After all, the world has transgender trouble. Philosophers have the same problems as everyone else and (I'd argue) a few extra to boot. So I want to reframe the question: are there unique features of analytic philosophy that at least partially explain why it has transgender trouble? In considering this question, my first thought was about the demographics of philosophy. Who, historically and at present, counts as a philosopher? Whose works are considered "paradigms" of philosophical inquiry? Who establishes philosophy's dominant imaginary—the shared assumptions, values, and beliefs that give rise to prevailing conventions, rules, and practices within our discipline?

No one will be shocked to know that philosophy long has been the dominion of (almost exclusively) men who perched atop nearly every imaginable social hierarchy. Even now, in 2020, it's common for a philosophy syllabus to be composed entirely of cisgender, straight-identified, white men from the global North. One effect is that socially dominant interests, standpoints, and modes of thought saturate philosophy's center. But beyond that, philosophy also has a longstanding tradition of using philosophical methods and tools for the purpose of justifying these social hierarchies. As Christia Mercer (2019) convincingly argues, the history of philosophy is filled with men using philosophical reasoning to justify their presupposition that women are inferior—morally and bodily—to men. Similarly, Charles Mills (1997) points out that philosophy is hostile to persons of color, as well as to discussions of concrete sociopolitical issues such as reparations, colonialism, and racism. The reason, Mills argues, is that white philosophers set up disciplinary boundaries that count these people and ideas as incompatible with "serious philosophy" (4). Similar arguments could be made regarding disability, class, ethnicity, sexual orientation, and, importantly for our purposes, gender identity. Transgender persons and issues have been not only missing from philosophy but systematically excluded by philosophers who use their training to justify dominant ideology about sex and gender, and who dismiss challenges to this ideology as unjustified, irrational, unreasonable, or (my personal favorite) counterintuitive.[3]

But this isn't yet a satisfying explanation. The overwhelming cis, straight, nondisabled whiteness of philosophy is important, but it isn't—at least, not historically—unique to philosophy. The academy long has been the stomping grounds of privileged white men. And while every field has problems, I regularly hear colleagues from other humanities disciplines express horror at the carelessness, cruelty, and ignorance on display in philosophers' public discussions of transgender issues. There remains an explanatory gap between the fact of philosophy's cisgenderness and the fact that philosophy can be and is used to devalue trans persons.

Talia Bettcher (2018) suggests a source of philosophy's transgender trouble that is somewhat orthogonal to its demographics. "It's more than a little heartbreaking," she writes, "to find an entire literature, a rich domain of philosophy, all of one's own hard work, completely erased—due to nothing but arrogance, dismissiveness, and laziness." While I agree with Bettcher, I still feel some dissatisfaction with this answer. Laziness, to me, suggests a blameworthy failure to care about the tasks or norms that one is expected to satisfy. I do not think philosophers are intellectually lazy in this respect. Philosophers are not irresponsibly failing to meet an expectation to engage existing philosophical (much less interdisciplinary) work on gender before opining about it.[4] There is no such expectation, particularly within my specialization, the subfield of metaphysics.[5]

Given this, it is predictable that philosophers who speak from ignorance about trans issues—and, typically, the metaphysics of gender specifically—negatively react to charges of laziness and hubris. These charges, to them, can seem like accusing a soccer player of double dribbling; for many, the operating rules of philosophy don't say that one must be informed about the literature on a topic prior to "doing philosophy" about it. It is no wonder, then, that when feminist, queer, and trans scholars charge these philosophers with intellectual laziness and hubris, we are countered with the allegation that we are "zealots" and "tin pot dictators" who are waging war against academic freedom.[6] Within philosophy, ignorant speech on trans issues is not generally perceived as lazy or arrogant (though I agree with Bettcher that, relative to broader scholarly norms, it is). To the contrary, it is considered academic speech, as opposed to speech uttered by persons who happen to be academics. It is considered philosophically serious speech.

Here again, we can ask: why? I suspect that an answer lies somewhere both between and below philosophy's cisgenderness and its intellectual laziness and hubris. The first part of the answer brings us back to the advice to "go think" rather than read. Thinking—and speaking—before reading is not merely tolerated in philosophy; it is advised. At the very least, it is assumed a standard way of doing serious and original philosophical work. Five minutes of reflection will tell us that this methodology creates a disciplinary culture in which so-called commonsense is self-justifying and universalized. Stephanie Kapusta helpfully summarizes philosophy's methodological reliance on commonsense as reliance on "clear, independent analysis" of presupposed concepts or terms, in which the targeted concepts or terms are "decomposed . . . into simpler units."[7] These presupposed concepts and terms are not only abstracted away from history and social context—they establish the boundaries around which views are philosophically serious.[8] Philosophical work is devoted to making presupposed concepts and terms precise, consistent, or explanatorily useful, and only rarely to challenging them or questioning the entire conceptual framework on which they rest. This methodology is philosophically legitimate, by which I mean it is generally accepted as a method for producing philosophical knowledge (or, at least, justified philosophical beliefs).[9] The philosophical legitimacy of thinking (and speaking) without reading—and, more to the point, of commonsense methodology—can help us understand why philosophers are permitted to speak ignorantly about trans issues, and do so with impunity. It also helps us understand why their speech generally takes dominant gender ideology for granted—again, with impunity. (After all, as Sally Haslanger [2017] among others have pointed out, a central tool of ideology is to pass itself off as commonsense.)

But this does not, by itself, wholly account for philosophy's transgender trouble. In particular, it does not explain two things: first, philosophy's general hostility toward transgender identifications and experiences, and second, its intolerance for those philosophers (primarily, feminist philosophers) whose intuitions clash with what we might call "cisgender commonsense"—the presupposed concepts and terms built into dominant, trans-exclusive gender ideology.

To account for this hostility and intolerance, we have to ask a further series of questions: Whose commonsense constitutes philosophically legitimate commonsense? Whose pretheoretical concepts and terms constrain philosophical inquiry? And whose intuitions are philosophical intuitions? It isn't simply that "Don't read—go think!" is a legitimate methodology within philosophy; it is legitimate only when the resulting thoughts adequately align with the commonsense of the culturally powerful.[10] By contrast, the commonsense of the racialized, poor, queer, transgender, or disabled is considered philosophically irrelevant "ideology," "activism," or "delusion." Their perspectives are automatically placed in what Salamon (2009: 228) calls the "realm of justification": in this realm, an unmeetable epistemological burden to prove their philosophical legitimacy is placed on already marginalized people and ideas. Speaking about a job interviewer's demand, years prior, that she justify her work on queerness as philosophical work, Salamon writes, "I am still not sure what kind of justification might have sufficed" (229).

I share Salamon's exasperation. No justification for trans philosophy will suffice when alignment with cisgender commonsense is necessary for work to be considered philosophical work. Not that justifications aren't available: a cursory search would turn up books, academic journals, and even popular articles that discuss the methodology of feminist, queer, and transgender philosophy. But this literature is brushed aside as politically motivated, unlike the objective and rational perspective of cisgender philosophers who have mastered the methodology of thinking without reading.

Excuse the sarcasm; I'm exasperated. My point, in short, is that uninformed (they would say "a priori") thought about trans issues is deemed philosophical only when it aligns with cisgender commonsense. What seems intuitive to gender-conforming philosophers who have never studied trans and queer scholarship sets the standards for what counts as legitimate, "objective" philosophical positions about trans issues. And this situation is not unique to trans issues: similar standards historically have ruled out the possibility of analytic philosophy of race, gender, disability, or class, as well as social critique more generally. While highly abstract arguments about the ideal form of justice are considered paradigmatically philosophical,[11] empirically informed arguments about local forms of racial justice are devalued as "lightweight" philosophy.[12] While the nature of mental content is assumed to clearly be a philosophical issue, the nature of gender identity is not. While philosophical debate over the source of happiness traces back to Aristotle, relevant insights from disability studies about well-being have been ignored. The list goes on and on.

To make this point concrete, let me describe a scene. In spring 2018, I gave a paper on genderqueer identification at a prestigious philosophy department. At the end of my talk, a senior faculty member asked the first question: "What do you think gender is?" I responded by explaining my pluralist stance on this question. He was not satisfied. "I just want to know the ordinary view," he said. "Ordinary for whom?" I replied. "Just the ordinary view," he insisted. "I honestly don't understand your question," I said. "Ordinary for whom?" He grew frustrated. "Just the ordinary view! What someone in the pub would say."

The fact that, to this philosopher, an anonymous cisgender person in a bar is an authority on gender speaks volumes. Even more does the fact that, in the space of an academic talk, it was unremarkable to presuppose not only that the so-called ordinary view is philosophically authoritative, but also that the ordinary view is the estate of persons who have never reflected on, much less lived, transgender or queer experience. In this story, we see the combination of both "Don't read—go think!" as a philosophically legitimate methodology, as well as the presupposition that cisgender commonsense sets the limits on what views about gender are immune from the otherwise inescapable "realm of justification." Analytic philosophy's transgender trouble will remain so long as philosophers continue to disregard trans studies and voices, and undeservedly legitimize cisgender commonsense.

Robin Dembroff is assistant professor of philosophy at Yale University. Their research focuses on feminist metaphysics, epistemology, and philosophy of language.

Acknowledgments

Many thanks to Elizabeth Barnes, Katharine Jenkins, Stephanie Kapusta, Laurie Paul, Jennifer Saul, and Susan Stryker for feedback during the development of this article.

Notes

1. My focus is on analytic philosophy, which is rooted and predominant in anglophone philosophy departments. Analytic philosophy is commonly (though not without difficulty) distinguished from continental philosophy, in which central figures (e.g., Foucault, Hegel, Heidegger, Derrida, Merleu-Ponty) typically come from mainland Europe and employ different analytical tools and methods than analytic philosophers. See Gutting 2012 for a critical survey of various proposed bases for the analytic/continental distinction.

2. See, for example, multiple amicus briefs in the case of *RG & GR Harris Funeral Homes v. Aimee Stephens* that cite Kathleen Stock (Carter 2019; McHugh 2019). In addition, Maya Forstater's (2019) witness statement in a recent UK case cites Kathleen Stock, Alex Byrne, and Jane Clare Jones, as well as an *Inside Higher Ed* open letter from twelve philosophers that defended philosophers' antitrans rhetoric in the name of "academic freedom."

3. "Whose intuitions?" is the obvious next question.

4. At a minimum, I think philosophers should engage the existing literature on gender within philosophy before confidently opining about it. Arguably, they also should engage relevant literature outside philosophy as well, such as literature from sociology, history, anthropology, and gender studies.

5. I think metaphysics is here joined by epistemology and philosophy of language. Other subfields, such as modern and ancient philosophy, seem to be far less susceptible to legitimizing this methodology.

6. These are terms actually used by senior philosophy faculty (Brian Leiter and Daniel Kaufman) to describe Susan Stryker, Rebecca Kukla, and myself in response to our decision to not coplatform with antitrans activists (Dembroff, Kukla, and Stryker 2019; Leiter 2019; Kaufman 2019).

7. Kapusta, email correspondence to author, January 6, 2020.

8. Katharine Jenkins (2014: 263) points out that this leaves feminist philosophers in a double bind, as their "research will involve violating, to some degree, the norms of the very institution that makes it possible for [them] to undertake that research in the first place."

9. Here I draw from Dotson (2012: 5), who defines legitimization as "practices and processes aimed at judging whether some belief, practice, and/or process conforms to accepted standards and patterns, i.e. justifying norms."

10. Here, some might object that many philosophical positions are far from commonsensical—for example, David Lewis's modal realism, Peter Singer's hard-line consequentialism, Kant's transcendental idealism, and so on. I have two things to say in response to this objection. First, in all these cases, these noncommonsensical positions were derived from commonsense intuitions. That is, they are—according to their advocates—necessary consequences of what are taken as incorrigible commonsense intuitions, such as commitment to the possibility of things being other than they actually are, moral intuitions, and human free will. Second, and relatedly, even within philosophy, not all commonsense beliefs and attitudes are taken as equal. Some are seen as more fundamental than others. When these beliefs and attitudes internally conflict, or conflict with received information, philosophers often disagree about what to hold fixed and what to give up. It is perhaps especially damning then, to see that "commonsense" ideas about gender are so fundamental to many philosophers that they are willing to disregard the scholarly merits of entire fields of study to maintain them.

11. The term *ideal form* is intentional, as well as skeptical. See Mills 1997.

12. See, for example, the exclusion of W. E. B. Du Bois, Frederick Douglas, and Angela Davis from the philosophical canon.

References

Bettcher, Talia Mae. 2018. "When Tables Speak: On the Existence of Trans Philosophy." *Daily Nous* (blog), May 30. dailynous.com/2018/05/30/tables-speak-existence-trans-philosophy-guest -talia-mae-bettcher/.

Dembroff, Robin, Rebecca Kukla, and Susan Stryker. 2019. "Retraction Statement by Robin Dembroff, Rebecca Kukla, and Susan Stryker." *Changing How the World Thinks*, August 26. iai.tv/articles/retraction-statement-by-robin-dembroff-rebecca-kukla-and-susan-stryker -auid-1256.

Carter, W. Burlette. 2019. "Brief of Amicus Curiae Professor W. Burlette Carter in Support of Petitioner." *Harris Funeral Homes v. Stephens*. No. 18-107. United States Supreme Court.

Dotson, Kristie. 2012. "How Is This Paper Philosophy?" *Comparative Philosophy* 3, no. 1: 3–29.

Flaherty, Colleen. 2019. "The Divide over Scholarly Debate over Gender Identity Rages On." *Inside Higher Ed*, July 19. www.insidehighered.com/news/2019/07/19/divide-over-scholarly -debate-over-gender-identity-rages.

Forstater, Maya. 2019. "Claimant's Witness Statement." *Medium*, November 22. medium.com /@MForstater/claimants-witness-statement-abe3e8073b41.

Gutting, Gary. 2012. "Bridging the Analytic-Continental Divide." *New York Times, The Stone* (blog), February 19. opinionator.blogs.nytimes.com/2012/02/19/bridging-the-analytic -continental-divide/.

Hancox-Li, Samantha. 2019. "Why Has Transphobia Gone Mainstream in Philosophy?" *Contingent Magazine*, October 1. contingentmagazine.org/2019/10/01/transphobia-philosophy/.

Haslanger, Sally. 2017. "I—Culture and Critique." *Aristotelian Society Supplementary Volume* 91, no. 1: 149–73. doi.org/10.1093/arisup/akx001.

Jenkins, Katharine. 2014. "'That's Not Philosophy': Feminism, Academia, and the Double Bind." *Journal of Gender Studies* 23, no. 3: 262–74. doi.org/10.1080/09589236.2014.909720.

Kaufman, Daniel. 2019. "Philosophy's Aspirant Tin-Pot Dictators." *Electric Agora* (blog), September 8. theelectricagora.com/2019/09/08/philosophys-aspirant-tin-pot-dictators/.

Leiter, Brian. 2019. "Zealots Working Overtime Now to Shut Down Gender Critical Feminists." *Leiter Reports: A Philosophy Blog*, September 1. leiterreports.typepad.com/blog/2019/09 /zealots-working-overtime-now-to-shut-down-gender-critical-feminists.html.

McHugh, Paul R. 2019. "Brief of Amicus Curiae Dr. Paul R. McHugh, M.D. Professor of Psychiatry in Support of Petitioner." *Harris Funeral Homes v. Stephens*. No. 18-107. United States Supreme Court.

Mercer, Christia. 2019. "The Philosophical Origins of Patriarchy." *Nation*, July 1. www.thenation .com/article/patriarchy-sexism-philosophy-reproductive-rights/.

Mills, Charles. 1997. *The Racial Contract*. Ithaca, NY: Cornell University Press.

Salamon, Gayle. 2009. "Justification and Queer Method; or, Leaving Philosophy." *Hypatia* 24, no. 1: 225–30.

Scheman, Naomi. 1997. "Queering the Center by Centering the Queer: Reflections on Transsexuals and Secular Jews." In *Feminists Rethink the Self*, edited by Diana Meyers, 124–62. Boulder, CO: Westview.

Tuvel, Rebecca. 2017. "In Defense of Transracialism." *Hypatia* 32, no. 2: 263–78. onlinelibrary.wiley .com/doi/abs/10.1111/hypa.12327.

Trans Studies and Resistance in an Academy Based on Masculinity Contest Culture

TRAVERS

Abstract Trans studies is a burgeoning and global interdisciplinary field of scholarship. Although trans people in general continue to remain on the margins of the academy in Canada and the United States, some of the trans scholars who contribute to the field of trans studies are in continuing faculty (tenure-track and tenured) positions. Trans women in general and trans women and trans feminine people of color, in particular, however, are particularly underrepresented in this labor pool. The author brings together a theoretical pastiche consisting of a Black feminist analysis of patriarchy as a layered phenomenon, trans necropolitics, and a masculinity contest culture paradigm to trouble this limit to representation within trans studies in Canada and the United States.

Keywords academic culture, trans misogyny, patriarchy, necropolitics, masculinity contest culture

In a session at the 2019 American Studies Association honoring the foundational legacy for trans studies of Susan Stryker's 1994 article "My Words to Victor Frankenstein above the Village of Chamounix: Performing Transgender Rage," an audience member challenged the room to attend to the relative scarceness of trans women in the academy, noting that folks who are presumably read as masculine—regardless of personal identity or intent—have had far more success in securing continuing faculty appointments. Trans studies is a vital but still emerging field, and a quantitative breakdown of the identities of people with continuing faculty appointments is neither available nor necessarily desirable. One of the many things trans studies does well is to call into question the construction of gender categories that can be measured in this way. But the overarching white supremacist, colonial, and antifemale/antifeminine logic of the academy's "masculinity contest culture" (Berdahl et al. 2018) draws attention to

TSQ: Transgender Studies Quarterly * Volume 7, Number 3 * August 2020   **407**
DOI 10.1215/23289252-8553062   © 2020 Duke University Press

the potential power of trans misogyny/misogynoir to shape the field—even as the field itself is substantially organized to resist and oppose these structures and processes of power.[1]

An important project for trans studies to undertake relates to the material and cultural conditions of its production—via the experiences of a range of trans people in the institutional contexts of the academy. Trans people of all genders tend to pay a nonnormative "tax" over the long haul in preparation for the tenure-track job market because of the emotional and practical labor involved in managing gender dysphoria, trans negativity, and the logistics of transition. These drains on well-being, energy, and productivity are radically compounded for those who experience racism, colonialism, ableism, and/or enforced poverty. The intense hatred directed at trans women in particular—whether by trans-exclusionary radical feminists or the Christian right or as a result of the garden-variety legacy of colonialism and white supremacy—is a dynamic widely reported by trans women and substantiated by the extreme discrimination and violence that trans women of color experience.

Hierarchies within the Academy in Canada and the United States

Despite the diversity and equity initiatives that have altered the almost exclusively white and cis-male demography of the professoriate in Canadian and US universities and colleges since the 1960s, current research indicates two important facts. First, those of us who are nonnormative (according to markers of gender, race, class, and Indigeneity) remain a numerical minority and experience discrimination with regard to salary, tenure, and promotion (James 2019; Jaschik 2019; Momani 2019; Stryker 2014; Wong 2017). In addition to hiring, earnings, and tenure and promotion differentials, minority faculty members experience greater formal and informal service workloads. Stryker (2014) observes that "the data show that in the higher education workplace, women and men of color, as well as white women, still face far more hostility, mistreatment and process-based inequality than their white male counterparts. These experiences can take place in everyday situations and culminate in substantial macroaggressions." Second, of those faculty who are nonnormative, it is white, cis women who have made the greatest gains (Thobani 2016). Despite leadership by scholars in the field of trans studies who actively work to promote both trans scholarship critical of these normative logics and the employment of racialized/marginalized trans scholars, compelling anecdotal evidence points to a continuing employment pool of trans scholars at Canadian and US universities and colleges that is skewed toward faculty members who are read as white and masculine. Granted, the sample size is both small and anecdotal, but I believe this to be the case in both universities in general and in the specific disciplines that contribute to trans studies. Given the relative absence of trans women from continuing faculty positions, it is ironic that two pieces widely considered to be foundational to trans studies are written by trans women: Sandy Stone's (1991) "The *Empire* Strikes Back" and Stryker's (1994) aforementioned article.

I trouble this inequitable dynamic in trans studies as a profession by drawing on a Black feminist critique of globalized patriarchy as a metasystem of violence that divides "persons" from "non-persons" (Perry 2018), trans necropolitics (Haritaworn, Kuntsman, and Posocco 2014; Snorton and Haritaworn 2013), and the framework of masculinity contest culture (Berdahl 2015; Berdahl et al. 2018). Drawn together, these theoretical perspectives allow for an analysis of academic cultures that are hostile to trans people in general and particularly hostile to racialized trans women/trans feminine individuals. This occurs via modern/neoliberal organizational logics that are proclaimed to be neutral by their proponents but in actuality are far from it.

Patriarchy as an Overarching Metastructuring Force

In *Vexy Thing: On Gender and Liberation* (2018), Imani Perry employs a Black feminist lens to characterize patriarchy as a metafoundation of modernity, describing it as a globalized and intersectional structuring force that emerged via the violence of the colonial order and finds its most recent expression in the current neoliberal iteration of the global division of labor. According to Perry, "who counts" today, that is, who is a person/patriarch, versus who is considered a nonperson and hence disposable "finds its point of origin in the logic of domination of the sovereign European nations in modernity" (89). To be a patriarch is to be afforded full personhood in legal, social, and political terms (19). Hatred and disparagement of the feminine and those assigned to it is central to modernity and was globalized through colonialism. Gender, from this perspective "was not only a simple binary applied to a reading of biological sex, but in terms of relations, it depended on a truncated reading of details of the form (of the body, of the society) that would instruct how the person would be treated. . . . The gender categories of humanity were disciplined by ascribing meaning to shades of flesh, national origin, or legal status" (55). For Perry, patriarchy is "layered" (75), and "the layers are thick" (115). One of the ways in which patriarchy functioned and continues to function is through acts and relations of domination that are publicly visible. "The public sphere, 'the commons' which are often described historically as part of the 'masculine realm,' also provided a structure whereby those who were legal persons were set against those who were not. . . . The public domain provided theatres of patriarchal domination that included non-persons" (26–27). The logic of patriarchy is extended through the current neoliberal order while disrupting "some of the stability to that structure as the global economy pushes against the borders and boundaries of sovereign nations" (99) and "consistently demands more competition in every area of our lives" (100). The university, whether private or public, operates as such a public theatre within which personhood and nonpersonhood are marked via the distribution of material and cultural resources.

Trans Necropolitics

Necropolitics is a radical critical race theory introduced by Achille Mbembe in 2003 that focuses on the ways in which state entities award some people with life-sustaining resources while either killing others outright or denying them life-sustaining resources. While Mbembe focuses explicitly on state atrocities on a large scale, trans necropolitics identifies "assemblages" of oppression that unevenly distribute resilience versus harm, life versus death, along axes of (cis) gender, race, class, sexuality, and colonialism.[2] Trans scholars C. Riley Snorton and Jin Haritaworn draw on Mbembe's theory of necropolitics, Lisa Duggan's (2003) analysis of (white, middle-class) homonormativity, and assemblage theorist Jasbir Puar's (2007) queer necropolitics and its central concept of homonormative nationalism or "homonationalism" to formulate an explicitly trans necropolitics that focuses on the day-to-day experiences of racism and poverty for trans people of color (in the form of policing, urban planning, the prison-industrial complex, borders, enforced poverty, the war on terror, and lack of access to health care). Indeed, trans necropolitical theorizing resonates powerfully with the findings of the 2011 report *Injustice at Every Turn: A Look at Black Respondents in the National [US] Transgender Discrimination Survey* (Grant et al. 2011), which concluded that trans people of color in the United States experience a relentless barrage of micro- and macroaggressions. Trans necropolitics shares Perry's (2018: 118) analysis of "premature death" as "the essence of marginality" and her critique of social change efforts that seek the assimilation of "nonpersons" into hierarchical structures of authority and privilege. Both Perry's theory of layered patriarchy and trans necropolitics are consistent with Ruth Wilson Gilmore's (2007: 28) definition of racism as "the state-sanctioned or extralegal production and exploitation of group-differentiated vulnerability to premature death."

In an article about patriarchal femicide against both cis and trans women and girls in Mexico, Sayak Valencia (2019: 185) applies a transfeminist lens to bring attention to the "necropatriarchy [that] is the (trans)femicidal machine that up to this day accounts for more than 53,000 femicides committed against women from 1985 to 2016 in the Mexican territory." The concept of necropatriarchy is powerful for linking trans necropolitics with Perry's definition of global patriarchy as a layered phenomenon that results in the higher rates of murderous violence against trans women of color in Canada and the United States. Analyses based on layered patriarchy and trans necropolitics support a reading of continuing faculty employment in terms of who is invested in full personhood, "folded into life" (Puar 2007: 10), or provided with life-sustaining resources—and importantly, who is not. An analysis of the academy as characterized by "masculinity contest culture" reveals some of the ways in which this necropatriarchal logic plays out.

Organizational Cultures as (Layered) Masculinity Contests

Masculinity contest culture theory defines masculinity in terms of domination and control of other people (Berdahl et al. 2018: 426). This occurs within a gender system whereby masculinity and femininity are opposed such that "(masculine) men have higher status, more power, and greater privileges than women (or less masculine men)" (425). Manhood, however, is not only about establishing male superiority over women but operates "to create hierarchies among men" (426), and these hierarchies are shaped by race, class, and sexuality (and cis-normativity). Berdahl et al. note, for example, the "'Teddy Bear effect,' whereby Black men need to do extra 'identity work' to ensure that White colleagues do not feel threatened . . . and the 'authority gap,' in which the gap in authority at work is greater between Black and White men than between Black and White women" (427). Drawing on Raewyn Connell's 1987 concept of hegemonic masculinity, Berdahl et al. (2018: 426) note that "the hegemonic masculine ideal for men is to be rich, White, heterosexual, tall, athletic, professionally successful, confident, courageous, and stoic. Even if very few men enact and embody all aspects of hegemonic masculinity, its idealization makes these dimensions widely normative." Within masculinity contest cultures, men—and others—who fail to achieve these ideals "may nonetheless appropriate, emphasize, or engage in some dimensions of hegemonic masculinity in how they act or think about themselves" (426). In so doing, these "hybrid masculinities reify dominant masculinity tropes and reinforce gender inequalities" (426). As Perry (2018: 84) observes, "Western imperialism continues to dictate global relations, including gendered ideas of control, conquest, extraction, and exploitation, and whose lives matter." This oppressive ethos shapes organizational cultures and reward systems, including the masculinity contest cultures at play in colleges and universities in Canada and the United States.

In a blog post titled "Did President Arvind Gupta Lose the Masculinity Contest?," University of British Columbia (UBC) professor Jennifer Berdahl (2015) employed masculinity contest culture theory to explain the (forced) resignation of UBC's first visible minority president in 2015. As an indication of the power of the masculinity contest framework to unsettle the business-as-usual of the academy, Berdahl's critical intervention prompted the chair of UBC's Board of Governors to interfere with Berdahl's academic freedom by attempting to silence her. [3]

A Logic at Odds with Trans Studies

> I have called the work of working *on* institutions *diversity work*: the work we have to do in order to be accommodated or the work we have to do because we are not accommodated.
> —Sara Ahmed, "Feminists at Work: Complaint, Diversity, Institutions"

Universities in Canada and the United States continue to be dominated by faculty members and administrative elites who are disproportionately white, male, heterosexual, and cisgender. The claim by universities to universality, grounded in the exclusive logics of liberal humanism, has provided feminist and antiracist social movements of resistance some leverage against these modern logics of layered patriarchy, to the extent that notions of "diversity" and "equity" have taken hold, at least performatively (Ahmed 2019). Perry (2018: 88) acknowledges that this change has allowed her, "a black woman born in the deep South, to be present within" the academy. Indeed, some of "us" who were not included in earlier iterations have made it as continuing faculty members, to the extent that faculty who are women/racialized/queer/trans/from working-class backgrounds/ from the global South are no longer de facto excluded and completely without power in these institutions.

Diversity at Canadian universities, however, has translated mostly into the hiring of white (cis)women into tenure-track jobs (Thobani 2016). While some white women have fought tirelessly for diversity and equity initiatives that challenge white supremacy in the academy, many white women view equity and inclusion through a single-issue gender lens that normalizes and reinforces white privilege. I am reminded here of a photograph of a white woman holding a protest sign that circulated on Twitter just after the 2016 presidential election. The sign declared, "If Hilary won we'd be having brunch right now." This message defines political success for many white women as compatible with the extensive layered patriarchal violence that the Obama administration, like all the presidential administrations before his, meted out to racialized, Native American, "undocumented" and "foreign" people.

Despite significant attention to striations of race, class, gender, and indigeneity and neoliberal globalization in the fields that contribute to trans studies, the academic job market and tenure and promotion processes are formally structured by performance requirements engineered in accordance with the masculinity contest cultures of the academy and informally structured in ways that may be unwelcoming to trans people in general and trans women in particular. It is no accident, for example, that several highly successful trans women scholars achieved success *before* transition—having made it through an undergraduate degree, graduate school, and the successful navigation of the job market while being read as cis men. The mental health consequences of enduring prior to transition are significant, but successfully navigating these environments as visible trans women may not have been possible. Writing about her own traumatic experience as a trans woman on the tenure-track job market, Alex Hanna (2016) makes this important point: "A tenure-track faculty interview, even though potentially anxiety producing and traumatic, is still a relatively privileged situation. Before getting there, there are significant barriers to entering the higher education pipeline, including proper K–12 education, parental well-being and income, and adequate housing." A dynamic reflected in subaltern knowledge generation practices in general is that the most privileged members of oppressed groups typically have the greatest access to voice and socioeconomic security. Trans necropolitics is at play throughout the life course, and trans women, particularly those who are racialized, are disproportionately vulnerability to poverty. As Salvador Vidal-Ortiz (2009: 100) observes, "We operate within institutionalized constraints and, whether we do gender successfully or not, are held accountable. Often, trans women are not given employment in formal economy jobs (and unlike transmen), might not if they transition." While not de facto excluded from the academy, trans women of color are absent, with exceedingly few exceptions that I know of, from continuing faculty positions. This results from factors both inside and outside the academy.

Barriers to the training and professional development necessary to compete in the tenure-track job market are raced and classed (Henry et al. 2017) and cisgendered (Hanna 2016; Vidal-Ortiz 2009). Black and Indigenous/Native American people of color in Canada and the United States have poorer educational outcomes (Henry et al. 2017) and are disproportionately subject to push-out measures via the school-to-prison pipeline (Travers 2018). Poorer mental health outcomes associated with nonnormative gender identities are also a factor in impeding school success (Travers 2018). These ongoing barriers impact the makeup of and success rates within cohorts of graduate students, with the result that racialized and/or poor trans people of all genders, even more so than their significantly socioeconomically disadvantaged cisgender counterparts, are extremely unrepresented in the academic job market.

As a reflection of a layered patriarchal neoliberal global order, masculinity contest cultures in the academy reward/render intelligible masculine people and masculine modes of discourse and behavior while penalizing/dominating female/feminized people and feminized modes of discourse and behavior. Challenges to the elitism of the academy from feminist, antiracist, postcolonial, Indigenous, queer, and trans scholarship and activism—although significant—have often been absorbed or contained via the inclusion of white women, the performance rather than actualization of diversity and equity, and the assimilation of nonnormative scholars within the hierarchical order of the academy. The prevailing logic of the academy works to ensure that exceptions to patriarchal order posed by individuals who are women/racialized/trans reinforce the layered patriarchal logic of masculinity contest culture rather than challenge its foundations.

Trans women offend the organizational ethos of the academy by rejecting masculinity; this is deeply unsettling to organizational cultures based on the celebration and elevation of norms of masculinity that are coded white and middle or upper class. Trans women are particularly subject to hatred for renouncing the "gift" of masculinity to embrace femaleness/the feminine. Andrea Chu states this clearly: "There is no object worse than a woman. That's an operating assumption in all of my work. The problem with the transsexual is that she—and paradigmatically she *is* a she, especially if we're talking about twentieth-/twenty-first-century US culture more broadly—carries all the baggage of gender with her" (Chu and Harsin Drager 2019: 109). A trans necropolitical lens reinforces this point: both cis and trans racialized women are viewed as disposable in Canadian and US society, as evidenced by high rates of imprisonment of, violence against, and murder of Black and Indigenous/Native American cis and trans women and girls.

Speaking specifically about the patriarchal ordering of the academy and the challenges involved in resisting/transforming it, Perry (2018) highlights the ways in which patriarchal organizations have resisted change by incorporating representatives from demographic groups of previously defined nonpersons into their power structures and logics without altering the overall distribution of power and resources. This, she insists, is a structural problem we all must reckon with:

> The politics of inclusion overwhelm our struggles. Moreover, having a "seat at the table" as a precondition for our assertions threatens to over determine the table. . . . Our calls for an expansion of who can be patriarchs and ladies are such that we find the argument against the terms of liberalism difficult. We should not be ashamed of this or to admit this. It is a product of how we arrive at the institutional spaces where we have the conversations. We operate in the terms of liberal democratic theory even when we think with the tools of mid-20th-century Marxian/poststructuralist or feminist thought, and our current economic model is another challenging matter altogether. We are constrained and implicated by that constraint. That is our condition. (94)

I urge trans studies to explore the impact of masculinity contest culture on trans scholars and scholarship, including charting pathways of resistance. How can we deepen the work of going beyond playing the game to changing its rules?

Masculinity contest cultures perpetuate and reinforce inequalities while appearing "neutral" despite the ways in which such organizational cultures are foundationally (cis)gendered, raced, classed, and colonial. Trans studies in its most critical iteration is powerfully situated to document the necropolitical/necropatriarchal footprints of masculinity contest culture.

Fields that produce trans studies scholarship—within the social sciences and humanities—have been significantly shaped by feminist and queer scholarship and activism and have varied and complicated subcultures that operate to encourage and exclude, all within the larger context of the masculinity contest productivity measures of the academy. The situation/experiences of trans masculine and nonbinary people in the academy are complex: the former may be better positioned to be understood according to the terms of the masculinity contests of the academy, while the latter are often made to feel that we are not "trans enough" (Garrison 2018). But the "gender-troubling" figures of nonbinary folks may fit more seamlessly into queer-informed gender studies cultures. While trans masculine and nonbinary folks are subject to cissexism, harassment, and discrimination, trans women are often outsiders to both organizational cultures.

Trans women often bear the brunt of queer discomfort with the "trapped in the wrong body" iteration of trans identity, and, although the hostility and attacks on trans women by trans-exclusionary radical feminists are less mainstream and devastating in Canada and the United States than is currently the case in the United Kingdom, antitrans social movements operate to harm and exclude in Canadian and US contexts, often successfully gaining platforms at public institutions under the dog-whistle banner of "free speech."[4] The rage Stryker expressed toward antitrans feminist and queer forces in "My Words to Victor Frankenstein" has not lost its object. There is still plenty for trans women—and those of us who see their inclusion and well-being as central to our own liberation—to be angry about.

Because visibility as a trans woman in particular is equated with increased risk of discrimination and violence, it makes sense that the emerging and new generation of trans women who will have had access to and desire for gender-affirming health care from puberty onward may choose to "go stealth" (Beauchamp 2018). This capacity for going stealth, for being intelligible according to binary gender norms vis-à-vis various state and nonstate surveillance practices, is both a mark of racial and economic privilege and often necessary for survival. White and/or relatively wealthy trans children with supportive parents are a privileged minority among trans kids in terms of their access to the puberty-suppression therapy that can enable transnormative embodiment (Gill-Peterson 2018; Meadow 2014, 2018; Travers 2018). A trans necropolitical lens shines an unrelenting light on the reality that racialized trans people in general and trans women/trans feminine people in particular who fail to conform are de facto the most disposable members of our communities.

The nature and purpose of trans studies is the subject of the entire volume of which this essay is but a small part. It is beyond the scope of this relatively short piece to engage with these questions in any depth. I present, instead, without argument or explanation, three characteristics of a critical trans studies that I value. First, as Stryker does, I draw on the critical disability slogan of "nothing about us without us" to anchor the field. This requires the "us" who are well paid to produce it to be endlessly troubled so that trans people in all our variation are able to engage as remunerated producers of situated knowledge (Haraway 1991; Radi 2019). Second, a central purpose of trans studies is to empirically document the ways in which cisnormative binary sex systems operate as part of larger assemblages of oppression to create oppressive realities for trans people (Namaste 2000, 2005; Radi 2019; Schilt and Lagos 2017), to document the socially constructed nature of cisnormative binary systems and to fight against trans oppression, that is, to try to make things better for *all* trans people. This suggests the need for research into the experiences of trans people within academic organizational cultures that privilege some trans people over others. A final purpose of trans studies is to provide a cultural and political space for trans scholars from a range of subject positions and scholars from related disciplines (queer studies, gender studies, feminist studies, critical race studies, Indigenous and tribal studies, anti- and postcolonial studies, and more) to theorize and critically engage with each other. The lack of inclusion of trans women/trans feminine folks of color/from the global South in continuing faculty appointments in Canada and the United States is a structural problem for trans studies.

As a white, middle-class, trans-masculine, nonbinary full professor, I have profited from an extraordinarily rich combination of privilege and exceptionalism to build my career in the academy. I functioned as a masculine-presenting/butch queer woman—and am still read as such by some colleagues whom I feel uncomfortable about correcting—until I felt secure enough to refuse the femaleness assigned to me. My life as a tenured professor is very livable. It feels good to have been "folded into life," I won't lie. Those of us with institutional privilege need to fight to change academic cultures away from the layered patriarchy/trans necropolitics of masculinity contest culture—in our departments, institutions, and broader social environments. Scholars from marginalized communities have been working at this a long time, and trans studies scholars are no exception. If we are not doing this work in our working environments, then our scholarship is not contributing to an antioppressive trans justice. Perry's (2018: 103) reminder here is particularly apt:

> I believe that for the critic, the intellectual, the student, and the activist . . . the posture of distance in which one is not implicated in the mechanics of domination because one is not at the top of the global capitalist heap is untenable and unethical. That is to say, to claim a "we" in this morass is to deliberately disavow innocence. We are deeply and terribly guilty. Guilt, of course, is not equally distributed. But seeking innocence is a distraction of the highest order to critical thought.

Humbled by this reality as always, and with the full knowledge that I have made mistakes and will make many more, I close by identifying two interventions I think are important and that I have been striving to make. The first intervention involves the epistemological centering of the most marginalized trans people among us in our theorizing, analysis, and strategies for social change. I endeavored to do this in my recently published book, *The Trans Generation*, for example, by insisting on the need to center the most precarious transgender children: those who are racialized/impoverished/Indigenous/undocumented/dis/abled/binary nonconforming, and so on. I did this to explicitly decenter the mostly white, relatively wealthy, binary-conforming trans children with supportive parents who tend to circulate most in popular culture and in the news. Attending to the well-being of the most marginal in a demographic group positively impacts everyone in that group. Promoting the interests of the elite within that group via a single-issue focus, on the other hand, produces little meaningful change. But this scholarly focus lends itself equally to the extraction of value from Black and Indigenous trans people of color in the service of career progress for those of us who are white/settlers if we do not trouble the conditions of our employment at the same time. The second intervention requires keeping the following questions at the center: what is required, and what are those of us with continuing appointments able to actualize, to enable the remunerated participation of trans women/people of color in the production of trans studies? Part of this work dictates the need to document the ways in which the masculinity contest culture of the academy has necropolitical consequences.

Combining the theorizing of trans necropolitics/layered patriarchy/masculinity contest culture can enable us to track both economic and cultural flows of resources that create striations of privilege within the academy: among undergraduate and graduate students and among faculty members, divided according to continuing versus noncontinuing appointments, and among continuing appointments by rank, salary, and professional reputation.

Many antioppression scholars, including those involved in the production of trans studies, advocate for and endeavor to distribute resources in ways that oppose the hierarchical, top-down pattern of the academy. In keeping with the need to center the most marginalized students and faculty members, rather than constantly asking them to engage in disproportionate formal and informal service to the academic community, resources should flow toward them, from the most resource rich to the least resource rich. This has obvious implications for mentoring the next generation of trans scholars via assisting undergrad and grad trans students of color, particularly those who are trans women/trans feminine, as a mechanism for resisting the normative effects of masculinity contest cultures in the academy as a whole.

Travers is professor of sociology at Simon Fraser University. Their recent book, *The Trans Generation: How Trans Kids (and Their Parents) Are Creating a Gender Revolution* (2018), situates trans kids in Canada and the United States, white settler nations characterized by significant social inequality. In addition to a central research focus on transgender children and youth, Travers has published extensively on the relationship between sports and social justice, with particular emphasis on the inclusion and exclusion of women and queer and trans people of all ages. Travers's first book, *Writing the Public in Cyberspace: Redefining Inclusion on the Net* (2000), is an analysis of the ways in which equity of participation is inhibited in public spaces fostered by new information technologies. Travers is currently deputy editor of the journal *Gender and Society*.

Acknowledgments

I thank Susan Stryker for encouraging me to go beyond the late night text conversation the two of us had at the 2019 American Studies Association meeting and write this piece for *TSQ*; Jules Gill-Peterson, for comments on an early draft and for encouragement to write this piece; Jennifer Berdahl, for introducing me to masculinity contest culture theorizing; and Alex Hanna for sharing her experiences of transfeminine exclusion in the academy; and, most of all, the numerous scholars of color/Indigenous scholars who have worked for generations to produce scholarship that powerfully demonstrates the integrated workings and impact of white supremacy, colonialism, and heteropatriarchy.

Notes

1. The term *misogynoir* was coined by queer Black feminist Moya Bailey (2010) to refer to the hatred and disparagement reserved for Black women in American culture.
2. *Assemblages of oppression* refers to integrated systems of oppression: an intricate web of social history/social forces that surround us and impact experience in embodied ways. See, for example, Puar 2007.
3. This blog post so enraged John Montalbano, the chair of UBC's Board of Governors, that he contacted her to insist she withdraw her remarks. An investigator appointed by UBC concluded that Montalbano had interfered with Berdahl's academic freedom. In light of this finding, Montalbano was forced to resign (CAUT 2015).
4. Over the objections of trans people and our many allies, antitrans activist Megan Murphy has been platformed in the past year by the Vancouver Public Library and the Toronto Public Library and was to be allowed to speak at my own institution, Simon Fraser

University, until concerns about security costs resulted in the faculty member hosting Murphy to move the event off campus. The main targets of Murphy and other trans-exclusionary radical feminists are trans women, whom they refuse to recognize as women and seek to exclude from women's facilities and spaces.

References

Ahmed, Sara. 2019. "Feminists at Work: Complaint, Diversity, Institutions." Lecture given at Malmö University, Sweden, October 17.

Bailey, Moya. 2010. "They Aren't Talking about Me . . ." *Crunk Feminist Collective*, March 14. www.crunkfeministcollective.com/2010/03/14/they-arent-talking-about-me/.

Beauchamp, Toby. 2018. *Going Stealth: Transgender Politics and U.S. Surveillance Practices*. Durham, NC: Duke University Press.

Berdahl, Jennifer. 2015. "Did President Arvind Gupta Lose the Masculinity Contest?" *Jennifer Berdahl's Blog*, August 8. jberdahl.blogspot.com/2015/08/did-president-arvind-gupta-lose.html.

Berdahl, Jennifer, Marianne Cooper, Peter Glick, Robert W. Livingston, and Joan C. Williams. 2018. "Work as a Masculinity Contest." *Journal of Social Issues* 74, no. 3: 422–48.

CAUT (Canadian Association of University Teachers). 2015. "Investigation Concludes UBC Leadership Violated Academic Freedom." *CAUT Bulletin*, October 15. www.caut.ca/latest/2015/10/investigation-concludes-ubc-leadership-violated-academic-freedom.

Chu, Andrea Long, and Emmett Harsin Drager. 2019. "After Trans Studies." *TSQ* 6, no. 1: 103–16.

Connell, Raewyn. 1987. *Gender and Power: Society, the Person and Sexual Politics*. Cambridge: Polity.

Duggan, Lisa. 2003. *The Twilight of Equality: Neoliberalism, Cultural Politics, and the Attack on Democracy*. Boston: Beacon.

Garrison, Spencer. 2018. "On the Limits of 'Trans Enough': Authenticating Trans Identity Narratives." *Gender and Society* 32, no. 5: 613–37.

Gill-Peterson, Jules. 2014. "The Technical Capacities of the Body: Assembling Race, Technology, and Transgender." *TSQ* 1, no. 3: 402–18.

Gill-Peterson, Jules. 2018. *Histories of the Transgender Child*. Minneapolis: University of Minnesota Press.

Gilmore, Ruth Wilson. 2007. *Golden Gulag: Prisons, Surplus, Crisis, and Opposition in Globalizing California*. Berkeley: University of California Press.

Grant, Jaime M., Lisa A. Mottet, Justin Tanis, with Jack Harrison, Jody L. Herman, and Mara Keisling. 2011. *Injustice at Every Turn: A Look at Black Respondents in the National [US] Transgender Discrimination Survey*. Washington, DC: National Center for Transgender Equality and National Gay and Lesbian Taskforce.

Hanna, Alex. 2016. "Being Transgender on the Job Market." *Inside Higher Ed*, July 15. www.insidehighered.com/advice/2016/07/15/challenge-being-transgender-academic-job-market-essay.

Haraway, Donna. 1991. *Simians, Cyborgs, and Women: The Reinvention of Nature*. New York: Routledge.

Haritaworn, Jin, Adi Kuntsman, and Silvia Posocco, eds. 2014. *Queer Necropolitics*. Abingdon, UK: Social Justice.

Henry, Frances, Enakshi Dua, Carl E. James, Audrey Kobayashi, Peter Li, Howard Ramos, and Malinda S. Smith. 2017. *The Equity Myth: Racialization and Indigeneity at Canadian Universities*. Vancouver: University of British Columbia Press.

James, Yvonne. 2019. "Closing Canada's Universities Gender Pay Gap. Women Professors Remain Underpaid." *Star* (Toronto), August 5. www.thestar.com/opinion/contributors/2019/08 /05/closing-canadas-universities-gender-pay-gap-women-professors-remain-underpaid .html.

Jaschik, Scott. 2019. "Rethinking Diversity Frameworks in Higher Education: Authors Discuss Their New Book on Race in Higher Education." *Inside Higher Ed*, November 22.

Mbembe, Achille. 2003. "Necropolitics." *Public Culture* 15, no. 1: 11–40.

Meadow, Tey. 2014. "Child." *TSQ* 1, nos. 1–2: 57–58.

Meadow, Tey. 2018. *Trans Kids: Being Gendered in the Twenty-First Century*. Oakland: University of California Press.

Momani, Bessma. 2019. "Canadian Universities Must Stop Undervaluing Female Academics." *Globe and Mail*, January 14, updated February 8, 2019. www.theglobeandmail.com /opinion/article-canadian-universities-must-stop-undervaluing-female-academics/.

Namaste, Viviane. 2000. *Invisible Lives: The Erasure of Transsexual and Transgendered People*. Chicago: University of Chicago Press.

Namaste, Viviane. 2005. *Sex Change, Social Change: Reflections on Identity, Institutions, and Imperialism*. Toronto: Women's Press.

Perry, Imani. 2018. *Vexy Thing: On Gender and Liberation*. Durham, NC: Duke University Press.

Puar, Jasbir. 2007. *Terrorist Assemblages: Homonationalism in Queer Times*. Durham, NC: Duke University Press.

Radi, Blas. 2019. "On Trans* Epistemology: Critiques, Contributions, and Challenges." *TSQ* 6, no. 1: 43–63.

Schilt, Kristen, and Danya Lagos. 2017. "The Development of Transgender Studies in Sociology." *Annual Review of Sociology* 43: 425–43.

Snorton, Riley, and Jin Haritaworn. 2013. "Trans Necropolitics: A Transnational Reflection on Violence, Death, and the Trans of Color Afterlife." In *The Transgender Studies Reader 2*, edited by Susan Stryker and Aren Z. Aizura, 66–76. New York: Routledge.

Stone, Sandy. 1991. "The *Empire* Strikes Back: A Posttranssexual Manifesto." In *Body Guards: The Cultural Politics of Gender Ambiguity*, edited by Julia Epstein and Kristina Straub, 280–304. New York: Routledge.

Stryker, Susan. 1994. "My Words to Victor Frankenstein above the Village of Chamounix: Performing Transgender Rage." *GLQ* 1, no. 3: 237–54.

Stryker, Susan. 2014. "Transgender Studies Today: An Interview with Susan Stryker." Interview by Petra Dierkes-Thrun. *b20*, August 20. www.boundary2.org/2014/08/transgender-studies -today-an-interview-with-susan-stryker/.

Thobani, Sunera. 2016. "After UBC Ousted Arvind Gupta as President, It Made the University Whiter." *Rabble*, March 4. rabble.ca/blogs/bloggers/campus-notes/2016/03/after-ubc -ousted-arvind-gupta-president-it-made-university-white.

Travers. 2018. *The Trans Generation: How Trans Kids (and Their Parents) Are Creating a Gender Revolution*. New York: New York University Press.

Valencia, Sayak. 2019. "Necropolitics, Postmortem/Transmortem Politics, and Transfeminisms in the Sexual Economies of Death." *TSQ* 6, no. 2: 180–93.

Vidal-Ortiz, Salvador. 2009. "The Figure of the Transwoman of Color through the Lens of 'Doing Gender.'" *Gender and Society* 23, no. 1: 99–103.

Wong, Jackie. 2017. "Equitable Campuses, but for Whom? Scholars Push for a Deeper Look at How Race and Racism Play out on University Campuses." *University Affairs*, November 8. www.universityaffairs.ca/features/feature-article/equitable-campuses-but-for-whom/.

Dear Trans Studies, Can You Do Love?

IAN KHARA ELLASANTE

Abstract This essay considers the origins, intentions, and potential of transgender studies. As the field becomes increasingly institutionalized, is transgender studies capable of honoring the embodied knowledges from which it originates and, if so, how? The author suggests orientations that foreground the relevance, reciprocity, and accessibility of transgender studies for the very people whose lives and experiences the field transmutes into scholarship. The author draws from Dora Silva Santana's *papo-de-mano* and *escrevivência* and Kai M. Green and Treva Ellison's "tranifesting"—approaches that demonstrate that, in fact, transgender studies can do redress, tenderness, and love in the service of both knowledge production and resistance.
Keywords transgender studies, theorizing, embodied knowledges, institutionalization

Dear Transgender Studies,

Remember when we first met? I was eager and intrigued. But then you promptly had me up all night reading Jean-François Lyotard. With my brow furrowed, I tried to locate your roots in that text. I started to doubt that I had actually even caught a glimpse of you yet. I guess I kinda thought we'd have more in common. Remember me attempting to chart your genealogy, poring over pages of soul-numbing theory? In my mind, you'd have a throbbing heart, infused and churning with life blood: real transgender people living and bearing witness to real transgender lives had birthed, grown, and nurtured you. How is it that, according to these pages, your roots were more entangled with the dusty theories of white cis men than they were suffused with the embodied knowledges of QT2BIPOC gender-expansive folks like me?

It began to occur to me that perhaps we were not going to get along so well—that maybe it wasn't going to work out between me and you. Me, with all of my praxis and being and doing. You, with all your theories and, well, just philosophizing at length. Remember when I turned a page and whispered, "Oh, I get it. I don't belong here. This is not a place where I belong"? Remember when I began to grow resentful of the theories you claimed as your distinguished pedigree, the foundation to which you clung? Not because I was struggling to understand them,

TSQ: Transgender Studies Quarterly * Volume 7, Number 3 * August 2020   **421**
DOI 10.1215/23289252-8553076   © 2020 Duke University Press

but mostly because I was struggling to understand why they mattered, how they could matter so much. Remember when that one classmate mistook my irritation for ignorance: "Yeah, you just have to work at it, Ian. It's like a muscle"?

Okay, I acknowledge that perhaps my perception of what matters when it comes to these topics is skewed. As you might recall, I'd rush in late to the evening seminar after spending the day alongside Black, brown, and Indigenous trans, nonbinary, and Two-Spirit young people in support groups: driving with them to their appointments for housing intakes or health care, shopping with them to pick up food at the grocery store or clothes at the thrift store, dropping them off at the queer youth center or the bus stop or wherever home was for the time being, and working and advocating beside them. With these young people on my mind, inevitably, I'd think, "Don't we, myself and my kindred, deserve to see ourselves, our lives, our stories reflected in these theories? Showing up in these pages? I don't recognize us in here. Don't we matter here?"

I was often reminded of Craig Womack's (2008: 369) questions: "What is the relationship between our theories and the people we are theorizing about? Do the subjects of our theorizing see themselves in the same way as we describe them in books, journal articles, classroom lectures, and so on? How do we bring their self-representations into our theorizing?" Ultimately, I would lay the matter to rest near Barbara Christian's (1988: 72) incisive observation of her own experience with the new "New Philosophers" of literary criticism, that "I was supposed to know *them*, while they were not at all interested in knowing *me*."

Here's what I do know. Transgender studies, you are born and reborn of dynamic tumult, sustained by movements, debates, and transgressions that are transnational and anything but monochrome. You are born of Black, brown, Indigenous, immigrant, genderqueer, and nonbinary folks; of activists and artists and addicts; femmes and fairies; butches and banjee girls; *leitis* and *faʻafatama*; aggressives and studs; queers and queens; Two-Spirits and travestis; street kids and sex workers; and, yes, scholars too. Many of us flock to and crowd under the umbrella of "transgender" or its equivalents. Many of us reject such designations out of hand. Our grit and glamour, our triumphs and traumas, our hypervisibility, our invisibility. Our saltwater tears and a vast sea of lived experiences: these stormy waters are your birthplace every time.

So, transgender studies, how are you doing? No, I actually mean what are you *do*ing? How are you doing what you're doing? And for whom are you doing it? What are you doing to honor and strengthen your relationship to your birthplace? How does an increasingly institutionalized academic field do love? Do healing? Do revolution? Can it?

Ever hopeful,
Ian Khara

*   *   *

Transgender studies, as Susan Stryker (2006: 13) observes, intends to "(de)sub-jugate knowledge" by engaging "previously marginalized forms of knowledge" with "erudite scholarship" to "recapture, for use in the present, a historical knowledge of particular structurations of power." These knowledges, those of lived experience and of embodied expertise, are akin to those Malea Powell (2002: 12) calls "ghost stories": "those rooted in other knowledges, other ways of knowing, other ways of being and becoming that frequently go unheard and unsaid in much scholarly work," including "the webs and wisps of narrative that are woven around, underneath, behind, inside, and against the dominant nar-ratives of 'scholarly discourse.'" Powell continues, "I think a lot about what ghost stories can teach us, how in telling them I might both honor the knowledge that isn't honored in universities and do so in a way that interweaves these stories with more recognizable academic 'theorizing' as well" (12).

In fields like transgender studies, our "previously marginalized knowl-edges," our "ghost stories," are drawn into academic discourse and granted access to the podium, the publication, the pairing with theories of renowned scholars and, in the process, perhaps made less marginal. But is this how we "honor the knowledge"? By offering to it a type of legitimacy, validation by the academy? What about the QT2BIPOC people from whom these knowledges arise? Are they then less marginalized because their embodied knowledges reach a broader, more intellectual audience? Dora Silva Santana (2019: 210) asks us to consider how "the embodied theorizing and call for action of black and trans people transnation-ally" can be rendered visible via the processes of knowledge production and how such processes must be changed for this to take place. Perhaps we do a better job of honoring these knowledges when we more intentionally honor the people and the labor of their lives as the sources of these knowledges.

L. H. Stallings (2015: 224) observes, "If transgender and transsexual history and culture depend upon what has been published, visible, legible, and authorized enough to be archived, then we might query what has been omitted as a result of the conditions of illiteracy, criminalization, or poverty." In its aim to center and recontextualize such previously delegitimated knowledges, transgender studies intends to reconsider who and what is positioned as intellectual. This approach, ideally, invites transgender studies scholars and practitioners to weave new knowledge drawn in part from the wisdom of lived and living experience and "embodied theorizing" (Santana 2019: 210), to spend less of our energy "wor-shipping at the altar of the wisdom of the Theorist" (Powell 2002: 15). In con-sidering the participation in such "alternative" approaches to discourses, Powell asks, "What discourse is the Other discourse alternative to?" (15). As she reminds us, "Academic discourse, after all, isn't at the center of the lives of most of the humans on the globe." In other words, most people do not use the opaque language of academia to contemplate, create, and communicate knowledge. When these ways of knowing are interwoven, even foregrounded, within relevant strands of theory and into scholarly discourse, how are we then ensuring that this reconstituted knowledge is applicable, available, and accessible to those from whom it emerges? And how do accessibility and access look? In other words, how do we ensure that transgender studies does more than gesture toward reciprocity?

As it becomes increasingly institutionalized and tightens its grasp on recognition as a field of rigorous scholarship, transgender studies must be mindful to avoid replicating the same insurmountable barriers and insider/outsider dichotomies that exist throughout the academy. This is an institution designed to deny access, drawing its value primarily from its exclusivity. Instead of prizing the tools that fortify such walls, transgender studies can take up among its many tools of engagement an intentional "about us, for us, by us" orientation—"us" being those with experiential expertise in a myriad of ways of "being trans" and certainly not just those of us who are academicians. Within such a facet of transgender studies—in which knowledges that are produced, configured, and assembled about us are written, created, or performed by us and for us as the primary intended audience—we are more likely to dispense with discourse and language that "mystifies rather than clarifies our condition" (Christian 1988: 71). In so doing, we dismantle some of the barriers that preclude many trans people from seeing themselves reflected and participating in transgender studies.

In this approach, we employ various and creative modes of theorizing and engaging critically that are elicited by our own experiences and those of our kindred. This is one way to attend to the necessity of relevance, reciprocity, and accessibility when scholars of transgender studies engage with otherwise disqualified ways of knowing, such as the range of embodied epistemologies of transgender and gender-expansive people. This approach invites richer, more authentic engagement with transgender studies by people who are living the types of experiences that the field transmutes into scholarship. If, as Powell (2002: 15) points out, "the only difference between a history, a theory, a poem, an essay, is the one that we have ourselves imposed," then by taking such an expansive outlook on who and what is positioned as intellectual, we can ensure that transgender studies is done by a diversity of practitioners, not just by a small collection of scholars.

Transgender studies has long aspired to do more than observe, study, and interpret transgender phenomena. To this end, the field has embraced a shift away from identitarian methodologies (i.e., knowledge production based in the being, doing, and social positioning of transness, such as trans ethnography and auto-ethnography) toward more critical engagements with the hierarchies and structures of power and the conditions within which gender is both normed and destabilized. Despite the necessity of this type of critical theory to the development of a scholarly field, transgender studies' identitarian cornerstone is yet vital, particularly as it privileges the field's access to intimate knowledge of trans lives and experiences. Such close familiarity should inspire practitioners of transgender studies to shape theories and methodologies of tenderness, empathy, and love regarding our kindred and ourselves.

Santana (2019: 220), a "black Brazilian trans woman warrior, scholar, activist, artist and story teller of experiences embodied in language and flesh," asks, "What are the strategies of resistance and care for ourselves and our communities in the face of the haunting and material presence of death?" (210). In response, she undertakes a methodology she calls *papo-de-mana*, or "sista talk": conversing with and facilitating conversations between Black women. This practice contributes to a "multisited archive" of the knowledge and experiences of Black trans women in Brazil. This archive constitutes a body of work that, as Santana explains, "is accessed and activated then by our embodied knowledge and . . . can mean, but is not limited to, the ways we care for ourselves and for our communities, our relation to our landscapes, the discourses we create, the artistic work we produce in different media, and the imaginaries and emotions that are precariously disembodied into language" (211). With access to this "multisited archive" of embodied knowledge, Santana theorizes *mais viva*: "It means 'being-alive-savvy,' it is not just being alive but more alive; it is transitioning in the world by transcending, trans-ing life" (216). Santana's (2017: 182) project—and, similarly, her investments in the practice of *escrevivência*, "the woven tissue of unsubordinated writing of our living, writing as our living, writing-living," in which she insists on her right to write herself and her kindred into the stories she chooses to tell—demonstrate how transgender studies can do tenderness and healing in the service of both knowledge production and resistance.

Outlining a praxis of epistemic redress, healing, and resistance, Kai M. Green and Treva Ellison (2014: 224) call for transgender studies to more thoroughly engage its many shared investments with Black feminisms. They encourage using the shared tools of Black feminisms and transgender studies to form strategies of transformation "to move beyond mere theorizing." As Green and Ellison explain, "Tranifesting enacts a resistance to the political and epistemic operations that would encapsulate, and capitalize for others, the fruits of our labor. It is a form of radical political and intellectual production that takes place at the crossroads of trauma, injury, and the potential for material transformation and healing" (223). Tranifesting, as outlined by Green and Ellison, calls for expansive ways of knowing and creating new knowledges. It also spurs transgender studies to engage its underacknowledged shared lineage with Black feminisms and thereby enrich who and what is represented in the genealogy of the field.

As transgender studies is increasingly institutionalized, it may seem that it will inevitably find itself entrenched among the tarnished fixtures of academe. We must be mindful not to allow transgender studies to be anchored to a heritage that shuns the origins of this promising field—a heritage that is exclusionary by design, that would refuse to know us while requiring us to thoroughly know it. If we are to claim this institutional heritage, let us do so as the illegitimate stepchild crashing the stuffy family dinner: deliberately and brazenly nonconformist, elbows on the table, and defiantly critiquing each flavorless forkful. Then let us selectively but shamelessly pack up copious amounts of these bland offerings into Tupperware. Let us take them home to the kitchen in the heart of our home where we will deconstruct, reconfigure, supplement, infuse, and season it, preparing nourishing meals for our kindred and ourselves. With care-full practice and intention, perhaps transgender studies is an academic field that can indeed do healing and love.

Ian Khara Ellasante is a poet and cultural studies theorist whose current research engages the peoplehoood matrix—a core theoretical construct developed by Indigenous scholars—to examine the persistence of Indigenous and Black cultural identities within the oppressive milieu of settler colonialism and its associated regimes. Ellasante holds a PhD in American Indian studies from the University of Arizona and is an assistant professor of gender and sexuality studies at Bates College.

References

Christian, Barbara. 1988. "The Race for Theory." *Feminist Studies* 14, no. 1: 67–79.

Green, Kai M., and Treva Ellison. 2014. "Tranifest." *TSQ* 1, nos. 1–2: 222–25.

Powell, Malea. 2002. "Listening to Ghosts: An Alternative (Non)Argument." In *Alt Dis: Alternative Discourses and the Academy*, edited by Christopher Schroeder, Helen Fox, and Patricia Bizzell, 11–22. Portsmouth, NH: Heinemann.

Santana, Dora Silva. 2017. "Transitionings and Returnings: Experiments with the Poetics of Transatlantic Water." *TSQ* 4, no. 2: 181–90.

Santana, Dora Silva. 2019. "Mais Viva! Reassembling Transness, Blackness, and Feminism." *TSQ* 6, no. 2: 210–22.

Stallings, L. H. 2015. *Funk the Erotic: Transaesthetics and Black Sexual Cultures*. Urbana: University of Illinois Press.

Stryker, Susan. 2006. "(De)Subjugated Knowledges." In *The Transgender Studies Reader*, edited by Susan Stryker and Stephen Whittle, 1–17. New York: Routledge.

Womack, Craig S. 2008. "Theorizing American Indian Experience." In *Reasoning Together: The Native Critics Collective*, by Janice Acoose et al., 353–409. Norman: University of Oklahoma Press.

Issued by Way of "The Issue of Blackness"

JOSHUA AIKEN, JESSICA MARION MODI, and OLIVIA R. POLK

Abstract In 2017, *TSQ* published its special issue on the convergence of blackness and trans*ness, "The Issue of Blackness." In their introduction, "We Got Issues," editors Treva Ellison, Kai M. Green, Matt Richardson, and C. Riley Snorton offer a vision of a black trans* studies that acknowledges twentieth-century black feminist thought as its primary genealogy. For Ellison et al., the move to make black feminism the intellectual center of black trans* studies not only resists black women's persistent erasure from institutional narratives of knowledge making but also opens the contributions of trans* studies onto new fields of possibility for thinking and feeling embodiment, sociality, and memory otherwise. Aiken, Modi, and Polk build on Ellison et al.'s vision for a black trans* studies by bringing the concerns of "The Issue of Blackness" into conversation with recent black feminist critiques of disciplinarity and representation to imagine again how a black trans* studies rooted in black feminism might take shape in the university today.
Keywords black trans* studies, black feminist theory, decolonial theory, critical university studies

The desire to index the entanglements of black feminist poetics, the advent of trans* studies, and the aesthetics of racial capitalism cannot be traced through intellectual method alone. It is surely in the ether, suffused with our feeling. Our study of that suffusion began as historiography—making sense of what had transpired in the interdisciplines as they relied on Marxist, black, queer, and women of color feminisms since the 1980s—to unsettle our senses of the current juncture. Following the provocations of "The Issue of Blackness," the 2017 *TSQ* issue edited by Treva Ellison, Kai M. Green, Matt Richardson, and C. Riley Snorton, we also approached these entanglements genealogically, seeking the "how so" of where black studies and trans* studies do and do not meet.

The three considerations we put forward here arose from collective study that has led us to underscore questions already being asked but pitched more often than not in different registers. These gestures rehearse the feeling of imbrication. Slipping between the individuated *I* and the collective *we*, each

TSQ: Transgender Studies Quarterly * Volume 7, Number 3 * August 2020 **427**
DOI 10.1215/23289252-8553090 © 2020 Duke University Press

gesture models the sense of entanglement, the "being singular-plural" that characterized the sociality of our study (Nancy 2000). While we gesture toward convergent moments of inquiry, it is not our task to name specific points where blackness and trans*ness intersect—they do, and not always in the ways we might think. It is our goal, rather, to push up against modern systems of knowledge-power that wish such meeting places, subjectivities, sensations, and people would simply disappear, if not conveniently align themselves with the machinations of knowledge-power. We seek to interrogate the disciplining that has taken place in recent decades that obfuscates entangled methods, theories, and practices. The three of us—through both divergent and convergent modes of thought, and from differing self-identifications that sometimes coincide—attend to prob-lematics that cannot be unstaked from the stakes of our lives.

Gesture 1 | Aiken

The provocations that end Hortense J. Spillers's (1987) seminal essay "Mama's Baby, Papa's Maybe" haunt us. We are haunted by what is possible, and by what we may most need. What is asked in trans* studies and questioned anew in black studies is why we want to know what we know; my assertion is that the historical a priori (Jackson 2018: 621; Foucault [1969] 2002) abyss identified by black feminist poetics must be the grounds for a discussion that vindicates the project of feeling-thinking-breathing the world otherwise.

What Zakiyyah Iman Jackson (2018: 628) calls "the black mater(nal)" demands interrogation of not just binary gender as a social arrangement but also the conditions by and through which gendered difference exists. When Spillers (1987: 80) makes explicit that black men have had the "specific occasion to learn *who* the female is within itself" in the context of New World slavery, she locates a site of encounter that still calls to those of us who know the stakes of this occa-sion; those of us concerned with a "racialized perception of reality" (Spillers and duCille 2018: 7) are concerned with how this racialized perception punishes non-normative gender and sexual subjectivities, skews life chances, and structures dominant epistemologies.

Jackson's "black mater(nal)" reflects an iterative itinerary: between 1492 and the present, a narrative of how gendered life in the antiblack world persists. One's relationship to the "sublime function of the black mater(nal)" or "black femininity" can be a way of describing one's relationship to that which exceeds modernity's discursive and material terms. New World slavery came to be para-digmatically defined by the idea that the only thing black women could bestow on their children was slave status. Thus as we live the "afterlife of slavery" (Hartman 2007: 6), ideas of gender, sex, and sexuality remain defined against all things associated with femininity as it is routed through black life.

How to describe that world? In "Theorizing in a Void," Jackson (2018) denotes a genealogy of black feminist poetics' interrelation with physics that precedes and exceeds a contemporary feminist materialism. Alongside Spillers, we are also concerned here with Sylvia Wynter (1990, 2001), Michele Wallace ([1990] 2016), Kara Keeling (2007), Evelyn Hammonds (1987, 1994), and Kimberlé Crenshaw (1991, 1992), all of whom call attention to material and symbolic paradoxes of "black female sex/uality" as "not-absent-though-not-present," and the inverse "absent yet-ever-present" (Hammonds 1994: 129). Proximate to this absence-presence are what Jackson (2018: 621) calls "standpoints"—cisgender and trans* standpoints that, it must be underscored as Jackson does, take material and symbolic forms.

Dominant discourses of race and gender become logics through which black cis people, black trans* and nonbinary people, and most especially black trans* women experience "incalculable and insatiable violence" (633). These representational schemas attempt to reduce black life to gratuitous violence and nothing more. The black mater(nal) underlies these representational terms. Thus as certain strains of black studies struggle with their own persistent tendency to overdetermine black women's arguments and minimize the specific claims made by specific moves in (at least) the last five decades of black feminist thought—certain strains that Jared Sexton (2018) and Jennifer Nash (2019) have both criticized—black studies writ large cannot afford in turn to obfuscate the trans*ness of the black past. Historical accounts that try to capture how things were in the past quickly turn into projects of captivity that misrecognize what Tavia Nyong'o (2019) calls "non-binary blackness: a blackness that asserts another temporality than that which is enforced within straight time." A restive methodological project must take place: one that refuses a universal dehistoricized black or trans* positionality, and that attends to, rather, the traces of identification as those traces flicker, appear, and confound. Moreover, as Snorton (2017) asserts, the question becomes how these traces manifest in context, under what conditions, and in which temporalities: how black trans* experiences have been made apparent or have been conspicuously disappeared.

How might black trans*/queer genders remind us that the objective of our lives may not always be to be understood? "Gender violence is a reality for everyone surviving antiblackness," Ashleigh Shackelford (2019) writes; "No one knows my gender but me. And you were always uninvited."

To return to the question of how trans* studies and black studies push us to interrogate our hunger to obtain and acquire knowledge: Saidiya Hartman (2019: 143) writes, "Negroes were drifters, nomads, fugitives . . . they had not been allowed 'me' and 'mine.'" This disallowance of a "me" and "mine," of personhood that acknowledges interrelation and plasticity, reflects the material, epistemological, and ontological preconditions of black trans* life. Black gender fugitive experience, as it has been, and as it has been studied in the field of black trans* studies, must always-already be where "the positionality of subterranean and submersed thought" (Snorton 2017: 197) attends to "the nameless so it can be thought" (Lorde 1984: 37). For black people, the trans*ness and queerness of our relation to gendered categories not only animates our past but is what makes "carrying it forward" possible: it is a power source for transgressive demands.

Even if articulated differently, the history of racial blackness and the history of New World slavery means that black male's[1] "specific occasion" (Spillers 1987: 80) is one of "interior intersubjectivity" (Spillers 1996: 83). It is "the heritage of the *mother* that the African-American male must regain as an aspect of his own personhood—the power of 'yes' to the 'female' within" (Spillers 1987: 80). Moreover, given that this inheritance is that of the "mother and the mother-dispossessed" (80), we must ask what is lost if the specific occasion of black men's personhood is ignored. Spillers's assertion warrants a conversation regarding the "how so" of black male personhood, rather than black male being, is entangled a priori with a figuration's monstrosity: the "how so" of fugitive life. Fugitive life, following Susan Stryker's (1994: 248) essay on trans* monstrosity, may well be "located at the margin of subjectivity and the limit of signification."

This calls attention to a second concern regarding who and what must be disavowed, and how that disavowal must take place, for intelligible gendered subjects to exist. We are, at the very least, forced to sit with Spillers's penultimate paragraph, in which she describes the specific occasion that the black American male embodies because of the legal terms of New World slavery. The black mater(nal) establishes the queerness of black genders, given the legal arrangement that both followed the womb (*partus sequitur ventrem*) and followed the entitlements of white patriarchs (paterfamilias), namely, the right to own property. While Spillers's argument here has certainly not been lost on black feminist scholarship, neither must this element of her insight be lost in black studies writ large, nor in trans* studies. What might we be provided with if we recognize the black mater(nal) as also a figuration for Wynter's (1984: 34) discussion of the "Ultimate Chaos": "that which throws the humanist project as we know it into crisis"?

New modes of inquiry are necessary, as black studies and trans* studies are in the midst of doing this work up against wholesale institutionalization: registering proximities to whom, what, and potentially how the black mater(nal) has the power to make meaning. Spillers (1987: 80) ends on exactly this point—the how of meaning—suggesting that "'Sapphire' might rewrite after all a radically different text for female empowerment" in the case of "actually *claiming* the monstrosity (of a female with the potential to 'name')." The monstrousness of the black mater(nal) claim does the work of stabilizing the "arrangement of gender and regulation of sexual expressivity" whereby "black(ened) female sex/uality is an abjected or voided, oblique signifier of that foreclosure" (Jackson 2018: 633). The black mater(nal) claim is how.

Black feminist poetics and "poethics" (Ferreira da Silva 2014), as I have relayed, have and continue to reflect this sentiment. Jackson (2018: 628) explains that "the sublime function of the black mater(nal), which I am calling black femininity, is *an antecedent* to both perception and knowledge of a thing in a post-1492 context" (emphasis added). It is crucial that, as Marquis Bey (2017) explains in "The Trans*-Ness of Blackness and the Blackness of Trans*-Ness," "transitivity" defines not just black trans* lives but also the myriad of black experiences that visual, representational, and historical schema seek to ensnare. This "prepersonal singularity" is "characterized by instability" such that trans*—with the asterisk—is a *"moving mattering"* (Hayward and Weinstein 2015: 206), "engaging in a kind of 'guerrilla' (em)bodying through" (Bey 2017: 286) that Sandy Stone (2014: 92) describes as "disrupting the smoothness and closure on which power depends."

Indeed, many of the ideas in this gesture come from the provocations of Jackson (2013, 2016, 2018), Ferreira da Silva (2014), Tina Campt (2017, 2019), Rizvana Bradley (2016), and others whose works are running a course concerned with the world of racialized representation and reality that moves—crucially—in relationship with black trans* studies. Before personhood lies a "raced and gendered" fugitivity that is "anoriginal" (Bey 2017: 276), as suggested by such scholars as Snorton (2017), Savannah Shange (2019a), Kai M. Green (in Green and Ellison 2014; in Sloan 2016), Elías Costenza Krell (2017), and V. Varun Chaudhry (2019). Trans* of color critiques insist on a fugitivity that exceeds historical narratives of how contemporary gender categories have taken form. Moreover, I would underscore Bey's (2017: 276) contention that the vital force of this fugitivity "move[s] through the abyss underlying ontology, rubbing up alongside it and causing it to fissure." Before ontological being, we could suggest, there is dispossession or there is a nothingness, or—fractally—there is virtuality and something more (Ferreira da Silva 2016a, 2016b, 2017). "Carrying it forward" (Rowell 1991: 89) here, in terms of interdisciplinary fields, means following a dissembling itinerary, a wayward way of asking questions and being prepared to question what exactly those questions are for.

To speak to the abyss that underlies is to return, at an angle, to Evelyn Hammonds's (1994: 137) question of "what is it like inside of a black hole." Not just in terms of the invisibility, hypervisibility, silencing, and distorting of black cis and trans* women, but also in terms of considering the un-represent-ability of black matter and the black maternal, such that we use "sensitive detectors of energies and distortions," such as "reading strategies that allow us to make visible . . . distorting and productive effects" (134–35). The very "difference without separability" (Ferreira da Silva 2016b) that marks the physics of touching—the site of intrarelated indeterminacies—marks scholars and students of trans* studies, black studies, and trans* of color studies; queer of color analyses; scholars and students of black, women of color, and lesbian feminisms; and feminist science studies. We must find a way to find our way toward what must be done, at the expense and disposal of nobody and nothing.

I thus do nothing more than vindicate the project of a grounded *we* that exists beyond the world as we know it. This means careful readings of conjunctures: spending time with the interventions of a range of scholars—those who weave together the exigencies of normative childhood, the historical-scientific materialities, embodiments, and significations related to the "human"; and the queerness, trans*ness, and blackness of space, futurity, and time (Bernstein 2011; Castañeda 2014; Cox 2015; Meadow 2018; Gill-Peterson 2018; Shange 2019b; Tolbert and Peterson 2013; Hayward 2012; Stone 2017; Durban-Albrecht 2017; Ferreira da Silva 2007, 2014; Moten 2013; Barad 2015; Jackson 2018; Springgay and Truman 2019). We have to take the time to feel how different ideas are the product of comingling legacies. Queer black feminisms, trans* of color critiques, and feminist science studies, for example, all provide ways of thinking about the world. But it is only through the close study of their unique genealogies that inevitably, at times, converge, that we find language to say what we actually mean. We find ways to express how what we think rubs up against what we feel. Again, the stakes are high: Is my gender what I say it is or is it what racialized gender arrangements allow for? This question requires that we think about what Hammonds (1994: 140) calls a "politics of articulation" that, in the context of black women's sexuality, "represent[s] discursive and material terrains where there exists the possibility for the active production of speech, desire, and agency." How might we embody, inhabit, or announce a proximity to such terrains? What lines of thought and flight might be possible there? Wherever we are, we are haunted by a ghost that cares—haunted always by the grounds we choose to ignore.

Gesture 2 | Modi

Trans* studies and black studies share an irreducible relationship to poetics as a mode of knowing. The modern world—its teleological thought, its fixed localities, its division of white/European male subjects from their "others"—privileges determinacy as a mode of knowing. If we follow the path set by Spillers's American grammar (1987, 2003), in which black bodies in the afterlife of slavery and binary-gendered subject positions "adhere to no symbolic integrity," we traverse the mutual indeterminacy of black and trans* studies and their poetic remaking of social and material formations. Keeling (2009) and Snorton (2017,

2019) suggest that the grammar of a queer black radical politics operates in the "future conditional," and they initiate a transition to trans* black praxis that I wish to continue here. What grammar might map how trans*ness and blackness converse and converge, and how might that grammar intervene in the straightness—linearity—of white, cis-centric, settler colonial worlding?

Whatever this grammar might be, it will not resemble the grammar of disciplinary knowledge as we know it. Wynter contends that in order to unsettle the colonial order of being in which the "ethnoclass of Man" holds sway, we must unsettle the biocentric order of knowledge that reifies it (Wynter 2003; Wynter and McKittrick 2015). The disciplinary divide between natural sciences on the one side and the social sciences and humanities on the other is a constitutive element in the colonial project of asking "who and what are human beings?" Recent scholarship in the social sciences and humanities reconstructs the medicalizing, gendering, and racializing functions of this divide (Gill-Peterson 2018; Schuller 2018). However, the divisive logic still predominates. Colonial determination of "who or what human beings are" requires a "bioevolutionary teleological logic" based on the same Malthusian-Darwinian trope of naturally determined scarcity that subtends the accumulative logic of racial capitalism (Wynter and McKittrick 2015: 65). That is, the logics that undergird biological essentialism and economic scarcity also discipline bodies and modes of being into racialized and gendered categories. They assume a present perfect tense in which being and embodiment have always already been fixed.

When black and trans* studies converse and converge, one effect is the dissolution of the ostensibly indissoluble divide that Wynter elucidates, often through entangled re-formations of life and language. As trans* studies and black studies transverse disciplines and trans*ness and blackness escape fixed categories, perhaps the question they collectively ask is: who and what will we have been being?

The multiple *to be* verbs grate on the ear; the syntax feels redundant, the meaning crowded and unwieldy. Yet the plurality and surplus of being and meaning articulated by the future perfect conditional tense is precisely what I mean. As fungible modes of being, both trans*ness and blackness interpellate the supposed determinacy of race and gender, generating indeterminacy. The multiplicity in the past, present, and ongoing future engenders a trans* black mode of being. The conjuncture of these fields lies in the generative indeterminacies of syntax and grammar, and trans* and black interdisciplines activate these language-capacitated entanglements (Spillers 2003; Moten and Harney 2013; Bradley and Marassa 2014; Barad 2015; Bey 2017; Ellison 2017; Gossett 2017; Tsang and Moten 2017; Jackson 2018).

The concomitance of trans* and black studies transforms the dictum "The social revolution cannot draw its poetry from the past, but only from the future"

(Marx [1852] 2008: 3). Frantz Fanon famously closes *Black Skin, White Masks* ([1952] 2008) with a version of this oft-cited passage from Karl Marx's *Eighteenth Brumaire of Louis Bonaparte* in which he calls for "introducing invention into existence" to destroy the current colonial temporality that disallows black liberation. Trans* and black studies maintain Fanon's insistence that future poetry be an original poetry, an act of imagination and creation that breaks with precedent. But, following work on black and trans* ontology by Karen Barad, Bey, Ellison, Jackson, and Fred Moten, trans*ness and blackness invoke anoriginality, an irreducibly plural presence at the origin, as the imaginative ideal to bring into being. A world otherwise needs anoriginal poetry. Or more precisely and more broadly, it needs anoriginal poesis. This is not to say that poetry as a literary genre is the only mode of expressing trans*ness and blackness together or that their institutional forms should emulate literature departments. Just as the work of poet-scholars like Alexis Pauline Gumbs (2016, 2018, 2020) makes a case for trans-medial expression, I seek here to think through the grammar of bringing a trans* and black world into being.

Barad's (2015) notion of trans* materialities, for instance, resonates with Denise Ferreira da Silva's (2016b) assertion of black being as "difference without separability." Barad conceives of trans* materialities as ways of being and living in a space of plenitude—of plural social and material forms. They are not utopian projections "of some future or elsewhere" to arrive at or achieve but "material existences in the thick now of the present . . . that entail superpositions of many beings and times, multiple im/possibilities that coexist." A poetics of trans* materialities will have been articulating the "mutual indeterminacies of being and time" (288).

In pursuit of a similar plenitude and indeterminacy, Ferreira da Silva (2007, 2014, 2016a, 2016b, 2017) delineates the difference between blackness as category and blackness as matter. In modern regimes of thought, blackness as a category exists as "always already a referent of commodity, an object, and the other, as fact beyond evidence" (Ferreira da Silva 2014: 81) and, as such, functions at once as subjugated commodity and as the violence, terror, and "Ultimate Chaos" (Wynter 1984: 34) that threatens the modern ordered world. It categorically serves the modern economy of fixed signification that justifies planetary "total violence" (Ferreira da Silva 2016b: 57), such as antiblack state violence in the United States and in Europe, capitalist expropriation in Africa and Latin America, and the "refugee crisis" unsettling the grammar of human rights. In short, and in Ferreira da Silva's (2017) words, "the category of blackness serves the ordered universe of determinacy and the violence and violations it authorizes." Blackness as matter—as formless, vital substance—nullifies ways of knowing that depend on determinacy (as well as, argues Ferreira da Silva, separability and sequentiality). As matter, it "invites the possibility of knowing without modern categories" under which difference among humans and matter registers as separability (Ferreira da Silva 2014: 84). As a way of thinking and knowing, it imagines the world not as the location for self-determination and "places of scarcity" but as a plenum and "spaces of plenty" (Ferreira da Silva 2017). Both trans*ness and blackness can disorder the ordered universe on which the modern world's investment in pure being depends. They activate and animate pluralist praxes of being human.

Through their discursive and material entanglements, the fields of black and trans* studies activate latent possibilities in Hammonds's (1994: 141) call to resist the white/European male axis of power by traversing the indeterminate "discursive and material terrains" of black queer female sexualities and by fostering "the active production of speech, desire, and agency." As Ferreira da Silva (2017) asserts, "Blackness's creative capacity first manifests as a disruptive force." Trans*ness and blackness, in other words, mobilize a creative capacity that—within the "ethnogenderclass" of Man (Wynter via Bey 2017) and its attendant ordering of difference into race and gender—registers as disruption.

Ferreira da Silva (2007) and Stryker (1994), among others, deploy a Frankensteinian trope—the conception of monsters as unnatural, disordered matter that threaten the modern order of being—to describe modern categorizations of material (bodily and social) difference. Ferreira da Silva (2007) traces the "analytics of raciality" through imaginings and ordering of matter. Dr. Frankenstein's creation of life, she argues, chronicles how nineteenth-century sciences of the mind refashion self-consciousness as an effect of the rational laws of nature. In so doing, they globalize the modern separation and determinations—of subject and object, of the self and its others, inside and outside—that subtend the analytics of race (93–95). In other words, a Frankensteinian science of self-creation exemplifies how self-determination is generated by and through difference (of, for example, gender or race) and by recreating relations to the "laws of nature." Stryker's performative text "My Words to Victor Frankenstein above the Village of Chamounix" (1994: 238) announces a political, material, and ontological affinity with the rage Frankenstein's monster feels at being "perceived as less than fully human" when attempting self-determination. This rage, Stryker demonstrates, is produced by language's inability to represent trans*-material forms of embodiment—its inability to signify "matter that simultaneously eludes definitive representation and demands its own perpetual rearticulation in symbolic terms" (248). Stryker concludes by transmuting this rage and the chaotic forces signified by trans* embodiment into the creative capacity, or poiesis, to constitute being on her own terms and against the natural order. Spillers (1987: 80) articulates a related creative power, a poesis, in "claiming the monstrosity (of a female with the potential to 'name')." In their moments of poetic making, both trans★ and black being anagram matter.

If trans★ness transverses lines of determinate time and space to creatively reimagine and restructure materiality and what matters, it does so along similar but distinct routes to the same anoriginal condition that blackness as matter registers and mobilizes. Jackson (2018: 630) theorizes this entangled mattering through her concept of the black *mater*(nal), which is "precisely not a standpoint (cis, trans★, or otherwise)." Rather, it is "a place in space that conditions standpoint. Its figuration is a matter of history and proximity" (630). When trans★ness and blackness register not as estranged but entangled differences that mark another mode of being in the world, they fracture the determinate category of Man under the universal order. Their intersubjective imaginative power—their power to create out of the *material*—short-circuits the repetition of the past and instead functions as poesis, as the maker of what will have been happening.

Trans★ studies and black studies recently have made major inroads as institutionalized forms of critique against the determinate modern subject and universal order. Each edifies the other's practice of not conflating a growing institutional form for flourishing forms of sociality. Just as black study acts as a model for and a check on its institutional analog black studies, trans★ness transverses and transforms trans★ studies. It nearly goes without saying that the formation of new programs, departments, or fields based on categories of (racialized, gendered, embodied) difference does not dismantle the old violence these categories authorize.

Nor are poetics a teleological endpoint. Instead they articulate the entangled modes of knowing that are already at play in both fields as they imagine the world otherwise. To twist the name of Ferreira da Silva's ethico-political program (2014), we might engage black trans★ poethics, a moment of radical praxis in which sociality indexes the entangled world. It's the beginning of the world as we will have been knowing it.

Gesture 3 | Polk

In an interview in 2016, reproduced in *Trap Door: Trans Cultural Production and the Politics of Visibility*, Che Gossett asks visual artist and DJ Juliana Huxtable, "Do you feel that there is a black trans radical tradition? And how might it be defined?" (Tourmaline, Stanley, and Burton 2017: 39). Huxtable replies, "Well, it's weird because, to me, the word 'tradition' implies a handing down, or rituals, or hand-me-downs, and traced languages, and documentation of all that. To me, that's what tradition goes hand in hand with. And so, I find it hard to say whether or not there's a black trans radical tradition" (40).

In this last gesture, as we explore Ellison et al.'s insistence in "The Issue of Blackness" that a black trans* studies derives its theoretical tools from black feminism, we build on Huxtable and Gossett's exchange to consider what we all have gestured toward in some fashion: can there be such a thing as the black trans* radical tradition, and what is its relation to black feminism?

The concept of a "black radical tradition" has shaped the genealogy of black thought since Cedric J. Robinson published *Black Marxism* in 1983. In the scope of Robinson's (Robinson [1983] 2000) work, the black radical tradition referred to the set of creative political, aesthetic, and everyday practices that resisted objecthood under the totalizing force of racial capitalism's expropriation of black people's lives and labor. For Robinson, the paradigmatic figures of the black radical tradition include W. E. B. Du Bois, C. L. R. James, and Richard Wright. Although the black radical tradition is a framework that has facilitated the production of other paradigm-shifting work in black thought (Kelley 2002; Moten 2003), the black radical tradition qua Robinson gives limited attention to gender, and the ways in which the malleability of black gender amplifies, and indeed subtends the radical appositionally of blackness (Quan 2005).

For those of us positioned within the academy over fifty years into the institutionalization of black studies, the question of the black radical tradition is particularly salient. How might our attachments to the ordering of our history through the lens of Robinson's paradigm find themselves kaleidoscoped and transfigured when reconsidered in terms of a black trans* radical tradition? How might this ubiquitous concept in the historical and cultural study of black life be stretched and perhaps made new when refracted through trans*ness? How might this allow us to consider how a black trans* studies, rooted in a black trans* feminism, might reshape our superstructural narratives of blackness, precisely through its articulation of black trans* radical thought?

The oft-quoted history of trans* woman of color radicalism that frequently begins with Sylvia Rivera and Marsha P. Johnson's work through Street Transvestite Action Revolutionaries, and the roots of black trans* intellectuals and artists like Gossett, Tourmaline, and Green, among many others in prison abolition and transformative justice work, already points to a genealogy of blackness and trans*ness that is grounded not just in black feminism but also in a materialist analysis of power. As David Scott (2013: 1) has argued, the draw of the black radical tradition as the frame for black studies and its subfields lies in that framework's ability to generate a feeling, an "an idea of belonging" that orients black intellectuals to a shared past and which might steer us toward a common aspiration for how knowledge making could reflect our desires for a world beyond racial capitalism. And yet, queer studies, trans* studies, and black feminist theory have all affirmed that the scope of our desire, and thus the scope of our knowledge production, can contain more plurality and alterity than could be comfortably consolidated into "tradition."

When we invoke the black radical tradition in a vision for the future of a black trans* studies, to some extent we are already discussing something other than the particular genealogy of black feminism. The work anthologized in *Trap Door* (Tourmaline, Stanley, and Burton 2017) makes evident the context of racial capitalism and settler colonialism that informs the theory and practice of black trans* cultural producers and activists (those folks who create the texts and histories for black trans* study). On the other hand, Ellison et al. (2017b: 163), in "The Issue of Blackness," however committed they are to situating the study of blackness and trans*ness firmly in a black Marxist frame, refuse to acquiesce to a "Black feminist studies without black women" and consequently to a trans* studies without black feminism (and we'd add, following Jackson [2018] and Keeling [2007], without the black femme in particular). Black trans* femininity explodes at the edges of the black radical tradition.

Why bother with tradition? It *matters*. Beyond making meaning, it lends materiality to knowledge, to subjects, and to history. Tradition, whether radical or hegemonic, is a technology of enfleshment. Even from the margins of the university, the desire to participate in its forms of social and epistemic reproduction through the practice of citation, and marking oneself within a linear tradition, remains strong. Thinking about how blackness and trans*ness interact with an intellectual genealogy that has suffused the institutional legacy of black thought since at least the 1970s enjoins us to resist the erasure of black women's theoretical contributions; it is also an occasion to consider again the precarious terms of black feminism's capture in the institution. As Ellison et al. (2017b: 163) make clear in quoting Grace Kyungwon Hong's (2008) essay "'The Future of Our Worlds': Black Feminism and the Politics of Knowledge in the University under Globalization," they recognize that foregoing tradition by declining to acknowledge the contributions of black (lesbian) women historians, poets, and critics to the theorization of trans*ness perpetuates the university formation's targeted epistemic violence. Both black and trans* studies share a fraught relationship to the desire to make their subjectivities known on their own terms and in the balance of the university's voracious efforts to incorporate and domesticate difference (Ferguson 2012; Gossett 2013; Stryker 2008). The mode of tradition that is incorporated and reproduced as canon, or discipline, would have us identify and remember ourselves through the means of patrilineage and (intellectual) property. Instead we envision a lineage of black trans* feminism that reproduces knowledge and transfers memory in the mode of black mater(nity), or fanning roots of rhizomes, or the infectious, undulating groove and "funky erotixxx" (Horton-Stallings 2015: 10) of our femme bodies in the club.

The provocation of whether there can or ought to be such a thing as a black trans* radical tradition produces a web of poethical considerations that can't be resolved here, and which may have no resolution at all. But it does return us to the contributions that black trans* studies and recent black feminist criticism have already produced, which offer other orientations to the question. For example, by reading beyond the limits of historical materialism, without effacing the role of colonial expropriation that initiates the dominant order of race and racial knowledge, Ferreira da Silva's (2014) "Black Feminist Poethics" operates on the same frequencies as Snorton's (2017) transitive approach to blackness and trans*ness. The notion of transitivity as a relation of exchange "requires that one become acquainted with the social life of things, which is also to consider how one's relationship to things and as a thing entails a confrontation and rethinking of the past as it has been rendered into History" (Snorton 2017: 6).

This is the same attitude that Huxtable articulates when she questions whether there is such a thing as a black trans* radical tradition. In lieu of a tradition, she feels out a poethics and aesthetics of relation in "nightlife." "Nightlife," she says,

> was really welcoming. It was a space that was diverse—way more diverse than any other self-identified creative, left-of-center space, you know? There were a lot of Black people, a lot of queer people. It felt really free, like a space for experimentation. I've always wanted to be an artist. But I suppressed that urge because I didn't think it was possible. Nightlife became a way to experiment and to feel like I had space to pursue myself, to pursue my work as an extension of myself. (Tourmaline, Stanley, and Burton 2017: 51)

To the extent that we can envision a "field" of black trans* studies, we view it less as a genealogy that sees, as Robinson did, through a deep linear history of capital's flow. Instead, in taking up Snorton's grammar of transitivity and Jackson's dense black mater(nal), we forgo a vision of black trans* studies that works to establish historical continuity in favor of instances of stickiness, exchange, transitive movement. The social world—its ephemerality, its emergence, and its virtuality—ought to continue to shape the ways in which a black trans* studies manifests.

More than anything else, developing the field according to Ellison et al.'s vision may entail what Jennifer Nash (2019: 131) has called a "letting go." This black feminist poethical practice must go beyond letting go of "woman" as the (cis)gendered subject of black feminism to enact an even messier letting go of academia. In gesturing toward the undisciplined nature of a "black trans radical tradition," we mean to suggest that a field of black trans* studies, to quote Hartman (2019: 347), must not be another "dance within an enclosure"—where enclosure is produced by the seductive will to index a definitive tradition or canon—within which blackness and trans*ness articulate their transitive exchanges. What might we labor toward instead, as we excavate archives of blackness, trans*ness, and femme-ness, if we let go of the disciplinary impulse to assert a tradition? The vibrant social worlding of trans* embodiment helps us feel all the more at ease in this practice of letting go.

What Huxtable describes as the absence of a "radical tradition" as such is a proliferated atmosphere of vibrancy that is just as able to resist and exceed the threat of social death. The grammar, historicity, and geography of black trans*ness simultaneously resist the consolidation or uniform tracing of tradition, while still enticing us into genealogical projects like the ones issued by "The Issue of Blackness." As Huxtable suggests, the nonentity of a black trans* radical tradition offers an object lesson in understanding the ephemeral and emergent sociality that informs how we in the field discuss our variously submerged genealogies, to shape the very thing we mean to study.

Joshua Aiken is a poet and PhD student in history and African American studies at Yale University.

Jessica Marion Modi is a poet and PhD student in English and African American studies at Yale University.

Olivia R. Polk is a PhD student in American studies and African American studies at Yale University.

Acknowledgments

Thank you to Susan Stryker for her generous editorial eye, and for the invitation to contribute to this issue. Thanks also to Elizabeth Ault, who offered valuable feedback on an earlier draft. This piece was completed in love and rage for the lives of Nina Pop, Tony McDade, Breonna Taylor, Ahmaud Arbery, and George Floyd.

Note

1.   Here, I follow Spillers's language in describing people sexed as black males in this historical context rather than describing black cis men.

References

Barad, Karen. 2015. "TransMaterialities: Trans*/Matter/Realities and Queer Political Imaginings." *GLQ* 21, nos. 2–3: 387–422. doi.org/10.1215/10642684-2843239.

Bernstein, Robin. 2011. *Racial Innocence: Performing American Childhood from Slavery to Civil Rights*. New York: New York University Press.

Bey, Marquis. 2017. "The Trans*-Ness of Blackness, the Blackness of Trans*-Ness." *TSQ* 4, no. 2: 275–95. doi.org/10.1215/23289252-3815069.

Bradley, Rizvana. 2016. "Living in the Absence of a Body: The (Sus)Stain of Black Female (W)holeness." *Rhizomes: Cultural Studies in Emerging Knowledge*, no. 29. doi.org/10.20415/rhiz/029.e13.

Bradley, Rizvana, and Damien-Adia Marassa. 2014. "Awakening to the World: Relation, Totality, and Writing from Below." *Discourse* 36, no.1: 112–31.

Campt, Tina. 2017. *Listening to Images*. Durham, NC: Duke University Press.

Campt, Tina. 2019. "The Visual Frequency of Black Life: Love, Labor, and the Practice of Refusal." *Social Text*, no. 140: 25–46. doi.org/10.1215/01642472-758503.

Castañeda, Claudia. 2014. "Childhood." *TSQ* 1, nos. 1–2: 59–61. doi.org/10.1215/23289252-2399605.

Chaudhry, V. Varun. 2019. "Centering the 'Evil Twin': Rethinking Transgender in Queer Theory." *GLQ* 25, no.1: 45–50.

Cox, Aimee Meredith. 2015. *Shapeshifters: Black Girls and the Choreography of Citizenship*. Durham, NC: Duke University Press.

Crenshaw, Kimberlé. 1991. "Race, Gender, and Sexual Harassment." *Southern California Law Review* 65, no. 3: 1467–76.

Crenshaw, Kimberlé. 1992. "Mapping the Margins: Intersectionality, Identity Politics, and Violence against Women of Color." *Stanford Law Review* 43, no. 6: 1241–99. www.jstor.org/stable/1229039.

Durban-Albrecht, Erin. 2017. "Postcolonial Disablement and/as Transition: Trans* Haitian Narratives of Breaking Open and Stitching Together." *TSQ* 4, no. 2: 195–207. doi.org/10.1215/23289252-3814997.

Ellison, Treva. 2017. "The Labor of Werqing It: The Performance and Protest Strategies of Sir Lady Java." In Tourmaline, Stanley, and Burton 2017: 1–22.

Ellison, Treva, Kai M. Green, Matt Richardson, and C. Riley Snorton, eds. 2017a. "The Issue of Blackness." Special issue, *TSQ* 4, no. 2.

Ellison, Treva, Kai M. Green, Matt Richardson, and C. Riley Snorton. 2017b. "We Got Issues: Towards a Black Trans*/ Studies." *TSQ* 4, no. 2: 162–69. doi.org/10.1215/23289252-3814949.

Fanon, Frantz. (1952) 2008. *Black Skin, White Masks*. Translated by Richard Philcox. New Nork: Grove Atlantic.

Ferguson, Roderick. 2012. *The Reorder of Things: The University and Its Pedagogies of Minority Difference*. Minneapolis: University of Minnesota Press.

Ferreira da Silva, Denise. 2007. *Toward a Global Idea of Race*. Minneapolis: University of Minnesota Press.

Ferreira da Silva, Denise. 2014. "Toward a Black Feminist Poethics: The Quest(ion) of Blackness toward the End of the World." *Black Scholar* 44, no. 2: 81–97.

Ferreira da Silva, Denise. 2016a. "Fractal Thinking." *Accessions*, no. 2. accessions.org/article2/fractal-thinking/.

Ferreira da Silva, Denise. 2016b. "On Difference without Separability." In *Incerteza Viva: Thirty-Second Bienal de São Paulo*, exhibition catalog, edited by Jochen Volz and Júlia Rebouças, 57–65. São Paulo: Fundação Bienal de São Paulo.

Ferreira da Silva, Denise. 2017. "1 (Life) ÷ 0 (Blackness) = $\infty - \infty$ or ∞ / ∞: On Matter beyond the Equation of Value." *e-flux journal*, no. 79. www.e-flux.com/journal/79/94686/1-life-0-blackness-or-on-matter-beyond-the-equation-of-value/.

Foucault, Michel. (1969) 2002. *Archaeology of Knowledge*. 2nd ed. London: Routledge.

Gill-Peterson, Jules. 2018. *Histories of the Transgender Child*. Minneapolis. University of Minnesota Press.

Gosset, Che. 2013. "Silhouettes of Defiance: Memorializing Historical Sites of Queer and Transgender Resistance in an Age of Neoliberal Inclusivity." In *The Transgender Studies Reader 2*, edited by Susan Stryker and Aren Aizura, 580–90. New York: Routledge.

Gossett, Che. 2017. "Blackness and the Trouble of Trans Visibility." In Tourmaline, Stanley, and Burton 2017: 183–90.

Gossett, Che, and Juliana Huxtable. 2017. "Existing in the World: Blackness at the Edge of Trans Visibility." In Tourmaline, Stanley, and Burton 2017: 39–56.

Green, Kai M., and Treva Ellison. 2014. "Tranifest." *TSQ* 1, nos. 1–2: 222–25.

Gumbs, Alexis Pauline. 2016. *Spill: Scenes of Black Feminist Fugitivity*. Durham, NC: Duke University Press.

Gumbs, Alexis Pauline. 2018. *M Archive: After the End of the World*. Durham, NC: Duke University Press.

Gumbs, Alexis Pauline. 2020. *Dub: Finding Ceremony*. Durham, NC: Duke University Press.

Hammonds, Evelyn. 1987. "Race, Sex, AIDS: The Construction of 'Other.'" *Radical America* 20, no. 6: 28–38.

Hammonds, Evelyn. 1994. "Black (W)holes and the Geometry of Black Female Sexuality." *differences* 6, nos. 2–3: 127–45.

Hartman, Saidiya V. 2007. *Lose Your Mother: A Journey along the Atlantic Slave Route*. New York: Farrar, Straus and Giroux.

Hartman, Saidiya V. 2019. *Wayward Lives, Beautiful Experiments: Intimate Histories of Social Upheaval*. New York: W. W. Norton.

Hayward, Eva S. 2012. "Sensational Jellyfish: Aquarium Affects and the Matter of Immersion." *differences* 23, no. 3: 161–96. doi.org/10.1215/10407391-1892925.

Hayward, Eva, and Jami Weinstein. 2015. "Introduction: Tranimalities in the Age of Trans* Life." *TSQ* 2, no. 2: 195–208. doi.org/10.1215/23289252-2867446.

Hong, Grace. 2008. "'The Future of Our Worlds': Black Feminism and the Politics of Knowledge in the University Under Globalization." *Meridians* 8, no. 2: 95–115.

Horton-Stallings, LaMonda. 2015. *Funk the Erotic: Transaesthetics and Black Sexual Cultures*. Champaign: University of Illinois Press.

Jackson, Zakiyyah Iman. 2013. "Animal: New Directions in the Theorization of Race and Posthumanism." *Feminist Studies* 39, no. 3: 669–85.

Jackson, Zakiyyah Iman. 2016. "Losing Manhood: Animality and Plasticity in the (Neo)Slave Narrative." *Qui Parle* 25, nos. 1–2: 95–136.

Jackson, Zakiyyah Iman. 2018. "'Theorizing in a Void': Sublimity, Matter, and Physics in Black Feminist Poetics." *South Atlantic Quarterly* 117, no. 3: 617–48.

Keeling, Kara. 2007. *The Witch's Flight: The Cinematic, the Black Femme, and the Image of Common Sense*. Durham, NC: Duke University Press.

Keeling, Kara. 2009. "Looking for M—: Queer Temporality, Black Political Possibility, and Poetry from the Future." *GLQ* 15, no. 4: 565–82.

Kelley, Robin D. G. 2002. *Freedom Dreams: The Black Radical Imagination*. Boston: Beacon.

Krell, Elías Costenza. 2017. "Is Transmisogyny Killing Trans Women of Color? Black Trans Feminisms and the Exigencies of White Femininity." *TSQ* 4, no. 2: 226–42. doi.org/10.1215/23289252-3815033.

Lorde, Audre. 1984. "Poetry Is Not a Luxury." In *Sister Outsider*, 36–39. Berkeley, CA: Crossing.

Marx, Karl. (1852) 2008. *The Eighteenth Brumaire of Louis Bonaparte*. New York: Cosimo.

Meadow, Tey. 2018. *Trans Kids: Gendered in the Twenty-First Century*. Berkeley: University of California Press.

Moten, Fred. 2003. *In the Break: The Aesthetics of the Black Radical Tradition*. Minneapolis: University of Minnesota Press.

Moten, Fred. 2013. "Blackness and Nothingness (Mysticism in the Flesh)." *South Atlantic Quarterly* 112, no. 4: 737–80. doi.org/10.1215/00382876-2345261.

Moten, Fred, and Stefano Harney. 2013. *The Undercommons: Fugitive Planning and Black Study*. New York: Autonomedia.

Nancy, Jean-Luc. 2000. *Being Singular Plural*. Translated by Robert D. Richardson and Anne E. O'Byrne. Stanford, CA: Stanford University Press.

Nash, Jennifer C. 2019. *Black Feminism Reimagined: After Intersectionality*. Durham, NC: Duke University Press.

Nyong'o, Tavia. 2019. "Non-binary Blackness: After the End of the World with Samuel R. Delany." *Art Practical*, November 21. www.artpractical.com/feature/non-binary-blackness-after -the-end-of-the-world-with-samuel-r.-delany/.

Quan, H. L. T. 2005. "Geniuses of Resistance: Feminist Consciousness and the Black Radical Tradition." *Race and Class* 47, no. 2: 39–53. doi.org/10.1177/0306396805058081.

Robinson, Cedric J. (1983) 2000. *Black Marxism: The Making of the Black Radical Tradition*. 2nd ed. Chapel Hill: University of North Carolina Press.

Rowell, Charles H. 1991. "Above the Wind: An Interview with Audre Lorde." *Callaloo* 14, no. 1: 83– 95. www.jstor.org/stable/2931438.

Schuller, Kyla. 2018. *The Biopolitics of Feeling: Race, Sex, and Science in the Nineteenth Century*. Durham, NC: Duke University Press.

Scott, David. 2013. "On the Very Idea of a Black Radical Tradition." *Small Axe*, no. 40: 1–6. doi.org /10.1215/07990537-1665398.

Sexton, Jared. 2018. *Black Men, Black Feminism: Lucifer's Nocturne*. London: Palgrave Macmillan.

Shackleford, Hunter Ashleigh. 2019. "You Could Never Misgender Me." *Medium*, December 16. medium.com/@ashleighshackelford_92618/you-could-never-misgender-me-d5e9687d8523.

Shange, Savannah. 2019a. "Black Girl Ordinary: Flesh, Carcerality, and the Refusal of Ethno-graphy." *Transforming Anthropology* 27, no. 1: 3–21. doi.org/10.1111/traa.12143.

Shange, Savannah. 2019b. *Progressive Dystopia: Abolition, Anti-Blackness, and Schooling in San Francisco*. Durham, NC: Duke University Press.

Sloan, Aisha Sabatini. 2016. "Darnell L. Moore and Kai M. Green in Conversation." *Guernica*, March 9. www.guernicamag.com/darnell-l-moore-kai-m-green-conversation-in-black/.

Snorton, C. Riley. 2017. *Black on Both Sides: A Racial History of Trans Identity*. Minneapolis: University of Minnesota Press.

Snorton, C. Riley. 2019. "The Temporality of Radical Potential?" *GLQ* 25, no. 1: 159–61.

Spillers, Hortense J. 1987. "Mamas Baby, Papas Maybe: An American Grammar Book." *Diacritics* 17, no. 2: 64–81. doi.org/10.2307/464747.

Spillers, Hortense J. 1996. "'All the Things You Could Be by Now, If Sigmund Freud's Wife Was Your Mother': Psychoanalysis and Race." *boundary 2* 23, no. 3: 75–141. doi.org/10.2307 /303639.

Spillers, Hortense J. 2003. *Black, White, and In Color: Essays on American Literature and Culture*. Chicago: University of Chicago Press.

Spillers, Hortense, and Ann duCille. 2018. "Expostulations and Replies." *differences* 29, no. 2: 6–20. doi.org/10.1215/10407391-6999746.

Springgay, Stephanie, and Sarah F. Truman. 2019. "Walking Research-Creation: QTBIPOC Temporalities and World Makings." *Mai Feminism*, May 16. maifeminism.com/walking -research-creation-qtbipoc-temporalities-and-world-makings/.

Stone, Amy L. 2017. "Gender Panics about Transgender Children in Religious Right Discourse." *Journal of LGBT Youth* 15, no. 1: 1–15.

Stone, Sandy. 2014. "Guerilla." *TSQ* 1, nos. 1–2: 92–96. doi.org/10.1215/23289252-2399704.

Stryker, Susan. 1994. "My Words to Victor Frankenstein above the Village of Chamounix: Performing Transgender Rage." *GLQ* 1, no. 3: 237–54.

Stryker, Susan. 2008. "Transgender History, Homonormativity, and Disciplinarity." *Radical History Review*, no. 100: 145–57. doi.org/10.1215/01636545-2007-026.

Tolbert, TC, and Trace Peterson. 2013. *Troubling the Line: Trans and Genderqueer Poetry and Poetics*. Brooklyn, NY: Nightboat.

Tourmaline, Eric A. Stanley, and Johanna Burton, eds. 2017. *Trap Door: Trans Cultural Production and the Politics of Visibility*. Cambridge, MA: MIT Press.

Tsang, Wu, and Fred Moten. 2017. "All Terror, All Beauty." In Tourmaline, Stanley, and Burton 2017: 339–48.

Wallace, Michelle. (1990) 2016. *Invisibility Blues: From Pop to Theory*. 2nd ed. London: Verso.

Wynter, Sylvia. 1984. "The Ceremony Must Be Found: After Humanism." *boundary 2* 12, no. 3–13, no. 1: 19–70.

Wynter, Sylvia. 1990. "Afterword: Beyond Miranda's Meanings: Un/silencing the 'Demonic Ground' of Caliban's 'Woman.'" In *Out of the Kumbla: Caribbean Women and Literature*, edited by Carole Boyce Davies and Elaine Savory Fido, 355–72. Trenton, NJ: Africa World.

Wynter, Sylvia. 2001. "Towards the Sociogenic Principle: Fanon, Identity, the Puzzle of Conscious Experience, and What It Is like to Be 'Black.'" *National Identities and Socio-Political Changes in Latin America*, edited by Mercedes F. Durán-Cogan and Antonio Gómez-Moriana, 30–66. New York: Routledge.

Wynter, Sylvia. 2003. "Unsettling the Coloniality of Being/Power/Truth/Freedom: Towards the Human, after Man, Its Overrepresentation—An Argument." *CR: The New Centennial Review* 3, no. 3: 257–337.

Wynter, Sylvia, and Katherine McKittrick. 2015. "Unparalleled Catastrophe of Our Species? Or, to Give Humanness a Different Future: Conversations." In *Sylvia Wynter: On Being Human as Praxis*, edited by Katherine McKittrick, 9–89. Durham, NC: Duke University Press.

Empire and Eugenics

Trans Studies in the United Kingdom

EZRA HORBURY and CHRISTINE "XINE" YAO

Abstract This essay offers an overview of trans studies in the United Kingdom in the current climate of transphobia in both academia and the public sphere. This report outlines how trans-exclusionary radical feminist scholars have co-opted the language of victimization and academic freedom following proposed changes to the Gender Recognition Act in 2018. The production of ignorance about trans issues and trans studies is a deliberate project abetted by the UK media even on the left. In response, the authors organized an interdisciplinary trans symposium to affirm trans lives and trans studies for students, scholars, and the wider community. The authors reflect on the successes and failures of the event in light of their institution's past as the origin of eugenics founded by Frances Galton and the broader scope of the legacies of the British empire.

Keywords eugenics, colonialism, empire, trans-exclusionary radical feminism (TERF), trans

"Sex is real," tweeted J. K. Rowling in her defense of transphobia at the end of 2019. This high-profile outburst bubbled out of the bigotry actually informed by, rather than ignorant of, the legitimization of transphobia in UK academia. We can begin with the catalyst that brought together the two writers of this piece as collaborators: an exhibition entitled *Rights for Women* hosted by the Senate House Library, one of London's major academic libraries, that ran from July 16 to December 15, 2018 (Senate House Library 2019). It chronicled the multifaceted histories of activism for women's rights—and included Sheila Jeffreys's *Gender Hurts*, a manifesto about the ideological dangers posed by trans people. The only acknowledgment of trans women in the exhibit, Jeffreys's (2014) text argues that "transgenderism" is a "conservative ideology that forms the foundation for women's subordination" and functions as a form of state and institutional power. Elsewhere she has argued that gender-affirmation surgery abuses human rights akin to the "political psychiatry" of the Soviet Union (Jeffreys 1997: 59), and that the 2005 Gender Recognition Act was passed by Tony Blair's government to eradicate homosexuality (Jeffreys 2006). These are bizarre claims, and a far cry

TSQ: Transgender Studies Quarterly ∗ Volume 7, Number 3 ∗ August 2020 **445**
DOI 10.1215/23289252-8553104 © 2020 Duke University Press

from the understanding of trans studies we would get from the vibrant research history of trans rights and studies in the United Kingdom. Understanding the landscape for the struggles of this burgeoning, rich field requires tracing the conditions for how such an open display of transphobia in an academic library has become a familiar aspect of institutionalized transphobia.

The complaint that trans rights has become a hegemonic ideological institution armed with the power of the state allows transphobic rhetoric to employ a narrative of victimization in line with the ongoing mobilization of fictions of white female vulnerability to justify violence against marginalized groups. Without a factual basis for claims about the dangers supposedly posed by trans people, criticism of trans studies in UK academia employs a strategic amnesia that calls for the need to do critical research on trans studies while simultaneously refusing to acknowledge or engage with the substantial weight of trans studies as a discipline. This strategy stretches back to the earliest transphobic manifestos by women such as Mary Daly and Janice Raymond, for whom the violent, Frankensteinian trans woman bogey always proved a more useful subject than the experiences of real trans women. While US academia has institutionalized trans studies to some extent, it has remained a minority discipline in the United Kingdom. Here, the transgender specter proves too useful a tool around which white women academics can position their fictional victimhood. Ignorance is not just bliss—it is useful, deliberate, and violent. There exists, then, within UK academia, a peculiar form of the Dunning-Kruger effect, the cognitive bias in which confidence is inversely correlated to actual competence; thus the legitimacy and authority to speak on trans studies is justified via deliberate ignorance of trans studies.

The year 2018 was a flashpoint in the mainstreaming of what many recognize as trans-exclusionary radical feminism (TERF) or what proponents themselves term "gender critical feminism." In 2018, the UK government held an online survey for public responses to proposed changes in the Gender Recognition Act: if passed, these changes might have allowed trans people to alter their legal gender marker without being subject to the dehumanizing process of a Gender Recognition Panel. A few days before the closure of that survey, the *Guardian* published a letter titled "Academics Are Being Harassed over Their Research into Transgender Issues" (Stock et al. 2018). In this article, a group of academics—many of whom have never published on trans studies in any capacity—argue "that it is not transphobic to investigate and analyse this area [transgender issues] from a range of critical academic perspectives." These academics "also worry about the effect of such definitions on the success rates of journal submissions and research grant applications"—another peculiar, unsupported claim. The article has no hard data to support its assertions; in the absence of data, sources, and evidence—elements that should be familiar to academics—the article traffics in worries and concerns under the guise of academic freedom.

Such vagaries, or even outright lies, are a popular tactic of the UK press when it comes to (mis)representing trans issues. To give a few examples, in an interview with the *Telegraph*, popular children's author Jacqueline Wilson is "very, very worried" about "young children taking any kind of drugs, hormones or whatever" and "having major surgery" (Wilson 2019). The interviewer does not bother to point out to Wilson that no UK trans health-care providers administer hormones or surgery to children. A *Sky News* article promoting The Detransitioner Advocacy Network (DAN) from Sally Lockwood deploys the headline "'Hundreds' of Young Trans People Seeking Help to Return to Original Sex" and includes the bald-faced lie that we have "no data" on "the number who may be unhappy in their new gender or who may opt to detransition to their biological sex." Not true: of 3,398 patients, 0.47 percent "expressed transition-related regret or de-transitioned," and only three patients made a long-term detransition (Davies, McIntyre, and Rypma 2019: 118). The founder of DAN allegedly left the organization six months later (Comerford 2020). Evans claimed the money raised in the wake of Lockwood's article was to be spent commissioning articles from "Psychologists / lawyers / therapists / medical professionals," but the website hosts no such articles (Evans 2019; *The Detransition Advocacy Network* 2020). Further money raised was spent on "English pubs, and movie nights" (Evans 2020). No news outlet followed up on DAN. Stories such as Lockwood's rarely, if ever, consult academics who specialize in trans studies or trans academics themselves who remain sidelined, silenced voices in these narratives that seek to define them as predatory figures.

Trans studies seems to exist in a bubble, unacknowledged by those who argue against it, unconsulted when the issues it has studied for decades become headline news. Intense and mendacious media outrage against trans people is widespread in the United Kingdom, with the *Times* having published 323 largely critical articles on transgender rights and lives in 2018 alone. Media platforms that support this agenda encompass leftist and progressive outlets as well as the right and the mainstream. The UK branch of the *Guardian* holds the editorial position that, ultimately, trans rights threaten feminism, a stance that provoked a rebuttal from the publication's US office (Levin, Chalabi, and Siddiqui 2018). It is indicative that a subsequent letter by a few dozen trans exclusionary academics published in the *Sunday Times* warranted widespread consideration, but the open letters signed by thousands of university colleagues affirming trans rights found little media attention (Pennock and Ashton 2019; Pennock et al. 2019).

That UK newspapers should profit on outrage and spin is no surprise. That the same deliberate ignorance should thrive in academia is more concerning. One major cause for the respect still accorded to transphobia among radical feminists in the United Kingdom has been explained by Sophie Lewis (2019) as the absence of any dialogue on "the effects of globalization and police brutality . . . on race, gender and class, and how they all interact"; because of this absence, "middle- and upper-class white feminists have not received the pummeling from black and indigenous feminists that their American counterparts have." We can see then that this manifestation of transphobia in the former heart of empire metastasizes out of fictions of white female vulnerability and institutional ignorance, if not outright suppression, of Black and women of color feminisms. Perhaps this explains the popular equivalence between being trans and the performance of blackface: the conflation weaponizes lip-service outrage against anti-Blackness bereft of historical consciousness or consideration for embodied experience. Akwugo Emejulu, professor of sociology at the University of Warwick who works on racial, ethnic, and gender inequalities, argued, "Any feminist worth his or her salt should be advocating for the most marginalised" (Strudwick 2018). Along with Vanita Sundaram, a professor in the Department of Education at the University of York, Emejulu argues for the similarity of the biological essentialism of transphobia with eugenicist racism. There is a gulf between the understanding of feminism as a means to help the most vulnerable and as a tool to affirm white women's purity and power.

Of course, the devil's advocate approach to academic transphobia does not confine itself to the intellectual sphere: it compounds the hostility inflicted on trans and nonbinary students and staff in higher education. According to the UK LGBT advocacy organization Stonewall (2018), more than a third of trans students faced negative comments or conduct from university staff and three in five from other students. Seven percent were physically attacked by university staff or a fellow student. Meanwhile, *Times Higher Education* spotlights trans exclusionary philosopher Kathleen Stock as a brave academic under attack because students display trans pride flags at her university (Grove 2020). Much like the alt-right, trans exclusionary feminists exploit concerns about academic freedom, labor, and debate to claim their right to platforms at institutions where they can profess that to be trans is pathology or even mutilation—and then melt under critique from trans students, staff, and their allies like the snowflakes they accuse them of being. Nonetheless, many trans scholars and trans-inclusive feminist allies rightfully remain wary of entering public debate when the already-biased media arenas fetishize antagonism, and such platforms themselves help legitimize transphobic views. Instead, they decide when, where, and how to communicate, while mindful that discourse should lead to policy and action.

While trans exclusionary academics self-martyr in academic and media publications, the UK transphobic movement comprises angry and ill-informed online users. Many stem from the online parenting website Mumsnet and the remnants of the UK Skeptics movement. The latter, which developed in reaction to the rise of Evangelical Christianity during the Bush administration, turned their attentions to criticizing leftist social movements in the late 2000s. YouTube has proved a popular congregating spot for this group, and their videos now serve as a notorious recruitment tool for the alt-right. Meanwhile, as Edie Miller (2018) writes, "Mumsnet is to British transphobia more like what 4Chan is to American fascism." This online transphobia has been spearheaded by former comedy writer Graham Lineham, who took to the trans exclusionary movement after an episode of his television show *The IT Crowd* was criticized for its offensive portrayal of a trans woman and who has since been warned by the police for his harassment campaigns. Lineham and Mumsnet's war deluged the funder of trans charity Mermaids, the National Lottery, with so many complaints that Mermaids had its funding reviewed and threatened (it was ultimately not revoked). Absurdity is best fought with absurdity: this culminated in a countermove by leftist YouTuber Harry Brewis, who raised $340,000 for the charity in a fifty-seven-hour marathon livestream playing the video game *Donkey Kong* that included an appearance from US millennial progressive politician Alexandria Ocasio-Cortez. This series of events perhaps better resembles a fever dream than a serious overview of the major events in UK transphobia, but this is our current landscape. This is the result of sidelining trans studies in favor of fear mongering, ignorance, and online hate mobs.

We cannot pretend that our respective research on theorizing trans in early modern studies or queer of color critique in long nineteenth-century America occurs in a vacuum. The Senate House Library is just down the street from our institution. Complaints by a more junior and precarious academic are more readily ignored than emails from a newly appointed faculty member. Policy can be a useful tool if you are strategic. Our university's policy on trans inclusion is more progressive than the government's: the challenge is to transform documents into action while always being aware of their limitations in the project of making a space more livable.

Together with our colleague Ella Metcalfe in Maths and Physical Sciences, we were successful in securing an internal grant to hold our institution's first symposium on trans issues and for trans people, "Trans Studies, Trans Lives: Past, Present, and Future." Our call sought to bring together academics, activists, and creatives. We hoped to create a visible counternarrative of community and affirmation fusing the often bifurcated efforts of the research versus social and advocacy groups. All would be welcome to come, discuss, and learn in a spirit of generosity. In many respects, the event was a triumph: excellent presentations of research from the medieval period through the present and many forms of artistic and literary production informed by lived experience; outstanding turnout from students, staff, and faculty; participation from nonacademics living in the wider community; and visible support from senior administrators. Our keynotes were trans legal scholar Stephen Whittle and nonbinary psychologist and writer Meg-John Barker, who have made major contributions to the landscape of twenty-first-century trans studies. We aimed to include a mix of senior scholars, junior scholars, artists, and activists. Papers were presented on medieval, Victorian, and early twentieth-century trans history and literature; trans and lesbian solidarity; nonbinary experiences and bureaucracy; embodied transness; and navigating transphobia.[1]

Nonetheless, there were failings we share here in the hopes that others can learn from them to do better.

In our pool of submissions, presentations by and on peoples of color were few. Insofar as trans studies in the United Kingdom is a nascent field, trans of color studies is further marginalized, even though, as scholars elsewhere have argued, one cannot responsibly consider trans in isolation from race (Aizura 2018; Snorton 2017). We procured additional funds to subsidize travel and accommodations for minoritized and precarious presenters; we also tried to compensate by earmarking funds explicitly for presenters of color. Although the final program had Asian and Black presenters, for a combination of reasons such as cancellations and illness, in the end our lineup was entirely white. Most egregiously, one of our speakers who was to present on the criminalization and pathologization of queer Black masculinity was misgendered by security, who then doubled down on abuse. They rightfully withdrew their labor, a move that forced immediate public reckoning with the limits of liberatory work that can be done within an institution and subsequent administrative discussions about better practices. They then became a target on Twitter for transphobic abuse for a reason we would not discover until the following day: a self-described gender critical feminist had infiltrated the all-day event and—using a profile picture of Ayn Rand—was derisively tweeting the proceedings until they saw the opportunity to direct their eager audience to attack a young Black trans academic.

There would be value in a crowdsourced, public document to circulate organizational strategies to make such events safer and more just; we sought feedback from attendees on ways to improve. For instance, beyond pronoun tags and information on gender-neutral toilets, it would be useful to recruit volunteers to help guide people to the toilets if they felt unsafe. We had talked to the security staff about our event and how to treat our guests. Overall, they were wonderfully supportive and welcoming to our attendees—except that when one of them went on break, the replacement flagrantly ignored the guidelines. Ideally, then, there should always be a volunteer present throughout the conference to help receive guests and ensure their safety. We had prepared statements about respect and community that we read out and included in the program. A major concern was anticipating possible disruptions, although we hadn't considered online trolling. Rules against tweeting can be instituted, though these may be ignored by hostile attendees (and banning devices entirely creates accessibility concerns). We planned our configuration throughout the room to keep an eye out for possible disruptions along with strategies for communication and minimizing attempts to hijack the environment. But there are no truly safe spaces: only safer spaces.

Ultimately, we are based in the birthplace of eugenics (early founders of eugenics, Karl Pearson and Walter Weldon, conducted this research at our institution) and located in the former imperial metropole. It is no coincidence that our outsourced security staff, with few benefits and poor labor conditions, are disproportionately people of color. We have buildings named after the founders of race science whose mark remains more subtly on programs and entire disciplines of study. A secret eugenics conference was held here in 2017 (UCL News 2018). In her most recent book *What's the Use? On the Uses of Use*, Sara Ahmed (2019) devotes a chapter to our institution as a case study for the confluences of colonial race science, utilitarianism in education, and neoliberalism—and earlier in the work she discusses debates about trans access to bathrooms. Race science's hierarchies inform the rigid gender binary. Transphobia, too, is eugenics: the same normative logics of biological determinism and reproductive futurity are driven by the familiar righteous rhetoric of worries and concerns mobilized readily for reactionary and faux-progressive ends. While galvanized by the Gender Recognition Act, one can situate the virulence of this wave of transphobia in relation to Brexit and the hostile environment policy introduced in 2012 by the Conservative government "to create, here in Britain, a really hostile environment for illegal immigrants," as stated by former Conservative Prime Minister Teresa May when she was home secretary (Hill 2017). British "purity" is under attack: the threats are both without and within the crumbling erstwhile seat of empire.

We are perhaps reaching a crisis point in UK transphobia. A recent lightning-rod case involved a tax researcher, Maya Forstater, whose contract was not renewed after she tweeted her commitment to (as the judge at her employment tribunal phrased it) "refer[ring] to a person by the sex she considered appropriate even if it violates their dignity and/or creates an intimidating, hostile, degrading, humiliating or offensive environment" (Bowcott 2019). This sets an important legal precedent for transphobia, preventing it from becoming a protected belief. The decision garnered much transphobic criticism, most prominently from J. K. Rowling, but drew a line between trans people's legal rights and the rights of transphobes to harass them.

Currently, the state of trans research at our institution is intensely ambivalent. On the one hand, funding was awarded for the Writing Trans Lives project, a series of workshops featuring established trans authors such as Travis Alabanza, CN Lester, and Juliet Jacques that aims to support aspiring trans writers' endeavors in a culture that frequently dismisses them in favor of cisgender voices. On the other, our university is also playing host to a Women's Place UK conference, a group that espouses feminist values alongside justifications for demonizing trans people and sex workers. Perhaps our symposium made our institution more of a target: a journalist from one of the aforementioned news outlets disingenuously tried to goad a response from one of us about this conference based on involvement with the trans symposium. It remains to be seen how these issues will play out at a broader institutional level. Nonetheless, we, alongside the thousands of UK academics who signed open letters to affirm trans rights, must continue to strive to further trans rights as inextricable from the project of feminist antiracist social justice. We cannot let transphobic eugenics foreclose our efforts when its logics always seek to delimit the possibilities of those it minoritizes.

Ezra Horbury is a British Academy Postdoctoral Fellow at University College London. Their first book, *Prodigality in Early Modern Drama* (2019), investigates excessive spending and riotous youths on the early modern stage. They have also published in *Harvard Theological Review*, *Renaissance Studies*, and the *Journal of Religious History* and have recently been awarded a Huntington Fellowship.

Christine "Xine" Yao is lecturer in American literature to 1900 at University College London. Her book *Disaffected: The Cultural Politics of Unfeeling in Nineteenth-Century America* is forthcoming. Her scholarly essays have appeared in *J19*, *Occasion*, and *American Quarterly*, the last of which was a finalist for the 2019 Constance M. Rourke Prize for best essay. Xine is the cohost of *PhDivas*, a podcast about academia, culture, and social justice across the STEM/humanities divide. Her honors include the ASA Yasuo Sakakibara Essay Prize, and her research has been supported by grants from the Social Sciences and Humanities Research Council of Canada.

Note

1.   Full papers included Stephen Whittle, "A Perfect Storm: The UK Government's Failed Consultation on the Gender Recognition Act 2004"; Meg-John Barker, "Trans: Adventurers across Time and Space"; Robert Mills, "Recognising Wilgefortis"; Katherine Inglis, "Trans Visibility in Late-Victorian English Publishing"; Ann Heilmann, "James Miranda Barry and the Conundrum of Historical Transgender Representation"; Pamela L.

Caughie, "Queer Modernism and Trans Lives: Lili Elbe's Life Narrative"; Susan Rudy, "On Gender Ontoformativity; or, Refusing to Be Spat out of Reality: Reclaiming (Trans and Cis) Lesbian Solidarity through Experimental Writing"; Meshach Yaa-Yaw Owusu, "Black Trans Masculinities: Redefinition as Survival" (this paper was withdrawn); LJ Thuringer, "Who Needs Gender"; Aiden Greenall, "Please Select One: Mr./Mrs.," "Mx.," and "Non-binary Resistance"; Lo Marshall, "Negotiating Gender Diverse Worlds Built on Binary Expectations: The Kenwood Ladies Pond"; Victoria Sin, "Embodied Narratives"; Lara Bochmann and Erin Hampson, *StepOut* (short film); and Felix Kawitzky, "The Changeling's Story: The Fantastic Duplicity of Queer Bodies in Sci-Fi and Fantasy Fiction."

References

Ahmed, Sara. 2019. *What's the Use? On the Uses of Use*. Durham, NC: Duke University Press.

Aizura, Aren Z. 2018. *Mobile Subjects: Transnational Imaginaries of Gender Reassignment*. Durham, NC: Duke University Press.

Bowcott, Owen. 2019. "Judge Rules against Researcher Who Lost Job over Transgender Tweets." *Guardian*, December 18. www.theguardian.com/society/2019/dec/18/judge-rules-against -charity-worker-who-lost-job-over-transgender-tweets.

Comerford, Aidan (@AidanCTweets). 2020. "Settle in for story time, and question why no media outlet is following up on this. In Oct 19, Charlie Evans went on Sky News and claimed there were 100s of people seeking help detransitioning. This was a blockbuster claim as all studies show detransition is rare." Twitter, May 12, 9:35 a.m. twitter.com/AidanCTweets /status/1260126476571217920.

Davies, Skye, Stephen McIntyre, and Craig Rypma. 2019. "Detransition Rates in a National UK Gender Identity Clinic." In *Third Biennal EPATH Conference: Inside Matters, on Law, Ethics, and Religion (Book of Abstracts)*, 35–36. European Professional Association for Transgender Health.

Evans, Charlie. 2019. "Website for 'The Detransition Advocacy Network.'" *Crowdfunder*, November 12. www.crowdfunder.co.uk/website-for-the-detransition-advocacy-network.

Evans, Charlie. 2020. "Sookie's Travel to UK (2nd Detrans Meet)." *Crowdfunder*, January 15. www .crowdfunder.co.uk/sookies-travel-to-uk-2nd-detrans-meet.

Grove, Jack. 2020. "Kathleen Stock: Life on the Front Line of Transgender Rights Debates." *Times Higher Education*, January 7. www.timeshighereducation.com/news/kathleen-stock-life -front-line-transgender-rights-debate.

Hill, Amelia. 2017. "'Hostile Environment': The Hardline Home Office Policy Tearing Families Apart." *Guardian*, November 28.

Jeffreys, Sheila. 1997. "Transgender Activism: A Lesbian Feminist Perspective." *Journal of Lesbian Studies* 1, nos. 3–4: 55–74.

Jeffreys, Sheila. 2006. Interview at "Andrea Dworkin Commemorative Conference," Centre for the Study of Social Justice, Department of Politics and International Relations, University of Oxford, April 7.

Jeffreys, Sheila. 2014. *Gender Hurts: A Feminist Analysis of the Politics of Transgenderism*. London: Routledge.

Levin, Sam, Mona Chalabi, and Sabrina Siddiqui. 2018. "Why We Take Issue with the Guardian's Stance on Trans Rights in the UK." *Guardian*, November 2. www.theguardian.com /commentisfree/2018/nov/02/guardian-editorial-response-transgender-rights-uk.

Lewis, Sophie. 2019. "How British Feminism Became Anti-Trans." *New York Times*, February 7. www.nytimes.com/2019/02/07/opinion/terf-trans-women-britain.html.

Miller, Edie. 2018. "Why Is British Media So Transphobic?" *Outline*, November 5. theoutline.com
/post/6536/british-feminists-media-transphobic.

Pennock, Caroline Dodds, et al. 2019. "Thousands of University Colleagues Support LGBT+
Rights—We Won't Turn Our Backs Now." *Independent*, June 19. www.independent
.co.uk/voices/letters/lgbt-pride-university-transgender-students-education-stonewall
-a8964886.html.

Pennock, Caroline, and Bodie A. Ashton. 2019. "Why We, as Academics, Created a Letter in
Support of LGBT+ Rights." *Independent*, June 23. www.independent.co.uk/voices
/transgender-lgbt-pride-letter-academics-transphobia-higher-education-a8971136.html.

Rowling, J. K. (@jk_rowling). 2019. "Dress however you please. Call yourself whatever you like. Sleep
with any consenting adult who'll have you. Live your best life in peace and security. But
force women out of their jobs for stating that sex is real? #IStandWithMaya #ThisIsNot
ADrill." Twitter, December 19, 12:57 p.m. twitter.com/jk_rowling/status/1207646162813
100033.

Senate House Library. 2019. *Rights for Women*. Exhibition, University of London. archive
.senatehouselibrary.ac.uk/exhibitions-and-events/exhibitions/rights-for-women.

Snorton, C. Riley. 2017. *Black on Both Sides: A Racial History of Trans Identity*. Minneapolis:
University of Minnesota Press.

Stock, Kathleen, et al. 2018. "Academics Are Being Harassed over Their Research into Transgender
Issues." *Guardian*, October 6. www.theguardian.com/society/2018/oct/16/academics-are
-being-harassed-over-their-research-into-transgender-issues.

Stonewall. 2018. "LGBT in Britain—University Report." April 25. www.stonewall.org.uk/lgbt
-britain-university-report.

Strudwick, Patrick. 2018. "Meet the Feminist Academics Championing Trans Rights." *Buzzfeed*,
December 22. www.buzzfeed.com/patrickstrudwick/meet-the-feminist-academics-champ
ion-trans-rights.

UCL News. 2018. "UCL Statement on the London Conference on Intelligence." January 10. www
.ucl.ac.uk/news/2018/jan/ucl-statement-london-conference-intelligence-0.

Wilson, Jacqueline. 2019. "We Still Have a Strange Way of Putting Girls and Boys into Different
Slots." Interview by Neil Armstrong. *Telegraph*, April 23. www.telegraph.co.uk/books
/authors/jacqueline-wilson-interview-still-have-strange-way-putting-girls/.

Bad Dads and Precarious Grads

On the "Trans ± Sex: Rethinking Sex/Gender in Trans Studies" Symposium

NICOLE SEYMOUR

Abstract This piece reports on the "Trans ± Sex: Rethinking Sex/Gender in Trans Studies" symposium held at the University of Arizona in September 2019. It focuses on two major themes that appeared throughout the symposium: cross-generational conflict and the death of the university.
Keywords symposium, trans studies, cross-generational conflict, critical university studies, precarity

In the summer of 2018, a letter of support for New York University (NYU) senior professor Avital Ronell—who had been accused of sexual harassment by one of her graduate students—was leaked on philosopher Brian Leiter's (2018) blog *Leiter Reports*. Some of the most established names in feminist/queer/trans theory, as well as critical theory more broadly, were signatories. Just a few months later, Pennsylvania State University senior professors Christopher Castiglia and Christopher Reed (2018) published a condescending response to Grace Lavery's critique of a manifesto that Reed had posted on his faculty web page. As Aren Aizura (2018) explained in a subsequent essay titled "Kill Your Dads: On Reed and Castiglia's Response to Grace Lavery," apparently grad students in one of Reed's classes had "objected to his listing of 'Judith' Halberstam [rather than 'Jack'] in the syllabus"—prompting him to craft a manifesto ridiculing, among other forms of so-called political correctness, concerns about "deadnaming" and the notion of preferred pronouns.

The vociferous backlash to both incidents—articulated most searingly by NYU graduate student Andrea Long Chu (2018) and most hauntingly by recovering academic Keguro Macharia (2018), in my view—revealed a deep and bitter divide. On the one hand we have certain established, elite intellectuals who are inclined to pull seniority and rank. On the other we have precarious, nonelite, or less-established intellectuals, many suffering the ongoing effects of the Great

TSQ: Transgender Studies Quarterly ★ Volume 7, Number 3 ★ August 2020   **455**
DOI 10.1215/23289252-8553118   © 2020 Duke University Press

Recession, and many of whom feel disillusioned by the former group after once revering them. (The radicals have come to appear reactionary.) Indeed, we might recall that the aforementioned letter defended Ronell on the basis of her "singular brilliance" and "international reputation," while Castiglia and Reed (2018) labeled the concerns of then-junior scholar Lavery as "adolescent." Insert "OK Boomer" joke here.

I recite these incidents, familiar as they may be to many readers, because they index two of the most prominent themes to crop up at the "Trans ± Sex" symposium held at the University of Arizona (UA) on September 5–7, 2019:[1] the contingencies of cross-generational relationships and the death of the university. These themes are deeply imbricated, as I will show, and their articulation points to a certain paradox: the once-upstart field of transgender studies is becoming institutionalized at a moment when academia's necrosis has become most painfully acute.

During the first panel, on "Trans ± ition," UA faculty Eric Plemons raised the topic of uterine transplants for trans women—a speculative prospect extrapolated from successful procedures on cis women (Cleveland Clinic 2019), and one that invokes the idea of cross-generational relationships quite literally. Plemons contemplated how advocacy for related research creates a "new horizon," or what I would call a moving goalpost, for what counts as transition. UA faculty Russell Toomey explored similar questions around transition with an even more explicit focus on cross-generational relationships. Referring to his work with Camp Born This Way, a summer program for trans and gender-nonconforming youth, Toomey reported that the steering committee recently decided for the first time to not invite pediatricians and to "decenter parents," figuratively and literally, such as by arranging their support meetings away from the main events area. Such moves potentially empower and depathologize trans youth; as fellow panelist Jules Gill-Peterson (University of Pittsburgh) quipped, approvingly, "Why does everything have to be a doctor's appointment?" Toomey also asked us to consider the ramifications of increasingly common contemporary scenarios in which very young children assert a gender identity that is accepted and validated by adults. To paraphrase: in such scenarios, can we really point to a discrete, dramatic event of transition, or are we simply speaking about identity?

Looking back at the symposium a few months on, I wish that Toomey and Gill-Peterson could have dialogued more directly on these points—especially considering that, as Gayle Salamon (Princeton University) later reminded us, Gill-Peterson's recent book *Histories of the Transgender Child* (2018) argues against the idea of trans childhood as a new phenomenon. But in any case, as Reed's manifesto and the response to Lavery's (2018) critique thereof indicate, certain people of a certain age nonetheless perceive the arrival of a new, and perturbing, wave of politicized trans youth. Indeed, in the postpanel discussion, Plemons claimed that Jack Halberstam's most recent book, *Trans*: A Quick and Quirky Account of Gender Variability* (2018), "sort of bemoans the loss of transition," or at least its "event-ness," explaining, "as Halberstam glosses it, trans identity is constituted through the fire of transition. You have to have had this act of suffering and then in the act of suffering come to know yourself." Most of us have probably seen similar sentiments splashed across social media from older LGBTQ+ folks, some heartened, some wistful, some bitter: "Kids these days have it so much easier." The more bitter versions can sound, perhaps not coincidentally, awfully similar to the sometimes-abusive dynamics of graduate mentorship, not to mention the often-callous responses from senior academics to those concerned about the collapse of the university job market: "I had to suffer, and now so shall you." Perhaps this link will seem like less of a stretch when we recall Chu's (2018) point that Ronell herself "writes of graduate school as a kind of indentured labor"—as "'cultish subjection.'"

To be clear, not all the cross-generational relationships considered at the symposium were antagonistic or agonistic. On the "Trans ± Sexual" panel, following presentations from his mentors Susan Stryker and Eva Hayward, Abraham Weil (California State University, Long Beach) warmly joked, "As our parents leave imprints on our lives, you will find me [locating my argument] in between th[eir] two papers." Importantly, then, this panel modeled collegial ways to critique recent intellectual developments without slipping into ad hominem attacks or a "damn kids, get off my lawn" mode. For example, Hayward critiqued what she perceives as trans studies' "abandonment of the transsexual" in favor of the supposedly more progressive figures of the transgender person and the nonbinary person—while stressing that she does "not mean individual identities; I mean the *logic* of nonbinarism." Meanwhile, Stryker countered that the lived experience of transsexual embodiment has functioned as the generative origin of the expansive field of trans studies. These differences notwithstanding, all three speakers considered in various ways what it might mean to return to what Weil, following Stryker, jokingly referred to as "the question of the 'old-fashioned transsexual.'" In the Q&A, Salamon justified this approach succinctly: "If we can return to . . . old questions, not by way of rejecting what is here now, but [by bringing them] into the present, I think we stand a better chance of being able to have this conversation in a multi-stranded way."

Other symposium presentations spoke to cross-generational concerns through specific case studies. On the "Trans ± Border" panel, Cole Rizki (Duke University) considered the reverberating memories of disappeared *travesti* in Argentina, while UA faculty Francisco Galarte shared Anthony Friedkin's 1970s photographs of a gender-nonconforming Latinx Los Angeles resident named Jaime Aguilar—while also offering some original theorizations of that new-fangled -*x* suffix that no doubt drives some Boomers crazy. And on the aforementioned "Trans + ition" panel, Gill-Peterson introduced her current research project on the history of "trans DIY": communities finding "unsanctioned and underground ways to transition." She discussed the example of Edith Ferguson, a Southern California trans woman who advertised her correspondence courses for other trans women in magazines in the 1950s. These courses aimed to help subscribers generate a "feminine ego" that they could project into the world, and which, as Ferguson promised, could also change one's material body—thus circumventing the medical model of transition that was coming to prominence at that time. Gill-Peterson's work on Ferguson is particularly interesting to me for how it resonates with my own work on the "organic" transitioning imagined in contemporary queer/trans environmental literature (Seymour 2013), and with Jeanne Vaccaro's (2015) theory of transgender as "handmade." Considering that the decentering of the medical model was a foundational move of trans studies, as Stryker reminded us with a nod to her 1998 introduction to *GLQ*'s "Transgender Issue," we can recognize here a generational continuity, rather than rupture, across the field.

Ferguson was not the only trailblazing "trancestor" invoked at the symposium. The weekend kicked off with a screening of two short films by artist Tourmaline at Tucson's independent Loft Cinema; a packed house was treated first to *Happy Birthday, Marsha!* (2018), a creative retelling of activists Marsha P. Johnson and Sylvia Rivera's activities in the hours leading up to the Stonewall Rebellion, and then to the more abstract *Atlantic is a Sea of Bones* (2017), featuring New York–based ball icon Egyptt LaBeija. Such figures also resonated across the later "Trans ± Visibility" panel featuring UA faculty Z Nicolazzo and Max Strassfeld and activist CeCe McDonald. Responding to Nicolazzo's question about "seeking past trans-ness," McDonald reported, "I didn't know about Marsha, and Sylvia, and Miss Major till I was an adult" because trans history has been so whitewashed. As she mused, "What strengths could black and brown trans, queer, and [gender-]nonconforming youth have if they had this information in their schools?"

Another question that continues to echo for me long after the symposium's close came from Hayward to the audience: "What do you think of 'cis' as a prefix? What do you think of 'cisgender' as really defining [in terms of] a politics of trans studies right now?" As she posed this question at the very end of her panel's Q&A, we did not have much time to explore it. In fact, one of my very few criticisms of this otherwise impressively generative and interdisciplinary symposium—the academic participants came from disciplines ranging from anthropology to English to religious studies—is that it danced around the category of "cis" in tantalizing but ultimately unsatisfying ways. (Another criticism is that the symposium ignored pressing contemporary issues such as the climate crisis, which I touch on below—even despite Hayward's extensive work on ecology and animality.) For example, Plemons acknowledged that advocacy for uterine transplants for trans women "doubles down on maternity as the essence of woman"—without explicitly considering how such ideologies oppress cis and trans women alike. Indeed, "all bodies are medicalized bodies," as Weil reminded us in an aside, and embodied gender is a moving target for everyone, as gender studies scholars have long suggested. I would have enjoyed hearing the panelists articulate how such insights can help us forge coalitional feminisms in the face of resurgent trans-exclusionary radical feminism (TERFism)—a phenomenon that A de la Maza traced from a Mexican perspective on the "Trans ± Border" panel. While a focus on "cis" could certainly risk recentering, well, cis people, we must also take at least somewhat seriously Hayward's wisecrack that "I've never met [a cisgender] person." As she continued, "For me, this is what the hope of trans studies was." I took this second comment to mean that trans studies, like queer studies, aims to reveal the universal impossibility of achieving gender or sexual norms, not (just) to affirm or render visible a discrete minority group.

At this point I should admit, first, that the aforementioned death of the university was more of a metatheme than one explicitly articulated in this symposium. Second, my perception of this metatheme is no doubt rooted in my own subjective view as someone who has been both traumatically impacted by this particular crisis and disappointed by the senior academics previously invoked. But as personal as this theme feels, I believe it deserves discussion nonetheless—especially as the field of critical university studies (CUS) rapidly expands just as trans studies has. Specifically, we need to consider how the death of the university ramifies for academics from marginalized backgrounds, including trans folks of color, working-class trans folks, and white trans folks. I would therefore point to Gill-Peterson's seemingly offhanded comment about her awareness, when coming to understand her trans identity, of what her employer's health plan would cover. We might also point to the fact that Toomey recently filed an American Civil Liberties Union–backed lawsuit against the state of Arizona over what journalist Rachel Leingang (2019) has explained as "an exclusion in the state's health-care plan that denies coverage for gender-reassignment surgery for him and all other transgender employees who use the state insurance program." This case, which is being argued on the basis of the equal protection clause of the US Constitution, has major implications for the future advancement of LGBTQ+ rights.

From this example, we can see how the institutionalization of trans studies has the potential to effect major structural changes—at the same time that, as Roderick Ferguson (2012: 4) describes of the neoliberal university and its fetishization of "diversity," "technologies of power . . . work with and through difference in order to manage its insurgent possibilities." Notably, Toomey told Leingang that he waited until he secured tenure before challenging the afore-mentioned exclusion: "'Tenure provides a little bit more protection.'" Here we must note that only 27 percent of university faculty jobs in the United States are on the tenure track (Flaherty 2018), that the majority of non-tenure-track faculty make less than minimum-wage workers (Kezar, DePaola, and Scott 2019: 1), and that the situation is likely to worsen. Thus we have to ask, what kind of a future do trans scholars face when health care is tied to academic employment, academic employment is scarce, and secure, well-paid academic employment even scarcer? What does it mean for trans studies more broadly to institutionalize when the institution is nearly extinct? Finally, to link (perhaps wackily) back to that topic of uterus transplants: what does it mean to pursue new means of reproduction in a world increasingly inhospitable to flourishing life, due to crises both economic and environmental? I can't help but note here that youth anxiety over such crises has fomented the cross-generational animus (see Lorenz 2019) that gave rise to "OK Boomer" jokes in the first place. That is to say, while all historical periods are marked by cross-generational conflict, the currently dire state of the planet in particular—rooted as it is in the decisions or lack thereof of older generations—is quite unprecedented.

But before my anxiety grows histrionic (insert "OK Doomer" joke here, with credit to climate scientist Kate Marvel [2019] for the punny formulation), I need to acknowledge the most obvious, and arguably most important, features of the "Trans ± Sex" symposium: it was held at an institution known, per Salamon, as "the epicenter for trans studies," and it would not have been possible without that institution's Transgender Studies Initiative (TSI). As Galarte's (n.d.) faculty website describes it, the TSI is "a collective of faculty that is the first of its kind in the world, that brings together scholars in Transgender Studies from various disciplinary backgrounds." Stryker put the TSI into motion in 2013—a massive undertaking that required coordination with multiple departments and colleges to allocate funds for several new tenure-line positions across the university. Such a feat is all the more heroic when we recall, again, the overarching trend toward contingency and precarity.

This is an opportune moment to return to a particular observation from Aizura's (2018) "Kill Your Dads" piece: "Instead of reflecting on what sense of *precariousness and exclusion* might move students to make such an objection [to Reed's alleged "deadnaming" of Halberstam], Reed doubled down and accused his students of political correctness and victimization" (emphasis mine). It is, again, this callousness toward the well-being of socially and institutionally pre-carious populations, in a time specifically marked by economic, environmental, and multiple other kinds of precarity, that makes positions like Castiglia and

Reed's so appalling. It's not surprising, then, that when I recently made a request on Twitter for a copy of Reed's manifesto—since scrubbed from his faculty page at Penn State—the first person to direct message me screenshots of an old version was a graduate student in queer and feminist studies who joked (?), "These . . . are not from me, probably."

I don't know if that graduate student will be able to find a job when they finish their PhD. I don't know what the climate will be like at that time, broadly or literally speaking. "Kids these days have it so much easier," except when they don't. At the same time, I see people like this student—doing cutting-edge work not dulled by "political correctness," as some might have it—as a glimmer of hope for the future. It's these kinds of contradictions that trans studies could engage with more deeply, in future symposia and perhaps in these very pages.

Nicole Seymour is associate professor of English and affiliated faculty in Environmental Studies and Queer Studies at California State University, Fullerton.

Acknowledgments
I thank Lily House-Peters, Susan Stryker, and Abe Weil for suggestions and conversation around this commentary.

Note
1. I was able to attend or view all symposium events save for the closing plenary on "Trans ± Publics"—featuring representatives from the immigration detention support organization Mariposas sin Fronteras, Tucson poet laureate TC Tolbert, and other trans and gender-nonconforming poets.

References
Aizura, Aren. 2018. "Kill Your Dads: On Reed and Castiglia's Response to Grace Lavery." *Medium*, December 13. medium.com/@aren.aizura/kill-your-dads-on-reed-and-castiglias-response -to-grace-lavery-28857b636a2c/.

Castiglia, Christopher, and Christopher Reed. 2018. "Conversion Therapy vs. Re-education Camp: An Open Letter to Grace Lavery." *Los Angeles Review of Books* (blog), December 11. blog .lareviewofbooks.org/essays/conversion-therapy-v-re-education-camp-open-letter-grace -lavery/.

Chu, Andrea Long. 2018. "I Worked with Avital Ronell. I Believe Her Accuser." *Chronicle of Higher Education*, August 30. www.chronicle.com/article/I-Worked-With-Avital-Ronell-I/244415/.

Cleveland Clinic. 2019. "For the First Time in North America, a Woman Gives Birth after Uterus Transplant from a Deceased Donor." *Health Essentials*, July 9. health.clevelandclinic.org /for-the-first-time-in-north-america-woman-gives-birth-after-uterus-transplant-from -deceased-donor/.

Ferguson, Roderick. 2012. *The Reorder of Things: The University and Its Pedagogies of Minority Difference*. Minneapolis: University of Minnesota Press.

Flaherty, Colleen. 2018. "A Non-Tenure-Track Profession?" *Inside Higher Ed*, October 12. www
.insidehighered.com/news/2018/10/12/about-three-quarters-all-faculty-positions-are-tenure
-track-according-new-aaup/.

Galarte, Francisco J. n.d. Faculty biography, the University of Arizona. gws.arizona.edu/user
/francisco-j-galarte-phd (accessed summer 2020).

Gill-Peterson, Jules. 2018. *Histories of the Transgender Child*. Minneapolis: University of Minnesota Press.

Halberstam, Jack. 2018. *Trans*: A Quick and Quirky Account of Gender Variability*. Berkeley:
University of California Press.

Kezar, Adrianna, Tom DePaola, and Daniel T. Scott. 2019. *The Gig Academy: Mapping Labor in the
Neoliberal University*. Baltimore: Johns Hopkins University Press.

Lavery, Grace. 2018. "Grad School as Conversion Therapy." *Los Angeles Review of Books* (blog),
October 29. blog.lareviewofbooks.org/essays/grad-school-conversion-therapy/.

Leingang, Rachel. 2019. "University of Arizona Professor Sues State over Access to Transgender-
Related Health Care." *Azcentral.com*, January 24. www.azcentral.com/story/news/local
/arizona-health/2019/01/24/ua-professor-russell-toomey-sues-arizona-over-transgender
-health-care-exclusion/2672432002/.

Leiter, Brian. 2018. "Blaming the Victim Is Apparently OK When the Accused in a Title IX
Proceeding Is a Feminist Literary Theorist." *Leiter Reports: A Philosophy Blog*, June 10.
leiterreports.typepad.com/blog/2018/06/blaming-the-victim-is-apparently-ok-when-the
-accused-is-a-feminist-literary-theorist.html.

Lorenz, Taylor. 2019. "'OK Boomer' Marks the End of Friendly Generational Relations." *New York
Times*, October 29. www.nytimes.com/2019/10/29/style/ok-boomer.html.

Macharia, Keguro. 2018. "kburd: Caliban Responds." *New Inquiry*, August 22. thenewinquiry.com
/blog/kburd-caliban-responds/.

Marvel, Kate (@DrKateMarvel). 2019. "Just did a search for 'ok doomer.'" Twitter, November 6,
7:03 a.m. www.twitter.com/drkatemarvel/status/1192095258215141376.

Seymour, Nicole. 2013. *Strange Natures: Futurity, Empathy, and the Queer Ecological Imagination*.
Urbana: University of Illinois Press.

Vaccaro, Jeanne. 2015. "Feelings and Fractals: Woolly Ecologies of Transgender Matter." *GLQ* 21,
nos. 2–3: 273–93.

Celebrating the Launch of the Lili Elbe Digital Archive

A Transfeminist Symposium

PAMELA L. CAUGHIE and EMILY DATSKOU

Abstract This article describes the launch symposium of the Lili Elbe Digital Archive held at Loyola University Chicago in February 2020. The Lili Elbe Digital Archive presents the life narrative of Lili Elbe, one of the most iconic figures in the history of gender variance, along with supplementary materials such as letters and newspaper articles. The symposium offered a queer-friendly, trans-inclusive space where trans, queer, and cisgender scholars and students across disciplines, universities, and generations came together to commemorate Lili's life and the work of the archive. This review examines the transfeminist pedagogy of the archive team and the symposium.

Keywords transgender, digital archive, feminist pedagogy, transfeminist, Lili Elbe

O n Friday, February 7, 2020, at Loyola University Chicago, we held a symposium to celebrate the official launch of the Lili Elbe Digital Archive (fig. 1; www.lilielbe.org). This digital edition and archive, hosted by Loyola University Libraries, is a companion to *Man into Woman: A Comparative Scholarly Edition*, coedited by Pamela L. Caughie and Sabine Meyer and published in Bloomsbury Academic's Modernist Archives series (February 2020). At a time when transgender scholars and trans folks face an increasingly hostile environment, both within and outside the academy, our symposium offered a queer-friendly, trans-inclusive space where trans, queer, and cisgender scholars and students across disciplines, universities, and generations came together to commemorate the life of one of the most iconic figures in the history of gender variance, Lili Elbe. Rather than simply an occasion to present our scholarly product, our symposium, in its structure and organization, embodied the collaborative feminist process by which the digital archive was created, and provided an occasion to celebrate the many scholars, students, and librarians who labored toward a shared goal. By the end of the day, as Professor Susan Stryker poignantly noted in her closing remarks, a

TSQ: Transgender Studies Quarterly ★ Volume 7, Number 3 ★ August 2020 **463**
DOI 10.1215/23289252-8553132   © 2020 Duke University Press

Figure 1. Splash page for the Lili Elbe Digital Archive, February 2020.

project organized around a transfeminine entity enacted a feminist ethos that constituted community and space in a new way. More than just the subject of this symposium, Lili Elbe served as a conduit for channeling mutual respect, gratitude, and love into a trans-inclusive, queer-affirming space.

For readers of this journal, Lili Elbe hardly needs an introduction, and yet readers may not know that her historical name was Lili Ilse Elvenes, though she used Lili Elbe in her life and in her life narrative. Or that she considered herself and Einar Wegener (Andreas Sparre in the narrative) to be two distinct beings. In the narrative, she asks her German friend: "Should I write a preface to the book, to explain why, when speaking of Andreas, I always use the third person, as in a novel? But, my dear friend, what other form of narrative could I have chosen?" (Hoyer 1933: 283); and in an interview with a Danish newspaper, the historical Lili flummoxed the reporter by stating, "Einar Wegener was a strange guy. He both went to the theatre and to cafés just before I had surgery" (Bast 1931). Nor may readers know that Lili Elbe's life narrative exists in four variant editions in three languages (Danish, German, and English), none of them authored solely by Elbe herself. *Man into Woman*—a title Lili disliked, preferring instead "How Lili Became a Real Girl"—is a fictionalized and highly edited collaboration.

These historical details—that Lili Elbe is historical and fictional, that she understood her identity differently than we would today, that the multiple editions are difficult to find and their languages not accessible to everyone— motivated us to produce a digital edition and archive. Importantly, the story itself contravenes the variant multilingual versions that seek to contain it, and this is precisely what our digital edition and archive instantiates. We do not produce an authoritative edition; instead, we gather together on a single interactive site the full range of materials making up the compositional and early publication history of Elbe's narrative. Transcribed and encoded facsimiles of each edition, linked at the paragraph level, enable detailed on-screen comparison of the different versions. The narrative is supplemented by archival materials, such as letters by Lili Elbe and the editor, Ernst Harthern (who used the pseudonym Niels Hoyer); articles from Danish newspapers of the 1930s; and chapters on Elbe from Magnus Hirschfeld's *Le sexe inconnu* (1935) and Hélène Allatini's memoir *Mosaïques* (1939). All materials in Danish, German, and French have been translated into English for wider access.

This was a prodigious effort. The very nature of this work necessitated creating a large team of contributors providing a range of knowledge and skills: knowledge of the editions' languages, of the history of gender variance, of gender and queer theory, of textual scholarship and digital tools. We worked together as a team to conceptualize and design a digital space that would be sensitive to the distinctive features of Lili's life story. Some sixty documents totaling over 1,400 images had to be photographed, transcribed, many translated, and all encoded in XML (extensible markup language), then converted into HTML (hypertext markup language), proofed, corrected, and retransformed for display on the site—a meticulous and highly iterative process. Approximately 1,680 paragraphs across six editions, including the first English-language translations of the German typescript and the Danish edition, had to be collated. Each document required nearly a dozen people to get it from original facsimile (fig. 2) to website rendering (fig. 3).

Encoding principles, collation guidelines, and a prosopography (essentially a list of people and place names with their key IDs) had to be created. The website had to be designed, pages produced, and a sustainability plan devised. And all of this had to be accomplished without major funding. None of our numerous applications to several US funding agencies (National Endowment for the Humanities, American Council of Learned Societies, the Andrew W. Mellon Foundation) was successful. Granted, the acceptance rate at such agencies hovers around 15 percent, yet in our case, there was typically one killjoy who deemed our project "trendy," accused us of trying to capitalize on the popularity of the 2015 film *The Danish Girl* (dir. Tom Hooper), or concluded there was little interest in such a project and, by implication, in such a historical figure. What might seem to be a mark of failure, however, has become a point of pride. That we were able to pull off this project without major funding owing to the enthusiasm, commitment, and diligence of our team members is, for us, the very definition of success.

The creation of the Lili Elbe Digital Archive has been a long time coming, over three years in the making, and we are not yet done. Originally, we had planned to be finished by July 6, 2019, when we went public with the website to

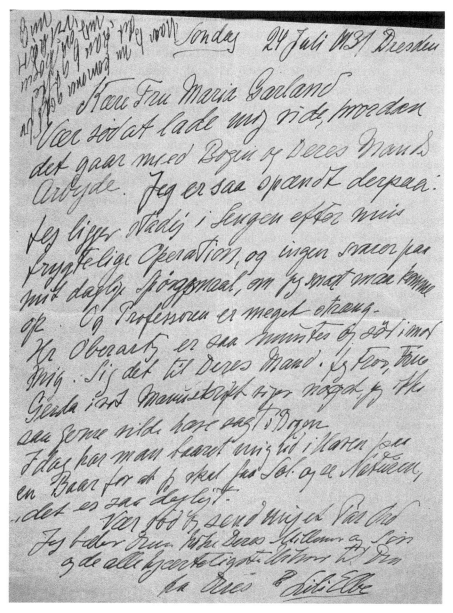

Figure 2. Example of an original facsimile from the Lili Elbe Digital Archive.

commemorate the one hundredth anniversary of the founding of Hirschfeld's Institute for Sexual Science. Then we hoped to be done for our official launch on February 7, 2020. But when you work as a large team, delays and diversions are inevitable. Collectively over the years we have lost loved ones, suffered illness and hospitalization, faced child-care and elder-care crises and bouts of unemployment; we have planned weddings and funerals, prepared for PhD and MA exams,

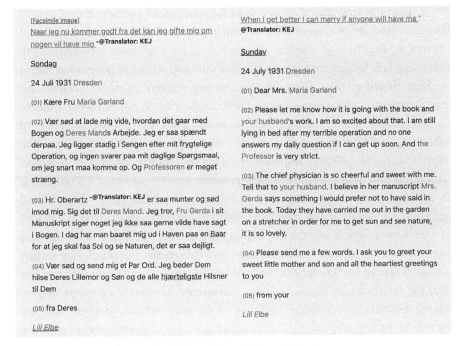

[Facsimile Image]
Naar jeg nu kommer godt fra det kan jeg gifte mig om nogen vil have mig -@**Translator: KEJ**

Sondag

24 Juli 1931 Dresden

(01) Kære Fru Maria Garland

(02) Vær sød at lade mig vide, hvordan det gaar med Bogen og Deres Mands Arbejde. Jeg er saa spændt derpaa. Jeg ligger stadig i Sengen efter mit frygtelige Operation, og ingen svarer paa mit daglige Spørgsmaal, om jeg snart maa komme op. Og Professoren er meget stræng.

(03) Hr. Oberartz -@**Translator: KEJ** er saa munter og sød imod mig. Sig det til Deres Mand. Jeg tror, Fru Gerda i sit Manuskript siger noget jeg ikke saa gerne vilde have sagt i Bogen. I dag har man baaret mig ud i Haven paa en Baar for at jeg skal faa Sol og se Naturen, det er saa dejligt.

(04) Vær sød og send mig et Par Ord. Jeg beder Dem hilse Deres Lillemor og Søn og de alle hjærteligste Hilsner til Dem

(05) fra Deres

Lili Elbe

When I get better I can marry if anyone will have me.*
@**Translator: KEJ**

Sunday

24 July 1931 Dresden

(01) Dear Mrs. Maria Garland

(02) Please let me know how it is going with the book and your husband's work. I am so excited about that. I am still lying in bed after my terrible operation and no one answers my daily question if I can get up soon. And the Professor is very strict.

(03) The chief physician is so cheerful and sweet with me. Tell that to your husband. I believe in her manuscript Mrs. Gerda says something I would prefer not to have said in the book. Today they have carried me out in the garden on a stretcher in order for me to get sun and see nature, it is so lovely.

(04) Please send me a few words. I ask you to greet your sweet little mother and son and all the heartiest greetings to you

(05) from your

Lili Elbe

Figure 3. Example of an original facsimile transformed into website text.

and coped with the numerous demands of our day jobs. Nevertheless, through it all, we have persisted. To borrow Maggie Nelson's metaphor of the Argonaut (in turn borrowed from Roland Barthes), our team may have morphed over the years, losing some members only to take on others, but we remain one entity, the Lili Elbe Digital Archive Project Team.

A model for interdisciplinary, collaborative scholarship and feminist pedagogy, the Lili Elbe Digital Archive could not be launched in the traditional format of the academic symposium, where senior scholars give papers on their singular accomplishments. Instead, our symposium showcased the work of a team of digital humanities and gender scholars, librarians and archivists, and graduate and undergraduate students in a range of disciplines and across Europe and the United States, who came together to conceive, design, and build the archive. We began our event with an evening showing of Tom Hooper's film *The Danish Girl*, serving pizza and popcorn as a way of creating community by breaking bread together. The film was followed by an energizing talk-back with David Ebershoff, author of the biofictional novel *The Danish Girl* (2000); Sabine Meyer, author of *Wie Lili zu einem richtigen Mädchen wurde* (*How Lili Became a Real Girl*, 2015) and a research consultant on the film; and Professor Susan Stryker, who, like Lili Elbe, needs no introduction for this readership. What emerged in the exchange among the guest speakers and the audience was a more nuanced, complex, historically grounded understanding of the film.

The following afternoon began with presentations by the two coeditors of *Man into Woman: A Comparative Scholarly Edition*, Sabine Meyer (Humboldt University, Berlin) and Pamela Caughie (Loyola University Chicago), both addressing how they came to study Lili Elbe's life and what this project has meant to them. Together they discussed the challenges Elbe's narrative presents for textual scholars and the ethical issues raised by their work, not just what it means for two scholars who are not transgender to edit Lili's text, but also the ethics of publishing Lili's personal writings when she could not give her consent. The responsibility that privilege imposed on us led to a mutual obligation to respect Lili's words and to honor, to the extent possible, how she saw her life's trajectory. To that end, our archive does not just preserve and memorialize this material against its future loss; it also reveals the resistance of the memorialized material to its own historicization and the way digital tools can better capture that resistance than the print medium. "Computer files are inherently unstable," says textual scholar W. Speed Hill (2006: 44); "they resist identity"—as do queer subjects. For Hill, the instability of digital archives "threaten[s] the work we invest in preserving the artifacts we cherish" (43). But for the queer scholar, to quote Matthew Burroughs Price (2015: 661), "the (re)making of queer worlds begins with the salvaging of these literary artifacts to be taken up in another queer time and place."[1] Our digital archive provides another queer space. The distributed authorship and fluid form of the digital archive mirror the narrative itself.

As Caroline McCraw, a technical editor on the project, noted in one of the roundtables, digital work is circular, iterative, and networked. The smallest emendation ripples through the entire site, affecting everything else and eliciting new ways of thinking about the representation of gender identity in this work. The digital archive is pulsing and alive, Caroline said, and its fluidity and simultaneity, its ever-evolving and shifting status, are the very qualities we need for our understanding of gender and sexual identity. Digital editor Rebecca J. Parker, taking us step-by-step through the process of archive building, pointed out the way encoding in markup language enabled us to capture the complex identification of Lili Elbe, who was at once a historical figure and a fictional character, who both *posed* as Lili by serving as Gerda's model and *was* Lili, Gerda's close friend. To encode Einar Wegener and Andreas Sparre using the same key ID as for Lili Elbe would distort the historical record and the narrative logic, conflating historical people and fictional characters and imposing our contemporary notions of transgender onto Lili. We found a solution through a collaborative discussion during which our digital editor came to understand Lili's identity through the lens of gender and queer theories, and the encoders and project director came to understand the promise, and limits, of digital tools for capturing the complexity of gender.[2] By using TEI (Text Encoding Initiative) guidelines, as

```
<person xml:id="wegenerE" source="historical" synch="#sparreAn #lili">
    <persName>Einar Wegener</persName>
    <persName>Einar</persName>
    <persName source="#danishSupp">Bé</persName>
    <persName source="#danishSupp">Hr. Wegener</persName>
    <persName source="#danishSupp">Maleren Wegener</persName>
    <persName source="#danishSupp"><persName key="wegenerG">Gerda Wegeners</persName>
        Mand</persName>
    <persName source="#danishSupp">Manden Wegener</persName>
    <persName source="#danishSupp">in tidligere Mand</persName>
    <persName source="#danishSupp">Mr. Wegener</persName>
    <persName source="#danishSupp">the painter Wegener</persName>
    <persName source="#danishSupp"><persName key="wegenerG">Gerda Wegener</persName>'s
        husband</persName>
    <persName source="#danishSupp">the man Wegener</persName>
    <persName source="#danishSupp">former husband</persName>
    <note>Einar Magnus Andreas Wegener (b. 1882), a Danish painter; married to Gerda
        Wegener; died as Lili Elbe in Dresden, 1931</note>
</person>
```

Figure 4. Encoding names in the American edition of the narrative.

Rebecca explained, we could give these figures separate IDs and yet link them in the prosopography, allowing the different identities to stand separately but remain connected. Transforming the prosopography notes (fig. 4) into pop-ups in the HTML reading views (figs. 5 and 6) also allowed these connections to be easily accessible and visible to readers of the archive.

Caroline's and Rebecca's comments draw attention to Project Manager Emily Datskou's discussion of the feminist pedagogy informing this project. Emily explained how we incorporate the narrative into a range of classes—from core-level classes in transgender history and literature, to major classes in transgender memoirs, to graduate courses in queer modernity and in digital humanities—eliciting participation from students at all levels. For example, the site was designed in the required practicum for the Master of Arts in digital humanities in Fall 2018. Pamela, as the project director, gave the students only one requirement: the site must encapsulate modernism and femininity. And so the students used Bauhaus colors and fonts, and Taylor Brown captured Lili's femininity in our logo as seen in figures 7 and 8.

Integrating Lili's narrative into these classes not only generated new ideas for the project (for example, the digital humanities practicum students performed a color-blindness assessment on the site) but also provided us with team members, many of whom stayed committed to Lili and the project throughout the years. Outlining her own journey on the project in the closing roundtable, Anna

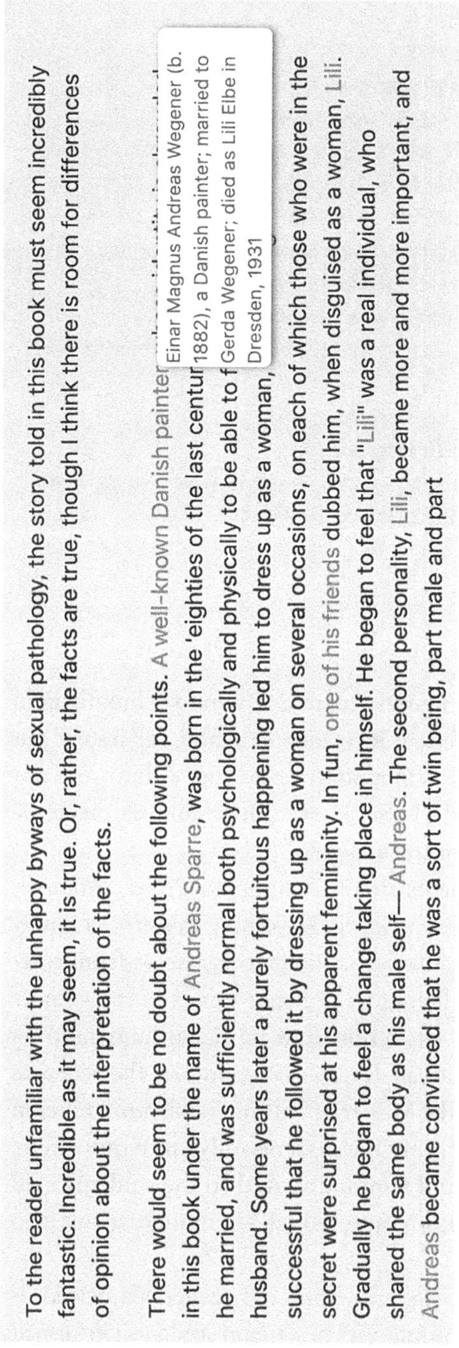

To the reader unfamiliar with the unhappy byways of sexual pathology, the story told in this book must seem incredibly fantastic. Incredible as it may seem, it is true. Or, rather, the facts are true, though I think there is room for differences of opinion about the interpretation of the facts.

There would seem to be no doubt about the following points. A well-known Danish painter in this book under the name of Andreas Sparre, was born in the 'eighties of the last century [Einar Magnus Andreas Wegener (b. 1882), a Danish painter; married to Gerda Wegener; died as Lili Elbe in Dresden, 1931] he married, and was sufficiently normal both psychologically and physically to be able to f husband. Some years later a purely fortuitous happening led him to dress up as a woman, successful that he followed it by dressing up as a woman on several occasions, on each of which those who were in the secret were surprised at his apparent femininity. In fun, one of his friends dubbed him, when disguised as a woman, Lili. Gradually he began to feel a change taking place in himself. He began to feel that "Lili" was a real individual, who shared the same body as his male self— Andreas. The second personality, Lili, became more and more important, and Andreas became convinced that he was a sort of twin being, part male and part

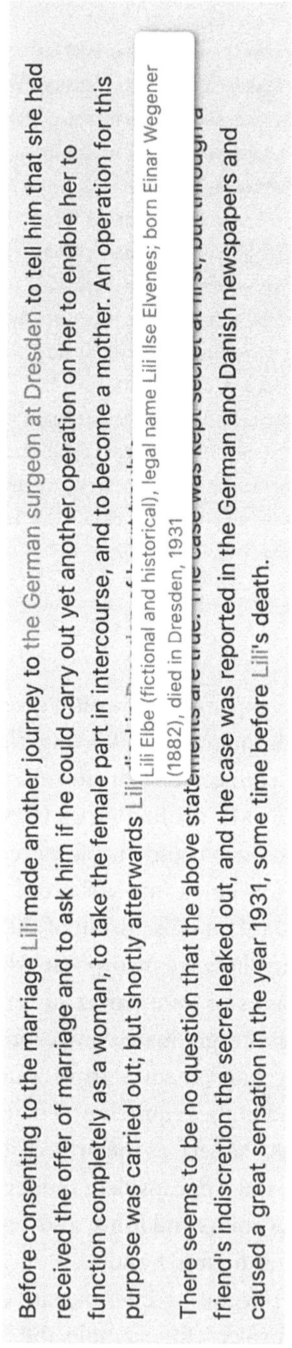

Before consenting to the marriage Lili made another journey to the German surgeon at Dresden to tell him that she had received the offer of marriage and to ask him if he could carry out yet another operation on her to enable her to function completely as a woman, to take the female part in intercourse, and to become a mother. An operation for this purpose was carried out; but shortly afterwards Lili [Lili Elbe (fictional and historical), legal name Lili Ilse Elvenes; born Einar Wegener (1882), died in Dresden, 1931]

There seems to be no question that the above statements are true. The case was kept secret at first, but through a friend's indiscretion the secret leaked out, and the case was reported in the German and Danish newspapers and caused a great sensation in the year 1931, some time before Lili's death.

Figures 5–6. Examples from the archive's prosopography and pop ups from the American edition of the narrative.

McCue, a technical editor who started on the project as a student in one of Pamela's core classes, recounted how she thought her participation would last only one year. But as she worked on each assignment, "somehow," she said, "Lili clung tight to me," and she remained on the project as a Provost Fellow for two more years and has continued after graduation as a volunteer. Lili's story will only wholly be known to her and the people who loved her, Anna acknowledged, but "my role on this project was to take pieces of her story, make them accessible for others, and allow new readings to emerge."

Emily further explained the collaborative atmosphere of our project as faculty, librarians, and students learn and work together as peers and come together regularly at team meetings. To foster collaboration and consistency, we pair experienced technical editors, like Danielle Richards and Xiamara Hohman, with new volunteers just learning XML, and we hold technical trainings as well as refresher sessions every semester. Using Google docs and spreadsheets, Emily keeps track of the multifaceted project work and a host of volunteers, and a GitHub repository allows a shared space for team members to work together, to track their contributions, and to assure accountability. Every engaged-learning student is named on the Git repo, with their pronouns and "handles" listed, just as everyone's contribution is documented in the metadata on the website. (See, for example, the Engaged Learning Fall 2019 GitHub repo on the Project Team page.)

Because the team is so large and the afternoon was too short, we invited undergraduate students to present their work during the coffee break. Ten students presented their group projects at digital exhibits stationed around the room, displaying their contributions—for example, social maps, time line, scene collation—and explaining their process and rationale to audience members, those familiar with digital archives or Elbe's life and those clueless about either or both. For many students it was their first professional presentation, and they relished the experience of playing expert to senior scholars.

Introduced by Caroline and Rebecca, who assisted Pamela in teaching the project in the undergraduate classroom, the closing roundtable, "Teaching and Learning with the Digital Archive," featured undergraduate students (some who have since graduated) who have participated as Provost Fellows, engaged-learners, and volunteers. Their remarks moved all of us as they spoke eloquently and from the heart about what their participation on this project has meant to them, personally as well as professionally. Orion Elrod, a first-year student, began by saying, "Here I am speaking at a symposium when I have never been to one before." Orion's remark brought out what Rebecca termed the "generationally collaborative" nature of the team, in which senior scholars support the professional development of emerging scholars and beginning students. The students' remarks captured as well what Emily had earlier outlined: namely, the many ways

Figure 7. Picture of Lili Elbe at the Women's Clinic from June 1930 found in the American edition of the narrative (1933).

we strive to give back to our team members. The students talked about the marketable skills they had acquired—not just technical skills but time management, teamwork, and critical thinking as well. They spoke of their satisfaction in seeing their work published with their names on the site and how they took pride in being able to point to something tangible as the product of their intellectual labor. In the digital world, we are all authors, blurring the line between literature and code, and shifting our understanding of work from product to process.

The students also addressed, as do students' blog posts on the Git repositories, how they came to know Lili Elbe and her narrative more intimately than they ever could by simply reading the text. Cristiana Bertola, a Romanian student who translated the French version of Lili's narrative published in *Voilà* in 1934, discussed how that opportunity to work extensively and closely with the language of another person led, as Caroline had earlier noted, to respect, appreciation, and affection. Remarking that her home country prohibits same-sex marriage, Cristiana said she hopes one day to translate Lili's story into Romanian and thereby speak back to her government's conservative notions of gender and sexuality. Coming from the Women's Studies and Gender Studies program, Anna explained how much she enjoyed working on a project that produced a lot of exceptions to rules, which required adding new rules to our guidelines, only later to have those challenged as well. This iterative process went on and on, Anna said, and made her proud to work on a project that adapted to the needs of the story: "It made me think about Lili, who was told she could only succeed by becoming 'a real girl' if she followed the correct rules of femininity and biology. Lili might have benefited from being allowed to break some rules, and it is this Lili whom I tried to consider as I worked on the project." As someone who identifies as transgender, Orion said he hoped

Figure 8. Logo for the Lili Elbe Digital Archive.

that someday some young person living in a remote area with family they cannot talk to will find this archive and thereby find some comfort and come to understand themselves and their history. All speakers conveyed the passion they felt toward the project, their gratitude for the opportunity, and, most touchingly, their love for Lili Elbe. As Professor Christine Froula from Northwestern University put it, the archive is a "collaborative labor of love." "I found it especially moving," she wrote after the event, "to hear the many Loyola students, from first-year undergraduates to advanced graduate students, all brimming with confidence, expertise, and eloquence, describe the parts they played, the skills they learned, and what their work on this project means to them" (pers. comm., February 23, 2020).

It was love that Susan Stryker identified as the overarching theme of the symposium. Love for a trans woman, love for our collaborative project, love for one another as a team. Lili Elbe was an important figure at the beginning of the transgender movement, Susan remarked, and now, as a new transgender movement emerges, Lili is, thanks to this project, once again an important figure, bridging the proverbial generation gap.

Earlier we invoked Maggie Nelson's *The Argonauts* (2015) as a metaphor for our variable project team. Here we want to close with a quotation from that work that we feel captures the nature of this love that filled the space of our symposium.

> Barthes describes how the subject who utters the phrase "I love you" is like "the Argonaut renewing his ship during its voyage without changing its name." Just as the *Argo*'s parts may be replaced over time but the boat is still called the *Argo*, whenever the lover utters the phrase "I love you," its meaning must be renewed by each use, as "the very task of love and of language is to give to one and the same phrase inflections which will be forever new." (5)

Pamela L. Caughie is professor of English and women's studies and gender studies at Loyola University Chicago. With Sabine Meyer, she coedited *Man into Woman: A Comparative Scholarly Edition* (2020). She is project director for the Lili Elbe Digital Archive and codirector of Modernist Networks, a consortium of digital projects in modernist literature and culture.

Emily Datskou is a PhD candidate in the English Department at Loyola University Chicago and the project manager for the Lili Elbe Digital Archive. Her dissertation explores the role of queer theory in nineteenth-century novels. She has publications in *Feminist Modernist Studies* and *Brontë Studies* and work forthcoming in *Creolizing Frankenstein*.

Acknowledgments
We are grateful to the Lili Elbe Digital Archive Project Team for all their hard work on the project and the symposium and for their contributions to this article.

Notes

1. These quotations are from Pamela L. Caughie and Sabine Meyer's (2019) "From Work to Tech: Digital Archives and Queer Narratives."
2. Pamela, Emily, and Rebecca coauthored an article on the possibilities and limitations of encoding standards for capturing new ontologies of gender in digital formats (Caughie, Datskou, and Parker 2018).

References

Allatini, Hélène. 1939. "Il et Elle" ("He and She"). In *Mosaïques*, translated by Anne M. Callahan, 198–237. Paris: Nouvelle Revue Critique. Lili Elbe Digital Archive. lilielbe.org/media/books/Allatini_chapter.pdf (accessed February 24, 2020).

Bast, Jørgen. 1931. "Lili Elvenæs, alias Einar Wegener, er afgaaet ved Døden. En tragisk Afslutning paa en fantastisk Livsskæbne" ("Lili Elvenæs, alias Einar Wegener, Has Passed Away. A Tragic End to a Fantastic Life"), translated by Marianne Ølholm. *Berlingske Tidende*, September 14. Lili Elbe Digital Archive. lilielbe.org/context/periodicals/1931-09-14_BT.html (accessed February 24, 2020).

Burroughs Price, Matthew. 2015. "A Genealogy of Queer Detachment." *PMLA* 130, no. 3: 648–65.

Caughie, Pamela L., Emily Datskou, Sabine Meyer, Rebecca J. Parker, and Nikolaus Wasmoen, eds. n.d. Lili Elbe Digital Archive. lilielbe.org (accessed February 24, 2020).

Caughie, Pamela L., Emily Datskou, and Rebecca Parker. 2018. "Storm Clouds on the Horizon: Feminist Ontologies and the Problem of Gender." *Feminist Modernist Studies* 1, no. 3: 230–42. doi.org/10.1080/24692921.2018.1505819.

Caughie, Pamela L., and Sabine Meyer. 2019. "From Work to Tech: Digital Archives and Queer Narratives." *Modernism/modernity*, February 1. doi.org/10.26597/mod.0087.

Caughie, Pamela L., and Sabine Meyer, eds. 2020. *Man into Woman: A Comparative Scholarly Edition*. New York: Bloomsbury Academic.

Ebershoff, David. 2000. *The Danish Girl*. New York: Penguin.

Hirschfeld, Magnus. 1935. "La manie androgyne" ("Androgyne Mania"), translated by Anne M. Callahan. In *Le sexe inconnu* (*The Unknown Sex*), 91–97. Paris: Éditions Montaigne. Lili

Elbe Digital Archive. lilielbe.org/context/chapters/HirschfeldChapter.html (accessed February 24, 2020).

Hooper, Tom, dir. 2015. *The Danish Girl*. Universal City, CA: Universal Studios Home Entertainment. DVD.

Hoyer, Niels, ed. 1933. *Man into Woman: An Authentic Record of a Change of Sex, the True Story of the Miraculous Transformation of the Danish Painter Einar Wegener (Andreas Sparre)*. Translated by H. J. Stenning. New York: E. P. Dutton. Lili Elbe Digital Archive. lilielbe.org/narrative/editions/A1.html (accessed February 24, 2020).

Meyer, Sabine. 2015. *"Wie Lili zu einem richtigen Mädchen wurde": Lili Elbe: Zur Konstruktion von Geschlecht und Identität zwischen Medialisierung, Regulierung und Subjektivierung ("How Lili Became a Real Girl": Lili Elbe: On the Construction of Gender and Identity between Medialization, Regulation, and Subjectivization)*. Bielefeld: Transcript Verlag.

Nelson, Maggie. 2015. *The Argonauts*. Minneapolis: Graywolf.

Speed Hill, W. 2006. "From 'an Age of Editing' to a 'Paradigm Shift': An Editorial Retrospect." *Text* 16: 33–47.

Trans | Acker

MCKENZIE WARK

Abstract The writer Kathy Acker (1947–97) is one of those few in the anglophone canon, or even near it, who opens a space for trans experiences. If trans literature, and literary studies, is to widen their ambits of aesthetic operation, one useful step would be to expand the critical study and literary experiment with such writers. The "Trans | Acker Symposium" at The New School in 2019 was a modest contribution to this project. This text introduces Acker and three of the texts from that event.
Keywords Kathy Acker, trans literature, trans theory

There is a fine literature by, for, and about trans existence, but it is not a large literature, and not many of its works and authors have made an impact on literary culture at large. For this and many other reasons, trans writers draw on sustenance from cis writers, including some who seem to make a space in their texts for us, and through that toehold, space for us in literature more broadly. One such writer is Kathy Acker.

Born in 1947, Acker was an avant-garde writer whose best-known work is *Blood and Guts in High School*, probably completed in 1978 but first published in 1984. It is still in print, still something of a cult classic, and of particular appeal to readers who find little place for themselves in literary culture, not least where questions of gender are concerned.

Since her untimely death from cancer in 1997, critical interest in Acker has slowly accumulated, finally flourishing into academic respectability. The novelist Chris Kraus's (2017) biography found a new readership for her. There's now two very fine critical studies, by Georgina Colby (2016) and Douglas Martin (2017). She was the subject of retrospectives in Karlsruhe and at the Institute of Contemporary Arts in London. Grove Atlantic is reissuing her major works, some with new introductions. A critical edition of her early work, edited by Justin Gajoux (2019), is now out in Paris. Meanwhile, the steady stream of scholarly articles, theses, and monographs continues to flow unabated.

The measure of a good writer is when their work will sustain multiple readings and rewritings. That really seems to be the case with Acker. There are just

TSQ: Transgender Studies Quarterly ★ Volume 7, Number 3 ★ August 2020 **476**
DOI 10.1215/23289252-8553146   © 2020 Duke University Press

so many Kathy Ackers. She has been read through the prisms of queer, punk, feminism, s&m, the avant-garde, postmodernism, and so on and so forth, with varying degrees of success. She has also been picked up by other artists and writers, from Laura Parnes (2009) to Linda Stupat (2019). For our own purposes, she is name checked in Imogen Binnie's *Nevada* (2013), a book with a key place in the emergence of a contemporary trans literature.

There's more to be said about Acker by trans writers and scholars. I mean trans here in the broad sense, including trans gender, transsexual, gender-nonconforming, nonbinary, and genderqueer people. Gender is a rich vein of material in her work, but trans writers have a lot to say about Acker beyond the question of gender.

That is why I organized a symposium on her work at The New School for Social Research on November 22, 2019, called "Trans | Acker," three of the papers from which appear in this volume. I'm interested in what we think about everything in her work. I wanted to make a space where we can speak, in the first instance to each other, about literature, our literature, and our place in literature as such.

I sometimes wonder if Kathy was trans. Kay Gabriel has warned me—more than once—about the dangers of this sort of projection, and rightly so. I don't think anything necessary or even useful for the trans encounter with Acker hangs on making her "one of us." But I can't help wondering if the sadness I feel about my own brief and failed encounter with Kathy has to do with both of us being trans and neither of us knowing it.

Of course, she hated categories and refused to abide by identities. The world according to Acker is a chaotic one of shifting sensations, of bodies prone to magical metamorphosis and yet also constantly throwing off visceral and confusing sensations (which, now that I put it that way, seems pretty trans . . .).

There's more than a few queer or feminist writers that trans people have been drawn to who in the end have let us down. I don't think Kathy would have been one of them. She didn't live to see trans culture emerge in its current form. I think she would have shown us love.

McKenzie Wark (she/her) is the author, most recently, of *Capital Is Dead* (2019) and *Reverse Cowgirl* (2020). She teaches at the New School in New York City. @mckenziewark.

References

Acker, Kathy. 2017. *Blood and Guts in High School*. New York: Grove Atlantic.

Acker, Kathy, and McKenzie Wark. 2015. *I'm Very into You: Correspondence 1995–1996*. South Pasadena, CA: Semiotext(e).

Binnie, Imogen. 2013. *Nevada*. New York: Topside.

Colby, Georgina. 2016. *Kathy Acker: Writing the Impossible*. Oxford: Oxford University Press.

Gajoux, Justin. 2019. *Kathy Acker 1971–1975*. Paris: Ismael.

Kraus, Chris. 2017. *After Kathy Acker: A Literary Biography*. Los Angeles: Semiotext(e).

Martin, Douglas. 2017. *Acker*. New York: Nightboat.

Parnes, Laura. 2009. *Blood and Guts in Hollywood*. New York: Participant.

Stupat, Linda. 2019. *Virus*. London: Arcadia Missa.

Cutting Up Words

Kathy Acker's Trans Locutions

MARQUIS BEY

Abstract This article argues that Kathy Acker articulates an understanding of transness through language. More than a meditation on gender-nonnormative characters in Acker's work, the article dwells on how Acker uses language as a vector through which to imply the residue of a certain understanding of trans. In short, examined here is Acker as a trans philosophical thinker, one whose thinking manifested in how she uses language.
Keywords Kathy Acker, trans, language

> That geography that is without verbal language: A marvelously luminous, viscid
> substance is left behind in me, defying words . . .
> —Kathy Acker, "Against Ordinary Language: The Language of the Body"

To be sure, this occasion to meditate on Kathy Acker demands attuned listening. More pointedly, it is because this specific occasion is one concerned with the trans in and around Acker, or the trans via Acker, that it demands listening, for only when we listen attentively might we glimpse—or rather hear—what I am deeming her trans locutions. My concern is not to find the moments in Acker's work when she mentions transgender people, though for another to have such a concern is undeniably, to my mind, valid and worthy. Nor is my concern, closer to what one might expect of a scholar trained in literature, to dwell on the moments in Acker's novels in which she discursively transgresses gender, though I may very well note, briefly, such a thing. (My refusal to meditate here on her novels, as might be more expected, comes in fact from a similar feeling Acker [2018: viii] has, namely, that "I don't give a damn about literature." It is writing, broadly understood in that Derridean sense, that *arche* sense, that I care about.)[1] My concern, rather, is a particular one, perhaps even a philosophical one: to

TSQ: Transgender Studies Quarterly ★ Volume 7, Number 3 ★ August 2020 **479**
DOI 10.1215/23289252-8553160 © 2020 Duke University Press

rummage around in those "little realms of handling language" (Acker 2018: 92) and find, in Acker's locutionary deployments, her manner of speech, or speech-ifying, that which bears the residue, as it were, of what might be called the trans.

In other words, I am interested, in these pages, in how Acker utilizes words and language as a modality of nonnormativity. For her to be "against ordinary language," as an essay (Acker 1993) of hers asserts, is, I argue, or rather bears, a trans relationship to the very grammar of language, which might be construed as a nonnormative or trans relationship to the circuitry of that which brings beings into the world. *Trans* here references, of course, genders transgressive of the purportedly immutable and mutually exclusionary gender binary; too, however, it references the ways that something different is done to and with language, how speech acts and words are deployed via a desire to interrogate their purported stability, and the manner through which language is lacerated. In short, I wish to suggest that Acker's relationship to language—what I understand in a Hei-deggarian fashion, in which "language is the house of being" and "language speaks man" (Heidegger 2008: 217)—is a trans one, a relationship that vitiates language's implicitly coherent grammatology and venerates the salvation implied by the force of the nonnormative.

Considered a cult figure in the punk movement and a key contributor to radical feminism and literary postmodernism, Acker has cultivated a notable aesthetic. Her corpus is full of sex, drugs, incest, and that which can only be called—lovingly and beautifully, to be sure—super duper weird. No doubt much of this is due to the influence of avant-garde poets of the day, with their exper-imentalism and disdain for linearity, for teleology, the master narrative—Acker and her influencers demonstrated remarkable adherence to Jean-François Lyo-tard's (1984: xxiv) axiomatic postmodernism: an incredulity to grand narratives.[2] Such an incredulity, for Acker at least, pervaded even the foundational level of the language. If there is a structure inherent to what we understand as language, an endemic structural coherence and assumption of naturalness, which might be best articulated through Noam Chomsky's attempt to develop a universal grammar, the trans of Acker's locutionary posture enters via the rejection of such a universality. Acker is irreverent toward language's rules, rules that demand to be followed for one's very legibility as even speaking language, which is also to say being sub-jectivated as a speaking thing. Language is forced to fail in Acker's corpus and, I might say, philosophical musings (my primary concern); thus she buttresses my subtitular claim, and the claim of this intellectual gathering, by echoing a position asserted by manuel arturo abreu (2016): that trans is a failure of language.

Transing Bodies

Acker (2018: 136) has said that, in her earlier works, her characters "changed gender a lot: I never got 'his' and 'her' right! And the dumb reason was: I just didn't remember, I didn't care, it meant nothing to me." She goes on: "I think the reason was probably my hatred of gender . . . a hatred of the expectation that I had to become my womb. My hatred of being defined by the fact that I had a cunt." Her work's disdain for gender is a hatred for how gender is used as a regulatory regime that coercively organizes bodies, reducing their breadth, and prohibiting mutability. She hates how gendered impositions ontologically reduce subjects, often genitally so, as she articulates, and writes toward a kind of subject that does not abide these impositions, or at least interrogates these impositions. This writing, I am asserting, is a trans locution.

It bears resemblance to Julia Kristeva's poetic and revolutionary language, as Susan E. Hawkins has argued. Hawkins argues that Acker's language, especially in *Blood and Guts in High School*—that novelistic "antigrammatical discourse that runs counter to ordinary language" (Colby 2016: 77)—exhibits an "experimental" (a term Acker abhorred) quality similar to Kristeva's articulation of poetic language, which Hawkins (2004: 644n4) describes as "nonsense" and "'musical' . . . effects [that] destroy not only accepted beliefs and significations, but, in radical experiments, syntax itself." Acker's language, following this reading of Hawkins (2004: 644n4), "disrupts through its very heterogeneity—shifting, fragmentary, often elliptical, and disjunctive." It is this sense of disruption I am thinking through the analytic of the trans because, indeed, Acker has as one of her chief aims an interrogation and disruption of gender, but also because there are implicit linkages of language to bodies, themselves fundamentally gendered, which intensify for me the utility of using trans specifically. In other words, not only is Acker seeking to experimentalize gender through her writing, which gives her work over to trans readings, she is, too, acknowledging how language, its very grammar and syntax, is mired in constructions of the body; and if her work is indeed alongside Kristeva's poetic language that "destroy[s] . . . syntax itself," a reading must be offered that designates such connections and destructions as vehemently, fundamentally, and unapologetically trans.

Hence when I say in this section's title that Acker is in the literary and discursive business of transing bodies, what I am attempting to suggest is a conversation, on her part, between language and what we have come to discern as the body. Language, partly at least, gives the body to us, gives it its shape and feel, its look. Thus through her transing of language—her irreverence toward gendered pronoun linearity, her troubling of syntax, her irruptions of form and genre (which, notably, is the etymological root for gender), her facilitation of trans discourse[3]—she also, in turn, transes bodiness.

She bodies language. Those familiar with the discourse pervasive in milieus from which I hail—those urban ghettoes full of Black English and linguistic innovation—know that this phrase is polysemous. On the one hand, to body something, in this instance to body language, is to give language to the body, to recognize a connection between the body and language, as I've alluded to above. In this sense there is a marked interaction between what language does and, in that Deleuzian parlance, what a body can do. But on the other hand, "to body language" also resounds in the sense of killing language. To body something is to exterminate it, to demonstrate its inferiority compared to the one who has done the bodying. (To be sure, this discourse traffics in masculinist, colonialist registers of conquest that lionize brutality and genocidal tendencies. Such a meaning must always be acknowledged, though I wish to use the term here anyway for illustrative purposes that Acker, undoubtedly, undermines.) Acker is bodying language in both these senses, and that gives way to a reading of her various and variegated locutions as hefty with trans significatory power. She produces, in this bodying of language, what Georgina Colby (2016: 6) identifies as Acker's "languages of the body," which gainsay ordinary, streamlined—perhaps I might say, running with my subtitular analytical framework, cis—language.[4]

Though Acker submits that she doesn't know why she refused linear narrative, gender continuity, and teleological orientation, I contend here that it is because she is a writer and thinker committed to trans locutions, modes of discourse, and narrative that index other ways of conveyance and livability. There is a tacit commitment to articulating, through writing and speech, what has been deemed outside legibility, outside narrative, outside the very criteria for existence and sense making. Her novels and interview responses demonstrate Acker's nonsensibility, as it were; in locuting through transness, which is to say expressing disorienting de-narratology and nonnormativity, Acker takes the word—that conduit for semiotic referentiality, or that biblical primordial givenness of things—and cuts it up, hacks it to bits, leaving only an un-language, which is precisely what might allow for other ways, trans ways, to be.

De-Narratives

Narrative, in simplistic terms, is the conveyance of a beginning, middle, and end. Narratives operate under an implicit teleology in which readers or listeners come to expect a certain flow of events that crescendo into a tidy resolution, a trajectory reminiscent of grade-school plot charts of exposition, rising action, climax, falling action, and resolution. But narratives are not innocent. They purport a naturalness and work to normalize certain modes of telling over others, deeming those others as invalid or, worse, unworthy of recognition as stories. Narratives construct the limits of narratology, so if one wishes to express a story, or "storyness," outside those limits one must effectively de-narrativize. And all of Acker's kooky, experimental tinkering with form is an attempt to write a de-narrative; "I guess what I wanted was to have a narrative that was a kind of 'de-narrative,'" she says.

"If there is such a word" (McCaffery and Acker 1991: 89). Of note are two things: first, of course, the desire to write a de-narrative, which I take to mean the kind of narrative that exceeds the implicit limits of an expected narrative, a narrative that is not properly a narrative. It is a narrative that undoes itself as narrative, which is to say a narrative that assumes its narrativity—if it can be called such—by virtue of its de-narrativizing. De-narratives become the "narratives" that they are by way of de-ing, if you will, narrative, narrativization, and narratology. Second, there seems to be something quite rich in Acker's ending statement, "If there is such a word." Admittedly I may be imbuing more weight into something meant to be a mere colloquial addendum or a trite turn of phrase holding little of substance, but I gather there is something to be gleaned from her concluding statement. To stage the statement as a conditional, as an "*If . . . ,*" posits that it is possible that such a word as *de-narrative* is not a word, which then means that it is not a word and falls outside language—*de-narrative* might hence be read as the language Hester, as I discuss below, wishes to be taught; de-narrative is a language that has meaning to those who might not be meaningful due to their "edginess," their existence and subjectivation—and writing—on the ontological edge. For a word such as *de-narrative* to have an existence only as an "if" marks it as a kind of nebulous para-language, a manner of speaking and writing from a language that does not exist or that exceeds the grammatical dictates of language. De-narrative, in short, is Acker cutting up words; de-narrative is, in a way, one of Acker's trans locutions.

And this then has the effect of bearing acutely on identity. Because Acker is quite bored with the question of identity, seeing it as "obviously" constructed and lacking any natural, essentialist moorings, she is drawn to the looseness—the possibility of transness and transitivity—of texts and language. Where she moseys toward is a disintegration of the consolidating, coherent *I*, that stand-in for the all of a byzantine complexity of multitudinous assemblages of subjectivity. Disintegrating the *I* is coming from a profound place of anger, surely, for Acker, but it is also coming from a significant desire to decentralize meaning. Where the *I* has long been proffered as the pinnacle pursuit of inquiry, Acker understands this tradition—which she locates, somewhat quintessentially, in Robert Creeley—as a decidedly male one. "I hated it because it was so male," she writes, following it up, crucially as I'll explain momentarily, with "and I didn't want that" (McCaffery and Acker 1991: 90). Rather than a departure from the phallogocentrism of the male lineage she describes as a sort of gynocentric place, or from a male lineage to the veneration of a female lineage that buttresses the gender binary, Acker deftly says, simply, she doesn't want "that." The refusal to designate what she does want, which would undoubtedly have been positioned in an oppositionally binaristic way, is a method by which she allows for the prefixal *trans* to take hold. This space of the trans refuses a "homing desire" that Nael Bhanji (2013) describes in terms

not so pleasant, a desire expressed when transgender people wish to find them
selves comfortably, normatively still within the binary, though at a pole they did
not begin at; rather, the space of the trans here echoes a nonbinary axiom, in
which the refusal of natal assignations does not lead to the "other" gender but to
an assertion of wanting, simply, not what has been given. Following Eva Hayward
and Che Gossett (2017), Acker expresses the transness of "that."[5]

Edginess

At least nowadays it seems like every so-called avant-garde artist of whatever
stripe claims their work is "edgy," which, by my albeit limited assessment, is often
simply code for saying non-"politically correct" things. Let's just not give such a
shallow edginess an attention it surely doesn't deserve. But Acker demonstrated a
kind of edginess that I can bounce to, an edginess that in fact resided on the edge,
which might be a way to describe a radical criticality and Fanonian "real leap"
outside the grammars that engender legibility. Acker's edginess manifested
through her language and how she mobilized language, the word, in such a way as
to find the limits, the norms, and push them.

The edge is where things are liable to get lost. The edge is an unmappable
non- or dislocation unable to be incorporated into the fold. It is where Acker
(2018: 8, 19) wrote from: "I wanted to work off the edges—being in between a
reading," she says in a 1976 interview with Barry Alpert. "I don't draw hard
categories, you know." Edginess, as I've titled this section, denotes a certain
proximity, or intimacy, with that which eludes thingness or intelligibility. On the
edge is where the cusp of understanding is blurred. Acker suggests a writing from
such a blurring, writing from the place where categories lose their hold and what is
birthed confounds what can be known. Writing and locuting from the edge, as
Acker seems to do, designates a trans sensibility in as much as there exists a desire
for a way to be and know outside current ways of being and knowing.

So Acker is edgy because she writes from the edge. It is not edginess in the
mere sense that she is remarking on taboo things or she is, as colloquially
expressed, "pushing boundaries." Acker's edginess resides in her expression of the
abysmal, the nonnormative, which is to say as forcefully as possible the subversion
of the violence that inheres in the normative (that discursive web of practices,
beliefs, protocols, and sensibilities not only deemed typical or normal but also,
importantly, forced onto the world and mapped onto others as coercively
mandated). Using myriad linguistic modes and strategies, Acker characterizes the
edgy through her attentiveness to linguistic breach, deformalizing form, and
interrogating genre. Her work and indeed her various locutions "slip" around
meaning, or established meaning, looking for something else outside what has

been determined as extant. Meaning cannot be gotten to, for Acker, directly or teleologically; meaning must be glimpsed sideways, arrived at askance, never settled but always unsettled and unsettling. Such a slippery methodology results in her never desiring or being able to define who or what she is—whether in terms of gender or literary niche or what have you (see Acker 2018: 31).[6]

And meaning hinges, it seems it is being argued, on language. Language inaugurates meaning that can mean, which is not all meaning, only meaning that is understood as meaning. In search of different ways to mean, one must search for different ways to use or unuse language, as it is language that gives meaning over to us—a language that is, again, broadly understood, more than the concatenation of graphemes and phonemes. This search finds expression in Hester's outburst in *Blood and Guts in High School*: "TEACH ME A NEW LANGUAGE, DIMWIT. A LANGUAGE THAT MEANS SOMETHING TO ME" (Acker 2017: 96). *Dimwit*, of course, is not an insult but the vocatively addressed character's name (though, Acker is saying something with this name). The new language Hester wishes to be taught bears another kind of meaning that would supersede the supposed meaning that has up until this point not been meaningful to her. This new language is one that has a meaning that is not, properly speaking, meaning. Ultimately, Hester wishes for meaning in a form, or nonform, that might finally mean something, which subtly interrogates the implicit hubris of what is often known as meaning as such, since here Hester is saying that meaning does not always mean or have meaning. The language that meaning is facilitated through is language that may not have as its recipient, or have as possible, the kind of being that needs and would be subjectivated by its grammar. Thus Hester requires some new language because she is a different type of person or wishes to be a different type of person, a person that is not hailed by the current grammars used for language and its meaning. So if in Heideggarian parlance language speaks us, and if Hester does not feel spoken—indeed, does not live in the residence that is the supposed house of being—then she needs a new language, for she is unhomed. What she is searching for, then, is not simply a language that will then comfortably place her within the ambit of normativity, interpellated easily into current grammars. She is searching for a language that means something to her, but "her" is a being in which meaning, in fact, disintegrates; and thus she is looking for a language that allows her to become a subject at the edge of language, on its outskirts, a language with a meaning she constantly slips away from, as that is precisely where the "me" of her request comes into being as "me."

Slipping away from meaning to find another kind of meaning, a meaning disallowed from the realm of normative meaning, which has been said to be meaning as such, toward meaning not as such, is Acker's way of stumbling out of bounds, where more interesting things happen. Conversant with her philosophizing on bodybuilding, she connects this movement toward the boundaries, at the edge, with the weightlifting usage of going "past failure." She says:

> ACKER: What you do, when you bodybuild, is work to failure. You put a frame around specific muscle groups, and you work each group to failure. Actually, I want to work past failure, which is negative work. And I think you're doing exactly the same thing with the text.
>
> LOTRINGER: What's "past failure" for a text?
>
> ACKER: To go into the space of wonder. (Acker 2018: 119)

As noted at the outset of this essay, the space of linguistic failure is a trans space. That is, rather than a space in which people or topics pertaining to identification with the gender known loosely as transgender, this trans space—purposely prefixal, as I and numerous other scholars have emphasized (see, for example, Stryker and Aizura 2013; Halberstam 2018; Bey 2017)—is one that initiates the failure of language, and with the affixation to bodybuilding, the failure of the notion of the body. Acker is correct: a negative rep (repetition, the lifting of the weight) in weightlifting is when one in fact can no longer lift the weight anymore and needs assistance to lift the weight, with the "negative rep" counted as the "lifting" downward, slowly. As someone who has done bodybuilding and competitive powerlifting, I can attest to the philosophical utility of such a practice. The work done past failure is, in some accounts of kinesiological literature, when muscles reach untapped growing potential. Trekking past failure, that trans and transitive space, is linked textually—or "extra-textually," to purloin Matias Viegener (see Wark 2019)—to wonder. Wonder is the realm of imagination. Imagination is precisely where failure is the precondition for inventiveness and newness. No longer the mark of poor GPAs and bad test scores, failure here is a generative call, since it marks the starting ground for what might be in excess of what we have currently.

The space of wonder is the place where one leaps from the edge; the place of wonder is the threshold leading to and from the edge. To wonder one must find themselves, at some point, at the edge, which makes the edge and edginess a precondition for wonder, which is, further, to say a precondition for the new, for knowledge, for experimentation, for the avant-garde. In Acker's work there is a reclamation of the chaotic and the strange, and there is value found in the departure from the normative, which we might rightly call a type of trans. And in some ways Acker worships this literarily. She worships the blood and guts spilled all over the floor because it is messiness that is, here, next to godliness. And "IF THERE IS A GOD," she writes in *Blood and Guts in High School* (2017: 126), "GOD IS DISJUNCTION AND MADNESS."

Marquis Bey is assistant professor of African American studies and English at Northwestern University.

Acknowledgments
I am astoundingly grateful to McKenzie Wark for her invitation to present this work at the "Trans | Acker Conference," as well as to Susan Stryker not only for her solicitation of this article for this issue of *TSQ* but also for her general kindness, support, intellect, and book recommendations.

Notes

1. For a write-up on Jacques Derrida's understanding of writing, see Reynolds n.d. If I may quote a summative passage from this source: "This is not writing narrowly conceived, as in a literal inscription upon a page, but what he terms 'arche-writing.' Arche-writing refers to a more generalised notion of writing that insists that the breach that the written introduces between what is intended to be conveyed and what is actually conveyed, is typical of an originary breach that afflicts everything one might wish to keep sacrosanct, including the notion of self-presence."

2. Famously, of course, Lyotard (1984: xxiv) defines postmodernism as "incredulity toward metanarratives."

3. There is an argument to be made that Acker's writing as well as her own gender expression are foundational to some contemporary transgender art and literary production. As D. Mortimer has noted, "Acker has certainly made it more possible for writers of the non-cis-straight-man variety to infiltrate the rigidly coded art and writing scenes" (see Cafolla 2019).

4. "I argue that Acker's experiments with language . . . produce in her later works modes of what Acker understands to be 'languages of the body' that run counter to ordinary language," Colby (2016: 6) writes.

5. Likewise, Acker is not trying to be definitive even in her refusal to move toward a demarcated destination. In Larry McCaffery's (1991: 90) "Interview with Kathy Acker," at the level of language, her locutionary transness manifests as her disinterest "in 'saying' anything in my work. The only thing I could use my works to say is 'I don't want to say things!' I couldn't say anything beyond that. I didn't give a damn if one character was another or not—I couldn't even remember who my characters were!"

6. She writes on this point: "I think I have this method of 'slippage,' where I will never talk directly about what I might be or who I am" (2018: 31).

References

abreu, manuel arturo. 2016. "Trans Is a Failure of Language. Poetry Is a Failure of the Body. Notes on TRANS PLANET Ep. 2." *Rhizome* (blog), April 19. rhizome.org/editorial/2016/apr/19/trans-is-a-failure-of-language-poetry-is-a-failure-of-the-body/.

Acker, Kathy. 1993. "Against Ordinary Language: The Language of the Body." In *The Last Sex: Feminism and Outlaw Bodies*, edited by Arthur Kroker and Marilouise Kroker, 20–27. CultureTexts. New York: St. Martin's.

Acker, Kathy. 2017. *Blood and Guts in High School*. New York: Grove.

Acker, Kathy. 2018. *Kathy Acker: The Last Interview and Other Conversations*. Edited by Amy Scholder and Douglas A. Martin. Brooklyn, NY: Melville House.

Bey, Marquis. 2017. "The Trans∗-Ness of Blackness, the Blackness of Trans∗-Ness." *TSQ* 4, no. 2: 275–95. doi.org/10.1215/23289252-3815069.

Bhanji, Nael. 2013. "Trans/Scriptions: Homing Desires, (Trans)Sexual Citizenship and Racialized Bodies." In *The Transgender Studies Reader 2*, edited by Susan Stryker and Aren Z. Aizura, 512–26. New York: Routledge.

Cafolla, Anna. 2019. "The Radical, Seducing Influence of Kathy Acker." *Dazed*, May 9. www .dazeddigital.com/life-culture/article/44381/1/the-radical-seducing-influence-of-kathy-acker.

Colby, Georgina. 2016. *Kathy Acker: Writing the Impossible*. Edinburgh: Edinburgh University Press.

Halberstam, Jack. 2018. *Trans∗: A Quick and Quirky Account of Gender Variability*. Oakland: University of California Press.

Hawkins, Susan E. 2004. "All in the Family: Kathy Acker's *Blood and Guts in High School*." *Contemporary Literature* 45, no. 4: 637–58. doi.org/10.1353/cli.2005.0005.

Hayward, Eva, and Che Gossett. 2017. "Impossibility of That." *Angelaki* 22, no. 2: 15–24. doi.org/ 10.1080/0969725X.2017.1322814.

Heidegger, Martin. 2008. *Basic Writings: From Being and Time 1927 to the Task of Thinking 1964*. Edited by David Farrell Krell. New York: HarperCollins.

Lyotard, Jean-François. 1984. *The Postmodern Condition: A Report on Knowledge*. Minneapolis: University of Minnesota Press.

McCaffery, Larry, and Kathy Acker. 1991. "An Interview with Kathy Acker." *Mississippi Review* 20, nos. 1–2: 83–97.

Reynolds, Jack. n.d. "Jacques Derrida (1930–2004)." In *Internet Encyclopedia of Philosophy*. www .iep.utm.edu/derrida/.

Stryker, Susan, and Aren Z. Aizura, eds. 2013. *The Transgender Studies Reader 2*. New York: Routledge.

Wark, McKenzie. 2019. "Kathy Acker: Get Rid of Meaning." *Brooklyn Rail*, February 5. brooklyn rail.org/2019/02/artseen/Kathy-Acker-Get-Rid-of-Meaning.

Nothing Until It Is Made Actual; or, Acker versus Growing Up

KAY GABRIEL

Abstract This essay argues for reading Kathy Acker in terms of what the author calls the "plasticity" of her sentences. These syntactic structures disclose Acker's attempt to expose and negate a bourgeois ideology of adolescence and maturity. The essay pursues this argument through a reading of Acker's novel *In Memoriam to Identity*, in particular its interest in Rimbaud as both biographical icon and literary precedent. The essay then argues that Acker's concerted literary attack on an ideology of maturity relates to the projects of trans literature at several critical junctures.
Keywords poetics, Kathy Acker, adolescence, theory

> What / industry do I practice? . . . / I practice no industry.
> —Amiri Baraka

> First there was the end of everything, and then there was childhood, a trap, and
> then there was that place between childhood and the world.
> —Mattilda Bernstein Sycamore

1.

Kathy Acker's novels displace the propulsion of narrative for the plasticity of the sentence.

It's not that Acker doesn't write narrative. She does, but not the kind you could pummel into a script for prestige television. In another decade, I'd remark specifically that Acker opposes linearity, but I dispute the metaphor of the "line." Recall the diagrams that Laurence Sterne proposed for his narrative in *Tristram Shandy*, which Viktor Shklovsky loved enough to reproduce in *Theory of Prose* (1990: 169): all those curlicues and loops are, topologically, linear. So too in Acker's novels: the problem that Acker has with the narrative course of literary realism isn't sequentiality. In *Blood and Guts in High School* (1984), Janey's

TSQ: Transgender Studies Quarterly ★ Volume 7, Number 3 ★ August 2020
DOI 10.1215/23289252-8553174 © 2020 Duke University Press

"breakup" with her father leads to her schooling in New York, her translations of the Persian poems, and her travels in Algiers with Genet. One thing becomes another, for Acker like anybody else.

But she specifically refuses the mode of novelistic realism that requires narrative as the social fiction of facing the consequences of your choices. This social fiction reduces to a kind of ethics—the kind of subjective behavior that's required of somebody who'll be trusted to pay back their loans, for instance. Fredric Jameson (2013: 212) submits that "for the most part an ethical literature has come to reflect the closure of class"; for Jameson, like for Acker, that's a comment on the received forms and possible genres of the European novel. "Ethical maxims and categories only work within a situation of homogeneous class belonging," he continues (212).

The form of ethics that Acker disputes is the fiction of maturity—facing the consequences of your choices, with better credit. The widely dissatisfying ground of that fiction proposes a subject with relatively unconstrained agency who develops from a plastic adolescent into a dependable adult. You open your mouth to say "Hallelujah, I'm a bum," and you bite down on your time sheet. Do I have to call it bourgeois? You already know.

The narratives of Acker's novels therefore specifically refuse not the form of sequential action but the ideology of a kind of causation rooted in the aberrations of an ethical subject. I think that's why reading Acker produces such a dizzying effect. The shifts between her scenes track the lateral direction of her compositional movement between the sources of her literary collage—lateral, that is, instead of the forward propulsion that a more standard realism requires, in the shift from significant action to consequential situation.

You could say she borrows that associative or connotational movement from outside the novel—from journaling, or poetry, or dreams—as well as from precedents like Jean Genet, Pièrre Guyotat or John Rechy. But I care less about where she got it from than the formal device she mobilizes to make it work: the sentence and its invertible, reversible structures.

Unlike some of her contemporaries who also specialize in a literature whose primary unit is the sentence—Bernadette Mayer comes to mind, or Lyn Hejinian, or a muscular prose stylist like Eileen Myles—Acker's sentences aren't especially virtuosic. (Acker's "greatness," as Robert Glück calls it [2016: 120–35], rests elsewhere than in being a highly original prose stylist. That follows from her fidelity to, say, David Antin: a writing whose claim is its derivative character, its ambitious retooling of culture authored by everybody else, can scarcely also boast the watermarks of a highly self-similar style.) Acker's sentences are neither especially hypotactic nor especially paratactic. Mostly they're pretty short, and syntactically simple. They're also syntactically complete. "Medea was a brat like me," from *In Memoriam to Identity*, is exemplary (1990: 83).

I will propose calling Acker's sentences "plastic." They're straightforward; their grammatical functions are easy to parse; and their content is, relatively speaking, contingent. By plastic I mean they're syntactically invertible and semantically reversible: they admit of inversions between subject and predicate, and the actions they narrate never really have the weight of finality. In one Acker sentence, your boyfriend can go back to his wife. In the next, he'll be with you in Brussels. You can be incarcerated, freed and arrested again in the space of a paragraph. You can probably be among the dead one hour, and back in New York in time to be scolded by your mother for masturbating.

I have two projects for this essay, building on the formal claim I am making here: that Acker's novels displace the forward propulsion of narrative in favor of the plasticity of the sentence. The first is to link that formal project to an ideological one—to establish that the form of her novel specifically rejects the fiction of maturity. The second is to make explicit, even undeniable, the latent connection between these formal and ideological levels, and the emergent formation of trans literature.

But you probably guessed that connection the moment I said "adolescent," or "plastic." In refusing the narrative of consequences and the fictions about the subject that it requires, Acker specifically obsesses over the problem of adolescence. At some level of abstraction, each of Acker's novels could be considered a perversion of a bildungsroman. Her literary world is all *Bildung* to the precise degree that it's adolescent, school without graduation. You can always recess to childhood, a state of legal or physical vulnerability wielded over you, a forfeiture of your capacities and agency into the hands of "parents, teachers, boyfriends" (1984: 165). On the other hand, there's the plasticity of adolescence, a delectable, fraught rebirthing of the self, a guided modification of the body that holds together reality and identification in an unstable and momentary unity.

Both—for Acker, and for you—coalesce in the double figure of Arthur Rimbaud.

2.

Okay, for me too.

Kristin Ross (1988: 49) writes:

> The genre of the "novel of youth" is formed out of the interplay between the transformational energies it derives from the energy of youth, and the formal limitations imposed by the necessity that youth must come to an end. Rimbaud, on the other hand, proposes the impossible: a narrative that consists of pure transformational energy, pure transition or *suradolescence*; a voice that speaks from the place of youth rather than ventriloquizes it; the movement of a thought

conjugated *with and in view of* (not after) the event; and the impossible notion that youth might not have to come to an end.

Acker's *In Memoriam to Identity* seizes on Rimbaud's "suradolescence." She makes the poet the subject of the first third of her novel, threading the tumultuous Rimbaud-Verlaine affair through, on the one hand, the history of the 1871 Paris Commune and the gutting revanchism of Thatcherite Britain on the other. By "double figure" I mean that Acker uses Rimbaud both for a literary and bio-graphical precedent: biographically, as the subject of an apparently inexhaustible adolescence; literarily, as immaturity's most adequate poet. *In Memoriam* renders as a concrete problem of narrative the principle that informs, possibly, all of Acker's novels: how to write a novel of acculturation for someone whose biog-raphy absolutely refuses maturity. "Quel siècle à mains!" Rimbaud (1960: 213) writes in *A Season in Hell*, "Je n'aurai jamais ma main." Ross (1988: 51) translates, "What a century of hands: I'll never learn to use my hands." In Ross's reading, Rimbaud specifically refuses to learn a trade. "In the time of good for nothings, bums, liberty will triumph," Acker (1990: 7) promises—picking up where her adolescent icon left off.

Acker rejects the telos of maturity as a matter of ideological refusal, washing her hands of professionalism's crud; *In Memoriam* emplots this refusal as a principle of its form. Adolescence is infectious, inescapable, and in vigorous opposition to the propertied unit of the family. Verlaine, or V, continually threatens to leave Rimbaud and return to his demanding wife. When he's with R he shrugs off his inconsistent maturity: "Through the night the two boys fucked each other," Acker writes (1990: 60). "'Our paradise'll happen as soon as we enter the magical world of childhood'"—a false promise: "R knew this was shit" (64). Even shit promises intimacy, all the more so from the undisciplined body of youth. When I was still in my teens a boyfriend pulled out to jerk off on my stomach, a scrim of my shit lining his glans. I didn't douche consistently before anal, really, until I was maybe twenty-two, twenty-three. Is that embarrassing? I fixate on the image, my shit, his cock, his hand going three or four strokes a second. Other details stick in my head, like: we were fucking in a hotel in Athens, on Euripides Street, and that this was around the time of the mass protests in Syntagma, the riot dog, though we didn't go to Athens to join the antiausterity movement. We were there on a travel grant from our university to see statues and vases; we went to Delphi, and I remember the bus lurching down the mountain, but I don't remember what he looked like when he came. Verlaine, anyways, "touched [R's] shit" (60).

Not that there's any romance of childhood as such—"IF YOU'VE GOT BAD BLOOD," she writes, "YOU'VE GOT BAD CHILDHOOD" (81). Acker riffs on Rimbaud's poem "Mauvais sang" ("Bad Blood") from *A Season in Hell.* In Ross's reading of that poem, Rimbaud (1960: 216–17) inhabits and satirizes a nineteenth-century discourse of racialization: "Je n'ai jamias été de ce peuple-ci; je n'ai jamais été chrétien; je suis de la race qui chantait dans le supplice" (I have never been one of you; I have never been a Christian; I belong to the race that sang on the scaffold). Ross (1988: 65): "The narrator's desires or investments are, quite simply, those of the 'inferior race.'" Pursuing Rimbaud's identifications, Acker introduces the slide of her conditional logic: anybody she cares to address has, in Rimbaud's sense, "bad blood"; so they've got "bad childhood," too. Note that Acker approaches Rimbaud from the creative position of producing a slant translation; Acker produces an effect in English impossible in French, squeezing a visual rhyme out of *blood* and *childhood.* Acker loops Rimbaldian themes into each other through the intervening moment of translation. She slices off a possible article from *childhood*, too, making it less like a condition ("a bad back") and more like an uncountable quantity, like blood or soup or yogurt, something you could be awash in.

Note, finally, Acker's tense. It's not like you had a bad childhood. You've got one right now.

And so do R and V. "I won't ever return to that desert called *childhood*, to the penurious country, the country in which I'm an orphan," she writes in R's voice, in a chapter titled "Translations of R's Poems" (1990: 66). If she's translating Rimbaud, she's doing it sideways. The poet did write, in his *Ouvriers* (*Workers*; 1960: 272), "Le sud me rappelait les misérables incidents de mon enfance, me desespoirs d'été. . . . Non! nous ne passerons pas l'été dans cet avare pays où nou ne serons jamais que des orphelins fiancés" (The south reminded me of the wretched events of my childhood, my summer despairs. . . . No! We won't pass summer in that miserly country where we'll only be orphans engaged to be wed). Rimbaud's prose poem, from *Illuminations* (1960: 272), displays contempt for a suburban space ("Nous faisons un tour dans la banlieue") where he and a companion took a dissatisfying walk on a "hot February morning" (cette chaude matinée de février). Rimbaud's poem oozes a kind of petty despair of the sort that characterizes his Charleville poems, and in fact he himself nods to "events of his childhood"; only his despair in the last paragraph inflects toward a possible marriage (*des orphelins fiancés*). Acker (1990: 66) ignores marriage—for now. Instead she doubles down on childhood as the refused object, transforming time into space, childhood into a desert; dropping Rimbaud's first-person plural for a first-person singular, she makes her poet promise to "be—forever—a refugee from my childhood."

Her slant translation echoes forward and backward in her chapter. At one point, R accuses: "You exiled me to another land, land that SHITS and REEKS, the land of childhood" (56). At another, he promises: "When our memories become actual, we'll be living in the world of childhood" (64)—actually that doesn't sound so bad. Acker's prose is alive to the ambivalences of childhood; her tense in that evocative sentence is more or less the future anterior, a point where the event that you desire will be in the past.

Acker is fond of these riddling pronouncements about the future. Here's a favorite, from *Pussy, King of the Pirates* (1996: 30): "'In these rooms of sleep and of dream,' she continued in another of her letters which will become famous after history has gone to sleep, 'we will walk around, brushing by each other, touching each other without actually touching. There we shall affirm everyone.'" Acker evokes a future nesting in quotations; I liked the bit about being famous after history has gone to sleep so much I wrote it into my own book. I bet she'd have approved, since she almost certainly lifted it herself, but I couldn't really say what it means, any more than I could expound on touching without actually touching, or the moment of a memory's becoming actual. I suspect it's pretty nice, though; I think she's thinking about the vanishing moment when an imagined or desired past becomes concrete and real. Is that deluded, fantasy, a perverse attitude? "Children who've no future or innocents whose innocence can have no future always believe in the future," she offers (1990: 66): a willful attachment, against and despite how fucking miserable you are right now.

3.

At some point you probably have to mourn your shitty youth.

In Memoriam both (1) affirms the universal violence of childhood and (2) intuits the asymmetry of that experience—you'd have to. Rimbaud's mother: "'I'll bring up my second kid by torturing him. That way he won't beget any infected children.' Her plan succeeded. R turned out homosexual" (4). And later: "Unable to bear or stop these tortures, R moved into the imaginary. The infinity and clarity of desire in the imaginative made normal society's insanity disappear" (5). R's torturers name a list of "parents, teachers, boyfriends"—the authorities in his life probably up to and including Verlaine. He's in the wrong century for high school, but getting closer all the time.

In an interview with Sylvère Lotringer, Acker (2018) disputed that the work of her mature career had much to do with the first-person singular: "Plagiarism," Lotringer asked, referring to Acker's signature method of literary collage, "was that something that came out of your exploration of the I?" She demurs: "I was no longer interested in the I. The I became a dead issue because I realized that you make the I, and what makes the I are texts" (93). Poststructuralist cant aside, I'm not sure I agree. Douglas A. Martin (2017: 52), reading the "Capitol" chapters of *In Memoriam*, writes, "It is here that 'I am an *other*' comes again, perennially relevant, in a parenthetical aside or realization." Martin is on to something: Acker never abandons the scandalous identifications of the first person, or its continual play.

I is another, *I* is someone else; the notorious scandal of Rimbaud's grammatically illicit sentence enacts something like the process of identification. But—from a different perspective—that process is another way of referring to what Acker calls "the infinity and clarity of desire": one effect of her "suradolescent" narrative would have to be the embrace of a continual plasticity of the self, an unsettled and introverted creativity that refuses a point of decisive maturation. A friend once commented on an essay I'd written: it's so teenaged, she said, every paragraph falls in love with something else. That process—unmaking and remaking, identifying and playing around—takes place between the first and third person, becoming, along the way, sentences you make up about yourself.

Maybe you're fibbing a little, but so what? Nobody short of a bureaucrat is asking you to stick to your fictions forever. Acker had her own, even for the basic components of her biography. Martin (2017: 7) writes, "How old my author was when she died is up for debate." Her driver's license says she was born in 1947; her library of Congress entry, 1948. "In one of Acker's last novels, *My Mother: Demonology*, one of her narrative strategies has become to *redo* her 'childhood,'" Martin continues. "The starting point for a life narration changes yet again: *I was born on October 6, 1945*" (4). There's something permissive about her lying and bluffing. She's George Clooney in the poker scene in Ocean's 11, and you're Brad Pitt: you so badly want her to win.

That's the point: I'm arguing that the plasticity of Acker's syntax enables the kinds of making and remaking of the self that characterize the sentences trans people say about ourselves, and that the ideological superstructure of *suradolescence* renders this excess of identification and desire uniquely visible. Or: I'm saying that if high school is a death trap, you have to scam your way out of it, like in eighth grade when I got busted for having gay sex with a classmate and had to see a therapist to avoid expulsion and that guy wouldn't release me from his supervision until I admitted I had, in fact, done something wrong. Or: I'm saying that the forces that compel you to return constantly to adolescence, and foreclose maturity in advance, are a matter of abstract and external determination rather than your own willful aesthetics. Ideology and the market chaperone you back to "the land that SHITS and REEKS, the land of childhood" (Acker 1990: 58)—if you don't or can't have kids, if your credit stinks. Or: that in the slippage between a first- and third-person account of yourself, you achieve something like a tenuous link between the "infinity and clarity of desire" (5) and the stone-cold sobriety of everyday life, and that's how anybody keeps living, but trans people sometimes know it a little better, since our motivation is so much more explicitly the discrepancy between embodiment and want. "The imagination is nothing unless it is made actual"—Acker again, but in quotation marks (95). She's talking about the Commune; I'm not, but I could be. I'm saying that the *suradolescence* of trans identity represents both a matter of objective imposition and subjective possibility, and I resent it almost as much as I resent the imperative to grow up. Sometime in my late teens I wanted nothing more than to look like Eliza Dushku on *Buffy*, and now if you squint hard enough I guess I sort of do.

4.

I kid, actually. If people are looking for a celebrity lookalike for me they usually say Geena Davis or Diamanda Galás.

Which kind of surprises me. Galás isn't trans, as far as I know, but she kind of looks it. I mean it's pretty hot. Acker herself tempts a biographical reading for her trans affinities, her evident departures from womanhood as a site of enthusiastic identification. I think those kinds of pronouncements are not, strictly speaking, possible. People like to do this kind of thing with, you know, Kurt Cobain or whoever, and I think you have to take people at their word instead of speaking for the dead out of one's own projections.

Acker's novels, on the other hand, have something to say to the emergent formations of trans literature. Consider:

1. In rejecting the fixity and telos of the bildungsroman, Acker's engagements and refusals align with the relationship that trans writing bears toward the much-maligned genre of the memoir. Nobody actually wants to write, and nobody really writes any longer, the kind of book that the memoirists wrote—but trans writing still faces down a social imperative to disclose one's status and its details. Viviane Namaste wrote in 2000 (1n3) that "autobiography is the only discourse in which transsexuals are permitted to speak," and that's still true. As a result, when we write, we write against the autobiographical imperative, without any hope of dismissing it just like that. One—Ackerian—device at our disposal is the writing of sentences in the first-person singular, without any commitment to the kind of realist depiction of the self that could pass muster with, for instance, a doctor.

2. Acker is a writer of and about the body without ever precisely saying what one looks like. As such, her bodies are malleable, subject to revision or modification. Engaged with body modification in its most literal sense, linked to the "infinity and clarity of desire in the imaginative" (1990: 58), she moves beyond the Deleuzian mode according to which the becoming of transsexuality is always a figure for something else entirely. Which matters for those of us for whom transformation is not a principle of allegory.

3. Martin points out that Acker compares the taste of her pussy to the vanilla lining the chocolate wafers of a Hydrox biscuit. I would call this technique identical to Dennis Cooper's (2009: 94) pornography, in which every scene devolves into a simile linking a body to the niche experience of a commodity: "I would have awarded his ass-crack the Oscar for Best Supporting Actor on the spot. I could have sold those jeans to scratch-and-sniff collectors on eBay and never worked another day in my life." Acker's alert to the commodification of the body—without ever opposing or rejecting it in the conservative mode of what Sophie Lewis (2018) calls the "school of wrong abolitionism." I don't need to tell you how that experience of the particularly commodified body bears with particular force on your life and your friends' and lovers' lives and mine. In writing or speaking sentences about the body, and it doesn't necessarily matter to whom but everybody wants us to and sometimes we want this for ourselves, Acker suggests devices for speaking of its mutations with and in view of and even against the commodity form.

4. It's unclear, biographically, how long Acker worked in strip clubs; it's clear that she treats it as a formative experience of gender and sexual relations— the axes along which each of her novels proceeds—on a par with or in excess of childhood, rearing, schooling. I'd go so far as to say that the kernel of sexual relations in Acker's world is its function as a form of exchange, inside or outside the family. Specifically, Acker demystifies the exchange relation of sex, the relation that a fiction like romance mystifies. That puts her work directly into contact with trans writing, and its narrative and social relationships to the world of sex work: "In her prison, the whore Louise Vanaen began to dream of a revolution, *a revolution of whores*, a revolution defined by all methods that exist as distant, as far as is possible, from profit" (Acker 1996: 30).

5. But I haven't even said anything about the city. Acker is a writer of the urban scale; even the Belgium that Verlaine and Rimbaud escape to looks, she says, like New York City in 1988. That's not, or not just, an aesthetic choice. Acker posits a spatial problem—fixating on the satisfaction and deprivation of human needs at the scale of the city. "Stealing was part of the city," she writes in *Pussy* (1996: 83). "Every city is born, continually being born, out of configurations of minds and desires: every city is alive." It's not a mysticism; she gets the Lefèbvrian thesis that capital produces space to satisfy its own oppositional needs, like concentrating labor in one place and pushing it as far as possible outside the wage. "After Ange had listened to O's dream, the two of them abandoned the now almost deserted city" (66). That's Rimbaldian, too. It finds an echo in trans writing, which might not take place in, but invariably belongs to, the city. Acker (1984) writes the urban scale shorn of a romantic urbanism; she satirizes the class that makes the city its playground, but she can't ever really kick the association.

"There's a very good artist who wants the world to be as it is in the center of his art. All the artists recognize this goodness. He's very animal especially his wiggling ass he's such a great fuck, all the women artists want to fuck him. He lives in Seattle. He's fucked every woman artist in Seattle" (215). Writing in satire of, and contempt for, the spatial scale she can't get away from, Acker suggests a possible writing of the city that doesn't produce just another *vie bohème*. Cyrée Jarelle Johnson (2019: 31): "The subway is also a boneyard."

I could go on guessing, but I suspect these intuitions will be tested in the practices of trans writing itself. Any minute now.

Kay Gabriel is a poet and essayist. She's currently a postdoctoral researcher at Princeton University.

References

Acker, Kathy. 1984. *Blood and Guts in High School, Plus Two*. London: Pan.

Acker, Kathy. 1990. *In Memoriam to Identity*. New York: Grove.

Acker, Kathy. 1996. *Pussy, King of the Pirates*. New York: Grove.

Acker, Kathy. 2018. *The Last Interview*. Edited by Amy Scholder and Douglas A. Martin. New York: Melville House.

Cooper, Dennis. 2009. *Ugly Man*. New York: HarperCollins.

Glück, Robert. 2016. *Communal Nude*. Cambridge, MA: Semiotext(e).

Jameson, Fredric. 2013. *Antinomies of Realism*. New York: Verso.

Johnson, Cyrée Jarelle. 2019. *Slingshot*. New York: Nightboat.

Lewis, Sophie. 2018. "'Not a Workplace': Julie Bindel and the School of Wrong Abolitionism." Verso Books blog. www.versobooks.com/blogs/3845-not-a-workplace-julie-bindel-and -the-school-of-wrong-abolitionism.

Martin, Douglas A. 2017. *Acker*. New York: Nightboat.

Namaste, Viviane. 2000. *Invisible Lives: The Erasure of Transsexual and Transgendered People*. Chicago: University of Chicago Press.

Rimbaud, Arthur. 1960. *Oeuvres*. Paris: Garnier Frères.

Ross, Kristin. 1988. *The Emergence of Social Space: Rimbaud and the Paris Commune*. Minneapolis: University of Minnesota Press.

Shklovsky, Viktor. 1990. *Theory of Prose*. Champaign, IL: Dalkey Archive Press.

Building the Pirate Body

K. K. TRIEU

Abstract When Kathy Acker writes about the body, it is frequently subjected to self-abnegation; there is a sense that the cohesion of self and body hangs on complete destruction and rebirth in terms of its material reality. The figure of the Pirate is an avatar through which Acker explores these tensions, particularly as they relate to her experience of femininity and gender, which, in many ways, aligns with experiences of gender dysphoria. In negotiating the ways in which she would like to be desired with the feminist knowledge that influenced her thought, Acker lays out a path in which the dysphoric body that is assigned female at birth may occupy a third space outside the gender binary. This article puts Acker's writing on the Pirate in dialog with Georges Bataille's figure of the Acéphale to explore the system of knowledge that comes from this subject — one whose articulation is in constant regeneration.
Keywords masochism, Acéphale, dysphoria, body

In the cephalic world, that is, the world that is related to the head, human's most consistent reaction to the fact that we must die is to dream up new worlds to die into. For if life had no meaning, all would be chaos, and we would be destined for nothing more than a primordial soup made of shit, piss, and cum. The body is nothing but a nuisance, its physiological functions a daily reminder of this reality. So it must be forgotten. The cephalic world makes for its god the Cartesian man, a model of knowing in which a self is constructed so that its own body may be left behind.

Out of all the ways to make money off dead bodies, philosophy is the most extra.

Under the sign of Descartes, there is possible knowledge and impossible bodies: the bodies that cannot be called other. The bodies, for example, that are made absent when the name "female" is assigned to genital flesh. A body like Kathy Acker's pirate body.

Thus for the people born under the sign of Descartes, gender operates on denying the existence of bodies. Since in the Cartesian world, seeing is knowing, being visible means being possible. A body is looked at, named "female," and makes absent the presence of women. Meaning is constructed through terms that highlight the differences between the observer and the observed. I see this female body: it is not me. I am not female. All that can be knowable is difference.

If I am not the body I have, the body I have is unknowable and therefore impossible. This body, since it is subject to chance, change, and death, is considered disgusting, horrific. It is unknowable because it exists on the other side of reason. A body that is absent, in making itself known, troubles the construction of being possible that hangs on seeing. In the cephalic world, Acker's pirate body seems a lot like the dysphoric body.

To give this body meaning, we must decapitate the Cartesian man in favor of a method of knowing that can affirm this impossible body. In exchange for a construction of meaning that relates a self to another, let's begin to think our bodies through self-related differences: a method of knowing that holds the colon, a labyrinth of shit, as its authority rather than the head.

Acker would like to affirm this self-related body, the body that exists without being knowable. The body that lives in wonder. But she has still not seen this body, any body at all. She has still not yet seen gender.

The Names of Nothing

Acker would like to be a pirate because she thinks that pirates, unlike women, get to have fun. Pirates live in a world of wonder, a world full of strange and unknown sights. Feminism tells us that woman is seen but does not see, which means that women don't get to be pirates. So for Acker, being born a girl means to be born in the wrong body, born dead, or born blind. The pirate body does not exist on either side of the gender binary, so according to reason it is impossible. But Acker's will is stronger than knowledge, so she works out a way to live life with death as her equal.

Acker grows up with a bossy mother and a weak father, so her model of gender already does not do what it should mean. Girl-Acker doesn't get to be a pirate because her mother tells her so, because the body that her mother sees is female. Grownup-Acker has been told that women do not see and thus cannot know, so she understands her female body to be unknowable. Woman is a lack: is nothing, is not fun.

"I am looking for the body, my body, which exists outside its patriarchal definitions," she writes, "of course that is not possible. But who is any longer interested in the possible?" (Acker 1997: 166).

Since we are still in the Cartesian world, the I who observes must remain sovereign to knowledge, for all that can be knowable is difference. To satisfy the conditions for thinking about this difference, what is subjective must be made in some way objective. It must be made possible. Acker would like to see this unknowable body, for to see is to make meaning, "*to be other than dead.*" (160). To do so she must first understand how it is that bodies come to be known. Knowledge penetrates the body and makes it female: woman is a lack that can be entered but cannot herself enter. To talk about gender is thus to talk about the feminine body.

In the Cartesian world where Acker is a girl who cannot be a pirate (in a world where she is dead) a body can be looked at and named female, a designation which makes the presence of women impossible. Wondering why her parents must still dress her up in white gloves and panty girdles (even though she is skinny) makes her wonder what being female really looks like. Since she knows that women are not allowed to see, she escapes into the world of books, where the ordinary world can be looked at through language.

Alice is in Wonderland: a dream where everything has no name. Where nothing does what it's supposed to: where everything is evil. Alice ran away to search for herself through fearful riddles and games. Acker, who reads this story so that she too can know herself, follows Alice into this labyrinth where reason is lost and, so too, "the meaning of words relating to the subject. To herself" (163). But dreaming is a gateway drug to being awake again.

In stories, woman is a plot device for male-on-male violence. The further away from reason that Alice strays, the more possible it becomes for her to see her own body. The more of a threat she presents to the he-who-is-dreaming-up Alice. And because plot dictates that we must be returned from chaos into the ordinary world, a knight appears, destined to save Alice from this labyrinth: "When these songs are over, Alice becomes a queen" (165).

Alice and Acker run into the world of books to find themselves, only to learn that language, like gender, has to do with death, since language reiterates what is knowable and denies what is impossible: the knowledge of one's own body. Acker, reading Alice through Judith Butler and Luce Irigaray, sees that, "as mirror mirrors mirror, she learns her proper place in the world as I, as Alice's reader, thus as Alice, learn mine" (165).

In the ordinary world, all that is unknowable is called the impossible. When Acker is returned from chaos, she is returned to the order of the possible. Language, like gender, operates on denying the existence of bodies. For the names "*girl* and *woman* were the names of nothing" (161). The dysphoria of the pirate body challenges the order of knowledge in which language must be mimetic. To find that which cannot be defined, Acker goes back into that labyrinth, where she last caught a glimpse of the body that escapes reason.

If under the sign of Descartes, the body of woman is unknowable, then we must castrate this model of man and remove the seat of reason that governs the body: the head. The cephalic world must become acephalic.

The Acephalic Man

Georges Bataille, the famously horny librarian, dreams of his daddy's syphilitic cock, and it tires him of meaning. He, like Acker, is sick of all the explanations of life that you can know through book learning.

Bataille sits in his room, sleeping or trying to sleep, feeling guilty about being alive. Having fucked his way through Paris during the height of the war, Bataille held on dearly to the call of decadence that promised transcendence through sex. Having been fucked out of one too many orgies, to stand and gaze upon amorphous balls of flesh long enough to smell the orgy farts, he realized that that promise of transcendence only made every being contained in those humans inconsequential. From this point on, Bataille makes meaning the patch of grass he pisses on for all of his life until, eventually, it becomes his grave.

But before he can pass on, Bataille must make for himself a new kind of god, a daddy that can fuck. He calls this god the Acéphale.

The acephalic god has no head. It is speechless. It holds in one hand a flaming heart and in the other a sword that is used for self-decapitation. Its myth is a sacred conspiracy to return the process of thought back to the body. In Bataille's version of the Acéphale, the skull sits in the place of the genitalia. Since skull represents thought, contemplation, and clarity, its placement here grounds knowledge within a self-related body: within a body that fucks (dies). Since the movement of decapitation is central to the formation of this body, thought becomes any physiological operation that empties the mind: like a sigh, orgasm, or falling asleep. The Acéphale is a god that affirms death, the materiality, "of that which must die. Us" (Acker 1997: 89).

Acker finds in the acephalic god a model through which she can learn to see, for the myth of the Acéphale unifies the I-who-observes and the eye-that-sees: an I with a cunt for its head.

In the ordinary world, the cephalic world, words make enemies of bodies because words are used to forget them: they turn bodies into male or female, into men and women through beliefs. With the castration of the Cartesian man, all that is knowable is the unknowable body. Now that Acker knows how to see her pirate body, she can begin to dissect the acephalic from the cephalic. Remember that for Acker, language is seeing. Thus her acephalic body cannot operate outside the language of the ordinary world—after all, "the word silence is still a sound" (Bataille 2014: 20). Acker cannot turn away entirely from language. She has finally seen gender but has not yet escaped its meaning.

To find the place where the body, and so gender, empties the mind, and thus its meaning, Acker looks for a style of articulation that negotiates between words and bodies. She finds this third language in myths, a story of the world where the gods who hold power over man also die, a story in which any meaning that comes from life is left up to chance.

In the cephalic world, human's most consistent reaction to the fact they must die is to dream up new worlds to die into; the horror of their physical death alleviated by psychic transcendence. There is a good way to die, in which a soul ascends to heaven, and a bad way, which leads it to hell. Remember that the body is where meaning becomes shit. So in the acephalic world, humans must make their myths out of evil.

At the center of the acephalic myth, at the center of this labyrinth, is of course Marquis de Sade, a man whose only purpose for writing is to destroy his self, to lose himself through sexuality. We know that this was not a purely critical stance because sex was not something that started in the head, but the ass. For he, who was a patriarch, was also fucked by patriarchy.

De Sade dedicates volumes of stories in which the reason that names bodies "male" and "female" come undone. Acker (1997: 69, 71) writes, "A woman can know freedom by choosing to counterfeit a man who selects the bottom power position. . . . Neither male nor female seem to be left." Knowledge penetrates the body and makes it evil. In the Sadean universe, you get to fuck death.

Acker makes de Sade a saint of the Acéphale and follows in his footsteps through a labyrinth in which the body that was female begins to forget itself. But Acker is tired of having the world explained to her by men. She dreams, instead, of "the labyrinth or the self that will lead us to languages that cannot be authoritarian" (91). She writes down these dreams in essays compiled in *The Languages of the Body*.

Acker's Masochism

Acker's dreams begin in the same way that stories do in the ordinary world: the name *female* makes absent, impossible, the presence of the pirate body. This absence is usually named "suffering," "pain," "fear," or "unbearable." But Acker wants to give it a different character—one with many names, but that which can never truly be named. For in the body that is unknowable, the self-related body, things can only be described and not defined.

In the story of the world told by its most fuckless philosophers, the thought that is best destroys its antecedents. In this theory of how knowledge meets the body, the I-who-observes will always be more accurate than the eye that can go blind. But in the acephalic world, the eye-that-decays precedes the I-who-can-ignore, since, through its adaptability, the eye that goes blind "is continuously seeing new phenomena, for, like sailors, we travel through the world, through or selves, through worlds" (Acker n.d.: 14).

For Acker (1993b: 303), "writers are, above all, readers: to write is to read and to hear accurately." The writers with all the answers are not the good writers, since the communicability of knowledge is never concerned with listening, and the absence she wants to understand would disappear once defined. In the self-related body, absence is merely the phenomenon of letting others speak first. Of writing and thinking through listening. The language of the body is a language that listens.

Phenomena that cause the eye-that-sees to engulf the I-that-observes allow us to glimpse a self-related difference: things like déja vu, or the feeling of being watched, or shivering when we're not cold. These things show us that this style of thought, which can be used to engage with the phenomena of absence, must be a physiological operation.

This sort of phenomenon speaks in a "language that announces itself as insufficient" (Acker n.d.: 14). While there are many experiences that create a self-related difference—like having a child, starting hormone-replacement therapy, or losing your memory—all of them cause a disturbance that makes us question the place of our selves in a totality. They put us in control, if only for a moment, of how our own bodies are formed.

This phenomenon tells us stories in "languages which contradict themselves. The languages of this material body: laughter, silence, screaming" (14). A language that erodes itself cannot be concerned with creating external relationships, such as that of self to other. Something that makes us scream does not necessarily mean it is fearful. The language of the body must speak to things that are true in their multiplicity. Its logic would be more concerned with tone over articulation.

"The languages of intensity. Since the body's, our, end isn't transcendence but excrement, the life of the body exists as pure intensity. The sexual and emotive languages," writes Acker (14). This truth is concerned with the inarticulate speech of bodies, all that cannot be processed only with the intellect.

In Acker's stories, the body always begins and ends whole. Though in the moments her characters begin to think through these phenomena of absence, they become a collection of bodily functions: the shit that ties death to life, blood that means you're dying, muscles that must be torn to grow stronger. In the acephalic world, the body precedes the mind because only its physiological functions can think through the impossible.

This is why in Acker, the body is dominated, rejected, abused by ordinary language. This is not a wish for punishment or for a redemption through pain. It is a masochist drive that insists on knowing what exists on the other side of what we readily dismiss as unbearable. It is an attempt to control the material reality of the body physically.

In this way of describing the body through the ways it seduces (that is, corrupts) the logos, she begins to describe the unknowable body—her pirate body. Remember that for Acker, language is seeing and becoming a self-related body. If the body expresses its consciousness through pain, writing, for Acker, is the intentional practice of her masochism.

Since the pirate body represents the phenomenological world of the body Acker wants to build from the confines of her dead feminine body, she must define its shape and thought through the ways feminine bodies engage with the unbearable. The actions that female bodies go through to think the phenomena of absence, such as abortion, divorce, or sleeping around, is where their bodies begin to remove themselves from gender, and where her masochistic practice begins.

If pain is how the body makes itself known, torture is a way of its speaking. Acker's short story, "The Language of the Body," opens on the scene of a wedding, which actually describes an abortion. The attending nurse asks if she'd like an anesthetic: "Since I knew that that type of voice meant that there would be a lot of pain, I chickened out" (1993a: 1). The self-related body understands there is tonality in silence: it's not what you said but how you said it.

The choice to shut out the ordinary world should begin here for this Acker, but the rational sensibility that is implicated in that type of voice leads her to take the anesthetic and push away the pain. But femininity, a language that listens, is conditioned to respond with what you want to hear: "I hate pain. I decided on anesthetic" (1). Since she has chosen to induce insensitivity to pain, this Acker remains in the ordinary world. But there must be some other way to listen to the body's loquacity without the presence of torture.

If the body is not going to be cut, then it's important that it be stripped, since nakedness is the condition that makes the body's thought possible. More than nudity, it invokes a vulnerability that allows the eye-that-sees to castrate the I-who-observes. Stripping humanity away from a man is just stripping him bare—to the impossibility of his weak nature in the face of patriarchy. Stripping humanity away from woman, who is already made to be nude, means to strip her down to her blood, for the pirate body must castrate the Cartesian man to be known.

In the cephalic world there is only lineage, no heritage. The project of sexuality is to create new bodies, and a new body is a disease that decays our flesh by adding it to an other. A fetus is a woman's flesh, the material that connects her to her heritage. It also contains generations of lineage: of its mother's blood, her mother's blood, and its father's blood. Marriage brings blood back into the order of reason because it relates heritage to lineage.

Abortion is the rejection of this return: the aborted fetus, stripped of its humanity down to its blood, is an object of lineage (baby) that relates blood back to heritage (dead flesh as for worms). "Suddenly, I had my period. This blood was brown and smelly. Actually, it looked like shit," writes Acker (15). The female biology removes itself from femininity on a monthly basis, its body contained in eighty milliliters of smelly blood that's deodorized and flushed away. The story of the pirate body is a story of sexual waste.

When Acker writes about female sexuality, the female body, which endures unbearable pain, becomes beautiful. Beautiful in an aesthetic sense, since aesthetics are concerned with making beautiful that which is in decay. But Acker doesn't care about being beautiful. "I don't want this sexuality," she declares, "I don't want to be diseased" (11). Her pirate body cannot be extracted through the reproductive (that is, heteronormative) sexuality, so she must look to one that is purposeless, a limitless expenditure. She must look to masturbation.

Masturbation, like dreaming, empties the content of the mind through a physiological function of the body. But unlike dreaming, masturbation begins in the body: "Irritation is happy to be touched, but if it turns too expectant or excited without relaxing, it will become rigid" (12). The body must be relaxed and responsive to touch for it to be excited. It must be naked. Masturbation helps you lose your language: making yourself cum is a knowledge that comes out of listening before you speak. It is here, in this foreign experience of a body for which there is no verbal language, that Acker starts to talk to her pirate body. Here, "at this point, still desiring where there's no body left to become desire, at this point of *failure*, the whole turns over into something else" (13).

Through sexuality, Acker has seen gender, she has seen her impossible body, and she has learned how to speak to it. All that is left is to understand how she can resurrect it from her dead world. Like dysphoric bodies, the pirate body must be played with to reveal its character. She does this through the practice of bodybuilding.

The Pirate Body

In bodybuilding, one must work a muscle group beyond the point of failure, beyond the point when the muscles can no longer perform their function. The body is where reason turns to shit. "Whenever anyone bodybuilds," writes Acker (1997: 148), "he or she is always trying to understand and control the physical in the face of this death. No wonder bodybuilding is centered around failure." Remember that we are now in the self-related body, where words do not do what they mean.

If language is the articulate form of thought, then bodybuilding is the articulate form of death. It is for this reason that bodybuilders are considered stupid. Since the body thinks existence through disease and decay, a practice that affirms this reality, that makes it beautiful, also makes it meaningful on the body's own terms. In bodybuilding, the muscles must be worked to failure, so that they can grow back stronger. Essence and meaning become one. The language of bodybuilding rejects ordinary language, in which meaning is drawn from external difference, and constitutes itself a language in which meaning is drawn from this self-related difference: "a method for understanding and controlling the physical which in this case is also the self" (148).

Acker builds her pirate body from this self. In the ordinary world, woman is a lack: is nothing, is not fun. Like the dysphoric bodies of transgendered humans, the pirate body shows us the limitations of asking what gender is, and it helps us consider instead what it does. The self-related body (dysphoric or pirate) castrates the cephalic god to resurrect a world reflective of its inner self. It does not transition from one side of the binary to another; it transitions out of the order of reason that names it impossible. When gender penetrates a self-related body, gender becomes shit.

In the acephalic world, where there is no such thing as philosophers and only writers, something that's made absent frees something else up. So when Acker is bodybuilding, she is not performing the strength of men, nor is she betraying her own gender. She is building a body—the body that was once called "female"—from death, from beyond the nothingness that was its name, to unearth, like pirates, a treasure from the labyrinth of shit that is this life.

K. K. Trieu is a writer of adult entertainment and promoter of nighttime events. He recently graduated from the New School for Social Research.

References

Acker, Kathy. 1993a. "The Language of the Body." *Canadian Journal of Political and Social Theory* 16, nos. 1–3: 1–15.

Acker, Kathy. 1993b. "Writing Praxis." In "The Credos Issue," edited by Bradford Morrow. Special issue, *Conjunctions*, no. 21: 303–4.

Acker, Kathy. 1997. *Bodies of Work*. New York: Serpent's Tail.

Acker, Kathy. n.d. "The Languages of the Body." Kathy Acker Papers, box 19, file 13. David M. Rubenstein Rare Book and Manuscript Library, Duke University, Durham, NC.

Bataille, Georges. 2014. *Inner Experience*. Translated by Stuart Kendall. Albany: State University of New York Press.

The Vulnerable Child Protection Act and Transgender Children's Health

SAHAR SADJADI

Abstract A recent spate of legislation such as South Dakota's HB 1057, known as the Vulnerable Child Protection Act, seeks to criminalize medical treatment for gender transition in minors under sixteen. This essay argues that these laws do not safeguard children's health but are part of a broader attack on transgender rights that uses the protection of children as a powerful pretense to scapegoat a minority. It suggests that the analyses and insights of the field of transgender studies could inform, enrich, and reconfigure current clinical and public-policy debates around gender-variant children. This essay also aims at drawing the attention of supporters of transgender children to aspects of current medical treatments and their potential implications for young people that might get lost in this explosive political climate.

Keywords children, puberty blockers, gender variant, transgender, South Dakota bill

These are dangerous times for those with a tenuous belonging to the nation. People whose lives disrupt the familiar and familial order of sex and gender have long held their place next to the racialized, the immigrant, the Jew, and the Muslim in attracting the fears and anxieties of their epoch. The situation can become absurd: following the July 2019 massacre in which a white nationalist traveled to a Walmart in El Paso, Texas, specifically to murder Mexicans, followed in turn by the mass shooting the next day at a bar in Dayton, Ohio, that left a transgender person dead among the other victims, a state legislator blamed these atrocities on "transgender, homosexual marriage and drag queen advocates," working to destroy the "traditional American family" (Miller 2019).

Transgender people are lightning rods for fearmongering such as this, and attacks on their rights have escalated in recent years. Protecting children is an old pretense for fomenting mistrust and panic around sexual minorities (G. Rubin 1984). Today these tendencies collide in efforts to "save our children" from a "transgender agenda," seen as designed to confuse young people about their gender identity, and to harm them through medically experimenting on their bodies.

TSQ: Transgender Studies Quarterly ★ Volume 7, Number 3 ★ August 2020 **508**
DOI 10.1215/23289252-8553202 © 2020 Duke University Press

South Dakota's HB 1057 is the latest legislative effort intended to save kids from the so-called transgender agenda. Known as the Vulnerable Child Protection Act, passed in the state House of Representatives on January 29, 2020, this draconian bill criminalizes medical treatment for gender transition in minors under sixteen, and it proposes prison time for doctors who provide such treatments. Wholesale attacks like these, on treatments as varied as steroids for sixteen-year-olds and gonadotropin-releasing hormone (GnRH) agonists (popularly known as puberty blockers) for nine-year-olds, are not informed by medical questions and concerns. Notably, the legislation's proponents make no mention of thousands of cisgender children for whom some of the same medical treatments are used, such as girls diagnosed with early puberty or children with short stature whose puberty is halted to delay the end of growth. Moreover, the bill excludes intersex children, who have often been subject to medically unnecessary interventions deemed appropriate by physicians and parents. This bill is not about protecting children's health. It is about protecting binary sex, even when children's bodies defy it, and it amplifies broader attacks on trans civil rights. It is no surprise that the same representative who introduced HB 1057 also authored a discriminatory bathroom bill in 2016.

Opposition to HB 1057 was robust and came from diverse stakeholders, including the American Civil Liberties Union, transgender rights advocacy groups, parents, medical professionals, "business leaders" anxious to avoid potential boycotts of the state, and even Republicans opposed to state practices they believe undermine "parental rights." The bill was defeated on February 10, 2020, in the state Senate's Health and Human Services Committee in a 5–2 vote, but other states, including Florida, Georgia, Kentucky, Missouri, South Carolina, and Texas are still considering similar bills.

Using the figure of the vulnerable child as a battleground for gender politics is not limited to the United States. Posters of children and slogans like "Don't Mess with our Children" abound in protests against "gender ideology" in Europe and Latin America. These posters often depict a conventionally gendered boy and girl, in the company of an adult man and woman, presumably cisgender heterosexual parents, and ostensibly in need of protection from gay or trans agendas. This explicitly right-wing movement increasingly finds common ground with a contingent of transphobic self-described "gender-critical" feminists or TERFs (trans-exclusionary radical feminists) who oppose "transgenderism" on the basis that it constitutes harm against (presumably nontransgender) girls and women. They ignore a robust body of transfeminist work, such as that of Emi Koyama, that expands our understanding of gender-based violence in ways that do not set cis and trans women in opposition. They oddly concur with conservatives that one is born and remains a man or a woman, as if Simone de Beauvoir's decades-old assertion, "One is not born, but rather becomes a woman," never happened. They do not understand that the long history of patriarchy and violence against women is entangled with a rigid gender binary that put women in their place, and they act as if high rates of violence against trans women by men doesn't merit feminist analysis and response.

I have been studying the clinical practices around childhood gender nonconformity for a decade as a medical anthropologist and have come to see that in the midst of this ideological warfare, there are actual children with actual lives and bodies—not just the rhetorically useful figure of the vulnerable child—whose interests might fall outside the polarized terms of contemporary discourse. The clinical debates in this rapidly changing field are politically explosive and emotionally charged, at times at the expense of careful assessment of children's condition. The attacks on the totality of trans health care have made researchers wary of critically investigating specific treatments, a practice that is important for improving the quality of care. Bills such as HB 1057 add fuel to the fire and contribute to a toxic climate for research and clinical care in this area. They severely limit access to treatment and available options for care of transgender youth.

In this climate, it is tempting to take the opposite position of one's enemy, by defending all medical interventions currently associated with gender transition in children and insisting that they are safe and save children's lives. Research on these treatments' effects are still in the early stages, however. Studies on the effect of *not* treating children are even more rudimentary and are overwhelmingly based on retrospective accounts rather than clinical observation. We need to understand more about how best to care for gender-nonconforming and transgender children. Acknowledging current uncertainties, I want to raise some questions about the received wisdom regarding the history and use of puberty suppression among advocates for transgender children. My goal is to draw the attention of supporters of transgender children to aspects of these practices and their potential implications for young people that might get lost in the political standoff. In doing so, I seek to highlight, as Kadji Amin (2018) has argued, that medical practices currently understood in a favorable light by trans people and their allies can have roots in beliefs that they might well oppose, while at the same time acknowledging that medical technologies can be taken up, reconfigured, and redeployed in ways that subvert the intentions of their originators.

When I began my fieldwork in 2010, puberty blockers had recently become available in the United States for treating children, often ages nine to thirteen, who had been diagnosed with Gender Dysphoria (then known as Gender Identity Disorder). Puberty blockers are agonists of gonadotropin-releasing hormone (GnRH); they are expensive drugs used in adults to treat prostate cancer and endometriosis, as well as in assisted reproduction procedures such as in vitro fertilization. While they are grouped together with steroid hormones in bills such as the Vulnerable Child Protection Act, GnRH agonists in fact do the opposite, by blocking the production of steroids. Puberty blockers can be beneficial to some children who are severely distressed about puberty, but they are not as neutral as often portrayed. Depriving the body of GnRH and steroids at a critical growth phase, particularly for an extended period of time, is a major medical intervention with potential systemic effects on the musculoskeletal and nervous systems.[1] The follow-up studies available for gender-variant/transgender children treated with puberty blockers investigate psychosocial adjustment (De Vries et al. 2011, 2014), not physical side effects, and they examine only those treated after age twelve. The only Food and Drug Administration (FDA)–approved use of GnRH agonists in children is for delaying puberty for those diagnosed with precocious puberty. The safety of the treatment for children who received Lupron (the same GnRH agonist commonly used for transgender children) for early puberty is contested, however, and the data are inconclusive.[2]

The main reason puberty blockers are considered preferable to steroids for younger transgender and gender-variant people by some clinicians is their reputation for being "reversible." Reversibility is defined in the clinical debates with regard to sex/gender appearance, in situations in which treatment is discontinued after a short period and natal puberty resumes. When GnRH agonists are started prepubertally and followed—as is standard protocol at many pediatric gender clinics—by steroids to achieve the physical characteristics of the other sex, reproductive organs and gametes don't mature, and loss of fertility results. On the other hand, adolescents who start hormone therapy after going through some stages of puberty *without* having received blockers are likely to preserve their fertility. The issue at stake here is not whether fertility per se is the highest value or that it must be preserved at all cost, but whether children are in a position to meaningfully consent to such a decision. In this respect, a nine-year-old and a fifteen-year-old differ significantly in their capacity to engage in medical decision making. Early GnRH agonist use also inhibits growth of genital tissue, which can in certain instances lead to more complicated future genital surgeries, if and when they are desired (culminating, for example, in a supply of penile skin insufficient for penile-inversion vaginoplasty, which might then necessitate a more complex vaginoplasty technique using a section of intestinal tissue). There are no data available about effects of the treatment on sexual health and function.

Today, puberty blockers are widely understood to be a crucial component of the "affirmative approach" to gender-nonconforming and transgender children. But the history of the relation of these drugs to the affirmative approach is more complex. Clinicians who, in the early 2000s, coined the term *affirmative approach* to depathologize and destigmatize childhood gender variance had a medically noninterventionist approach to young children (Menvielle, Tuerk, and Perrin 2005). Pioneers of the treatment of puberty suppression, unlike the clinicians who favored the affirmative approach, still operated within the established psycho-medical paradigm of a "Gender Identity Disorder" (Zucker and Cohen-Kettenis 2005).[3] Prior to 2010, Kenneth Zucker (2010), the psychologist whose practice of discouraging children's gender-nonconforming behavior or gender transition has been vigorously criticized by trans activists, had reportedly referred more gender-variant young people for puberty blockers than any other clinician in North America.

In the US context, however, puberty blockers soon became closely associated with supporting transgender children, within a clinical and cultural field shaped largely by cisgender parents and clinicians.[4] Well before a substantial discussion of the clinical practice of administering puberty blockers had taken shape among adult transgender activists and scholars, these treatments had already come under sharp attack by antitrans feminists such as Sheila Jeffreys and conservative groups such as the American College of Pediatricians. As a consequence of this constellation of ideological forces, the space for discussion and evaluation of these practices shrank significantly and became politically risky. As Emmett Harsin Drager has noted, legitimate disagreement over these medical treatments has become politically implausible in circles that affirm the lives of transgender children (Chu and Harsin Drager 2019).

Decades of vibrant debate among transgender intellectuals highlighting the diversity of trans lives—with or without medical treatment—have uniquely positioned transgender studies to intervene in these fraught circumstances. Such thought has resisted the reduction of trans experience to clinical narratives, and it has openly explored the dynamics and tensions in the relation of (adult) trans people to medicine (Stone 1991; H. Rubin 2003; Spade 2006; Aizura 2011). Moreover, the field of transgender studies has from the outset recognized the specificity of Euro-American formations of personhood and of the relation of the self and the body (Stryker 2004, 2006)—a notion entirely absent from the contemporary clinical discourses about children's sex/gender embodiment and identity. Decolonial and trans of color scholars have addressed the exclusions produced by universalizing the hegemonic Euro-American notions, and histories, of sexual/gender identity (Dutta and Roy 2014; Wesley 2014; Snorton 2017). Recent work by Jules Gill-Peterson (2018) on the medical archives and racialized young trans bodies, and Dora Silva Santana (2020) on black transgender childhood in Brazil, account for difference and inequality across race, class, and place among transgender youth. Travers (2018) has explored the social transformation driven by trans kids' experiences, while showing how this shift is marked by unequal access to affirmative care. This recognition of the sociohistorical situatedness of trans identities could be analytically extended across life stages to account for change and difference in trans embodiment among children and adults. Trans reproductive justice advocacy and scholarship (Nixon 2013; Strangio 2016; Cárdenas 2016) could also make a crucial contribution to current debates by providing tools for investigating the medical treatment of children and its implication for their reproductive health, rather than simply ignoring the issue in the face of its weaponization by transphobic forces.

Despite the discursive and ideological conundrums of addressing trans and gender-variant childhood, transgender studies has in fact undertaken this work. The inaugural "keywords for a 21st-century transgender studies" issue of *TSQ* in 2014 not only included entries for children (Meadow 2014) but also offered a critical perspective on the normalizing role of medical treatment of children (Castañeda 2014). In that single issue alone, there are essays on "Bio/logism" (Van Anders 2014), "Depathologization" (Suess, Espineira, and Walters 2014), and "Intersex" (Morland 2014), each offering important insights that could be brought to bear on contemporary clinical and public-policy debates about the medical treatment of gender-variant children. The authors' analyses would complicate some of the beliefs common in the clinical field today—for instance, that transgender children are "born this way,"[5] or that there are direct causal relations between trans identity and mental illness and suicide. (The fear that puberty per se can be a threat to life for transgender children permeates pediatric trans care, while the claim that puberty blockers reduce suicidality was central to arguments in the media against HB 1057.) A turn to intersex children's history, which has a longer record of research stretching back to the 1990s, would invite us to reflect further on the particular complexities inherent to informed consent and medical decision making for young children, as well as parental discomfort and worries about sex/gender ambiguity of children (Karkazis 2008).

In the strange political times in which we find ourselves, we need to preserve the space necessary for research, analysis, and debate over these issues, while adamantly holding open spaces in which young trans and gender-variant life is valued and can unfold along multiple pathways. Researchers who are not professionally and financially invested in medical treatment of gender-variant children need to conduct robust studies on the long-term health effects of puberty suppression, particularly for younger children who might not yet have the cognitive tools, life experience, and knowledge to evaluate the risks and benefits of these treatments. Justice for transgender children does not equal unexamined acceptance of all pharmaceutical offerings, just as it does not equal banning all care. While opposing harmful legislation like South Dakota's HB 1057, the care and treatment of children calls for caution, not because children cannot be transgender—as some of their opponents claim—but because transgender children's health matters.

Sahar Sadjadi is an anthropologist and medical doctor with the McGill University faculty at the Department of Social Studies of Medicine and a 2019–20 fellow at the Princeton University Center for Human Values. She is completing a book based on an ethnography of clinical practices around childhood gender nonconformity in the United States.

Acknowledgements

I am grateful to Susan Stryker for generous feedback and editorial suggestions on this essay. Thanks to Rosza Daniel Lang/Levitsky, whose reproductive justice perspective has informed my analysis of pediatric trans care.

Notes

1.   For a randomized clinical trial on the effect of pediatric use of GnRH agonists on bone mineral density, see Yanovski et al. 2003.

2.   In recent years, for example, there has been emerging evidence in the form of reports to the FDA, as well as on patient forums, of near- and long-term skeletal and neurological adverse effects experienced by women who were treated for precocious puberty in childhood with Lupron. They include depression, seizures, and degenerative disc disease, chronic pain, and bone fractures later in life. See the Kaiser Health Report (Jewett 2017).

3.   Peggy Cohen-Kettenis and her colleagues in the Netherlands were the first to use puberty suppressants in the treatment of children and adolescents (above age 12) diagnosed with Gender Identity Disorder.

4.   See *Trans Kids* (Meadow 2018) on the formation of a cisgender parent movement.

5.   For an analysis of the politics of a biodeterminist notion of transgender identity, see Wuest 2019.

References

Aizura, Aren Z. 2011. "The Romance of the Amazing Scalpel: 'Race,' Labour, and Affect in Thai Gender Reassignment Clinics." In *Queer Bangkok: Twenty-First-Century Markets, Media, and Rights*, edited by Peter A. Jackson, 143–62. Hong Kong: Hong Kong University Press.

Amin, Kadji. 2018. "Glands, Eugenics, and Rejuvenation in Man into Woman: A Biopolitical Genealogy of Transsexuality." *TSQ* 5, no. 4: 589–605.

Cárdenas, Micha. 2016. "Pregnancy: Reproductive Futures in Trans of Color Feminism." *TSQ* 3, nos. 1–2: 48–57.

Castañeda, Claudia. 2014. "Childhood." *TSQ* 1, nos. 1–2: 59–61.

Chu, Andrea Long, and Emmett Harsin Drager. 2019. "After Trans Studies." *TSQ* 6, no. 1: 103–16.

De Vries, Annelou L. C., Jenifer K. McGuire, Thomas D. Steensma, Eva C. F. Wagenaar, Theo A. H. Doreleijers, and Peggy T. Cohen-Kettenis. 2014. "Young Adult Psychological Outcome after Puberty Suppression and Gender Reassignment." *Pediatrics* 134, no. 4: 696–704.

De Vries, Annelou L. C., Thomas D. Steensma, Theo A. H. Doreleijers, and Peggy T. Cohen-Kettenis. 2011. "Puberty Suppression in Adolescents with Gender Identity Disorder: A Prospective Follow-Up Study." *Journal of Sexual Medicine* 8, no. 8: 2276–83.

Dutta, Aniruddha, and Raina Roy. 2014. "Decolonizing Transgender in India: Some Reflections." *TSQ* 1, no. 3: 320–37.

Gill-Peterson, Jules. 2018. "Trans of Color Critique before Transsexuality." *TSQ* 5, no. 4: 606–20.

Jewett, Christina. 2017. "Women Fear Drug They Used to Halt Puberty Led to Health Problems." *Kaiser Health News*, February 2. khn.org/news/women-fear-drug-they-used-to-halt -puberty-led-to-health-problems/.

Karkazis, Katrina. 2008. *Fixing Sex: Intersex, Medical Authority, and Lived Experience.* Durham, NC: Duke University Press.

Meadow, Tey. 2014. "Child." *TSQ* 1, nos. 1–2: 57–59.

Meadow, Tey. 2018. *Trans Kids: Being Gendered in the Twenty-First Century.* Oakland: University of California Press.

Menvielle, Edgardo, Catherine Tuerk, and Ellen Perrin. 2005. "To the Beat of a Different Drummer: The Gender-Variant Child." *Contemporary Pediatrics* 22, no. 2: 38–39.

Miller, Joshua Rhett. 2019. "Ohio Lawmaker Candice Keller Blames Gay Marriage, 'Drag Queen Advocates' for Dayton Shooting." *New York Post*, August 5. nypost.com/2019/08/05 /ohio-lawmaker-candice-keller-blames-gay-marriage-drag-queen-advocates-for-dayton -shooting/.

Morland, Iain. 2014. "Intersex." *TSQ* 1, nos. 1–2: 111–15.

Nixon, Laura. 2013. "The Right to (Trans) Parent: A Reproductive Justice Approach to Reproductive Rights, Fertility, and Family-Building Issues Facing Transgender People." *William and Mary Journal of Women and the Law* 20, no. 1: 73–103.

Rubin, Gayle. 1984. "Thinking Sex: Notes for a Radical Theory of the Politics of Sexuality." In *Pleasure and Danger: Exploring Female Sexuality*, edited by Carole Vance, 143–78. Boston: Routledge and Kegan Paul.

Rubin, Henry. 2003. *Self-Made Men: Identity and Embodiment among Transsexual Men.* Nashville: Vanderbilt University Press.

Santana, Dora Silva. 2020. Presentation at the panel "New Directions in Trans of Color Scholarship," New York University, February 11.

Snorton, Riley C. 2017. *Black on Both Sides: A Racial History of Trans Identity.* Minneapolis: University of Minnesota Press.

Spade, Dean. 2006. "Mutilating Gender." In *The Transgender Studies Reader*, edited by Susan Stryker and Stephen Whittle, 315–32. New York: Routledge.

Stone, Sandy. 1991. "The *Empire* Strikes Back: A Posttranssexual Manifesto." In *Body Guards: The Cultural Politics of Gender Ambiguity*, edited by Julia Epstein and Kristina Straub, 280–304. New York: Routledge.

Strangio, Chase. 2016. "Can Reproductive Trans Bodies Exist." *City University of New York Law Review* 19, no. 2: 223–45.

Stryker, Susan. 2004. "Transgender Studies: Queer Theory's Evil Twin." *GLQ* 10, no. 2: 212–15.

Stryker, Susan. 2006. "(De)Subjugated Knowledges: An Introduction to Transgender Studies." In *The Transgender Studies Reader*, edited by Susan Stryker and Stephen Whittle, 1–17. New York: Routledge.

Suess, Amets, Karine Espineira, and Pau Crego Walters. 2014. "Depathologization." *TSQ* 1, nos. 1–2: 73–77.

Travers. 2018. *The Trans Generation: How Trans Kids (and Their Parents) Are Creating a Gender Revolution.* New York: New York University Press.

Van Anders, Sari M. 2014. "Bio/Logics." *TSQ* 1, nos. 1–2: 33–35.

Wesley, Saylesh. 2014. "Twin-Spirited Woman: Sts'iyóye smestíyexw slhá:li." *TSQ* 1, no. 3: 338–51.

Wuest, Jo. 2019. "The Scientific Gaze in American Transgender Politics: Contesting the Meanings of Sex, Gender, and Gender Identity in the Bathroom Rights Cases." *Politics and Gender* 15, no. 2: 336–60.

Yanovski, Jack A., Susan R. Rose, Giovanna Municchi, Ora II. Pescovitz, Suvimol C. Hill, Fernando G. Cassorla, and Gordon B. Cutler. 2003. "Treatment with a Luteinizing Hormone-Releasing Hormone Agonist in Adolescents with Short Stature." *New England Journal of Medicine* 348, no. 10: 908–17. doi.org/10.1056/NEJMoa013555.

Zucker, Kenneth J., Susan J. Bradley, Allison Owen-Anderson, Devita Singh, Ray Blanchard, and Jerald Bain. 2010. "Puberty-Blocking Hormonal Therapy for Adolescents with Gender Identity Disorder: A Descriptive Clinical Study." *Journal of Gay and Lesbian Mental Health* 15, no. 1: 58–82.

Zucker, Kenneth J., and Peggy T. Cohen-Kettenis. 2008. "Gender Identity Disorders in Children and Adolescents." In *Handbook of Sexual and Gender Identity Disorders*, edited by David L. Rowland and Luca Incrocci, 376–422. Hoboken, NJ: Wiley.

Sustaining Trans Life

JAMES MCMASTER

Trap Door: Trans Cultural Production and the Politics of Visibility
Edited and with an introduction by Tourmaline, Eric Stanley,
and Johanna Burton
Cambridge, MA: MIT Press, 2017. 419 pp.

After the Party: A Manifesto for Queer of Color Life
Joshua Chambers-Letson
New York: New York University Press, 2018. 299 pp.

Trap Door: Trans Cultural Production and the Politics of Visibility is not your typical edited volume. Rather than conduct business as usual by gathering established academics into a single publication to address this or that gap in the field, Tourmaline, Eric Stanley, and Johanna Burton have commandeered the resources of elite cultural institutions like the MIT Press and the New Museum to achieve something else. These editors, as if in an effort to live up to the lived realities of trans intellection and imagination, have made their book into a gathering place within which trans academics, artists, and activists—as well as cis authors who write out of an "affinity" with such persons, as Sara Ahmed puts it in her contribution to the volume—might really reckon with the culture war that both takes and makes trans life in the present. In this way, *Trap Door* operates according to an antidisciplinary ethos, which is most evident in the two round-table discussions published in the volume's pages, one hosted by Tavia Nyong'o, the other by Dean Spade. The volume models coalition and collaboration among academics, artists, and activists in its construction, and, at the same time, it offers other models to this end, as when Fred Moten and Wu Tsang, friends and collaborators, bridge art and academia by discussing the interplay of beauty and terror in the latter's filmic work and in minoritarian performance more generally.

TSQ: Transgender Studies Quarterly ∗ Volume 7, Number 3 ∗ August 2020 **517**
DOI 10.1215/23289252-8553230 © 2020 Duke University Press

It is as rare as it is refreshing for a volume to so capably hold high theory alongside movement genius, but *Trap Door* has space for both, for Eva Hayward, whose essay experiments with "transposition" as a frame through which to understand sexual transition in relation to space, and for CeCe McDonald and Miss Major Griffin-Gracy, who are featured in an interview conducted by Toshio Meronek about what it is to live the hypervisibility of black trans womanhood. It's an interview that gets to the heart of the volume's organizing inquiry. "We are living in a time of trans visibility," the editors write in their introduction, "Yet we are also living in a time of anti-trans violence" (xv). What are we to make of this paradox? How are trans people to survive it?

As you likely know, the text accompanying Laverne Cox on the cover of *Time Magazine* in 2014 deemed this moment of seeming contradiction "the transgender tipping point." Readers of *Trap Door* who are ambivalent about this characterization can take comfort, though, in the fact that many of the volume's contributors have taken it upon themselves to complicate this view of contemporary trans reality, which would position this decade of the twenty-first century as the apotheosis of trans progress. Treva Ellison, for example, forwards a compelling reading of "the protest and performance strategies" of Sir Lady Java in the 1960s to make the claim that antitrans violence and trans visibility have always been tied to capital in ways that ensure their cyclical reappearance throughout history. This point is echoed, albeit in different tones and with different stakes, in the contributions by both Abram J. Lewis and Morgan M. Page. That none of these scholars' arguments undercuts the frame provided for these essays by Tourmaline, Stanley, and Burton is testament to that frame's nuance, which is also, eloquently, evident in the volume's title. Visibility is a *trap*, on this point the editors agree with Michel Foucault. But the editors also know that representation matters insofar as it opens *doors* for future folks to walk through on their way to becoming their best selves. The collection's title is an acknowledgment of this contradiction, an escape hatch in the stage of everyday life through which "the very notion of *being* itself" might be challenged in favor of "new modes of recognition, identification, and collective endeavor" (xx).

The trap door of the volume's title, then, is what enables *Trap Door* to be about much more than its central conceit. And there's space for this, too—419 pages of it. Though page count will make it difficult to read *Trap Door* cover to cover, this matters less than the various strands of thought that one can track (and teach) across the volume's chapters. Alongside authors who directly take up the twinned trends of trans visibility and antitrans violence, others position the internet as a central site of trans and gender-nonconforming life-making. While Juliana Huxtable, in conversation with Che Gossett, gestures to Tumblr as a kind of soil in which queer and trans subjects can begin to seed and sprout, Mel Chen looks to YouTube for an "Asian FTM archive." This archive acts both as a how-to guide for "the art and craft of gendered living" (150) and as an incitement to move "beyond thinking merely in terms of spectacle or visibility" to spend time with "the *kinds* of presences that may be carved out in a given medium" (149). Notably, too, micha cárdenas offers a poetic/performative investigation into the relationship between algorithms and affective, antitrans violence on social media, one that seems to share in Chen's desire to move past the problem of trans visibility (161).

Indeed, it is to *Trap Door*'s credit that it enables readers to think *through* the problem of trans visibility *into* other thought experiments that are unnamed by the editors but that are nevertheless given in what they've gathered together. Here's the question that I found myself thinking with while working my way through the book: what sustenance can trans cultural production yield for trans life? It's a question that, like a guardian angel, should follow any invocation of antitrans violence, and I ask it partially inspired by the time I've spent recently with Joshua Chambers-Letson's moving and stylistically bold *After the Party: A Manifesto for Queer of Color Life*. What Chambers-Letson offers with this second book is a survival guide, a collection of strategies for sustaining imperiled lives that is drawn from the intellectual reservoirs of black studies, queer studies, Marxism, performance studies, and other areas of minoritarian thought. As Chambers-Letson puts it at the end of his preface, *After the Party* "is about minoritarian subjects who keep each other alive, mobilizing performance to open up the possibility for new worlds and new ways of being in the world together" (xxii).

In each of the book's chapters, Chambers-Letson helps us see this process in action. Chapter 1, which is stunningly structured as a mix tape, takes an admiring look at Nina Simone to theorize "the pedagogy of performance" as "the transmission and sharing out of the feeling of freedom" (49). And Chambers-Letson shows us why we need such a feeling when he reckons with both Simone's relationship to suicide, as well as the suicide of one of his friends in 2013. It's a reminder of the intimate relationship that minoritarian subjects—and here we might say trans subjects especially—have with death. Other chapters in the book tell stories about other artists, like Felix Gonzalez-Torres, Eiko, and Tseng Kwong Chi. We learn that Gonzalez-Torres has much to teach us about what the late José Esteban Muñoz, following the philosopher Jean-Luc Nancy, called "the commons of incommensurability," in which what is irreducible and singular about any of us is to be seen and shared (out). We also learn that Eiko, through her slow and subtle choreography, when read through Rey Chow's thinking, can teach us something about entanglement that is not captured in the meanings imbued in the term by feminist science studies.

My favorite of Chambers-Letson's chapters, though, is his second, which sets out to revise the way we think about the category of reproduction within critical theory. Performance studies scholars will recognize this chapter as a return to field-forming debates about the ontology of performance, while feminist theorists will welcome it as a queer perspective on old conversations about care and motherhood (the author's specific interest is with the relationship between mothers of color and their queer sons). The chapter's point, which Chambers-Letson makes through close readings of various works by the Vietnamese artist Danh Vō, is ultimately this: "Performance's mode of reproduction," in other words, performance's capacity to remember and reanimate, "can facilitate the reproduction of imperiled life; it can sustain life" (85). This is significant not only because it is a theory of living on while dying, but also because it is nothing short of a theory of life after death, one that is exemplified by the written performance of mourning and melancholia that is, in many ways, *After the Party*'s beating bleeding heart. The book begins and ends in direct address to Muñoz. We learn that the "party" of the book's title is not just the Communist Party but also the party that ended when José died. "I wrote this book for you," writes Chambers-Letson to his mentor, whose influence is everywhere in *After the Party*'s pages, "And I wrote it to keep some part of you alive and with me (with us) in order to take you with us to the various battles that we will wage in your name—and in our own" (xxii).

"Death stalks people of color": Chambers-Letson repeats this phrase over and over in his book (76). And death stalks trans and gender-nonconforming people of color most of all. Having said this, do I even need to explain the value of a theory of life after death for trans studies and for those who mourn trans lives lost? After all, the idea that writing is one performance among others, one methodology among others, for extending trans and gender-nonconforming life is already coursing through *Trap Door*'s arteries. It's what Roy Pérez is doing when he writes about proximity in the work of trans and Filipina artist Mark Aguhar, whom we lost to suicide when she was just twenty-four years old. And, as we know from their contributions to *Trap Door*, it's what Chris Vargas, Stamatina Gregory, and Jeanne Vaccaro are doing when they engage in the work of curating— etymologically, a kind of care work—trans history, art, and existence into the view of those who seek out such treasures. What is needed as trans people continue to endure attritional and exceptional suffering is "More Life," as Chambers-Letson might put it (80). Thankfully, this is precisely what *Trap Door* and *After the Party* make possible.

James McMaster is assistant professor of gender and women's studies and Asian American studies at the University of Wisconsin–Madison.

Deinscribing Gender in Research across Global Contexts

D-L STEWART

Starting with Gender in International Higher Education Research:
Conceptual Debates and Methodological Considerations
Edited by Emily F. Henderson and Z Nicolazzo
New York: Routledge, 2019. 252 pp.

In *Starting with Gender in International and Higher Education Research: Conceptual Debates and Methodological Consideration*, Emily Henderson and Z Nicolazzo bring together an international group of authors to think about what it means to do research with and on gender in and about postsecondary institutions. This research focuses not just on institutions but also their participants: faculty, administrative staff, and students. As Henderson and Nicolazzo write in the introduction, "This text is specifically targeted at researchers who are grappling with the challenges of researching in/around/with/through gender in the current moment of higher education" (2). More specifically, they point readers to the book's central question, "When we say we are doing gender research, what do we mean we are researching?" (4). This is not only an important question but also one rife with implications for scholars and policymakers within and beyond the academy.

 Starting with Gender in International Higher Education Research is organized roughly by collectives of associations, but these collectivities are not discrete. Rather, as the editors note, "each chapter reaches into other chapters, whether by conceptual or methodological congruence" (5). Chapters 1 and 2 consider gender (Emily Henderson) and feminism (Susan Marine) as theoretical frameworks guiding postsecondary research. The authors of chapters 3 and 4 trouble what is meant by "women" (chapter 3, Kate Jönsas) and "men" (chapter 4,

Rachel Wagner, Chase Catalano, and Dan Tillapaugh) as presumably discrete categories through (re)considerations of and ethnographic inquiries into their own empirical research. Chapter 5 (Andrés Castro Samayoa), chapter 6 (Michael Woodford, Jessica Joslin, and Jack Marshall), chapter 7 (James Burford and Louisa Allen), and chapter 8 (Z Nicolazzo) engage the methodological implications of centering gender-related and gender-impactful social identities of sexuality and gender(s) as variables and axes of analysis.

Nicolazzo and Henderson, in the introductory chapter, rightly describe chapter 9 (S. L. Simmons and T. J. Jourian) as a transition point in the text. Simmons and Jourian's discussion of the concept of communities as contested space(s) illuminates the experiential implications of the conceptual and identitarian troubling of the first eight chapters. By doing so, this chapter also shapes how the reader approaches the discussion of gender-related and gender-impactful policies brought to bear by Madhumeeta Sinha, Genine Hook, and Talita Calitz in chapters 10, 11, and 12, respectively. These authors demonstrate how sexual harassment (chapter 10), institutional policies for "mothers" (e.g., parental leave; chapter 11), and Black student experiences (chapter 12) not only presume homogenous communities of gender but also fail to acknowledge the ways that institutional policies instantiate restrictive and binarist understandings of gender. These institutional policies then function as forms of what Nicolazzo (2017) has coined "compulsory heterogenderism," in which not only are people gendered along the binary, but those binarist assumptions lead to and are enclosed within assumptions of a (hetero)sexuality that embraces normative assumptions of desire and relationship. The book closes with a critical review of the book itself offered by Mary Lou Rasmussen (chapter 13). Rasmussen's chapter functions as an afterword and offers a compelling consideration of the issues and questions raised in the text as a whole.

Alongside Rasmussen's considerations, I was left pondering several issues after engaging with the authors of this text. I'll share just two of them here. First, as the authors consistently reinforce, the mainstream literature about gender in higher education (I prefer to name it *cisstream*, extending Sandy Grande's [2004] concept of *whitestream*) reflects normative understandings of gender (binarist and heteronormative). However, this literature base also informs policy and practice beyond higher education as it is used to support and advocate for gender equity on both national and global levels. For example, Bernice Sandler's (1999) scholarship on "chilly climates" has supported a great deal of the policy and practice interventions for women in STEM fields. Deinscribing cisheteronormativity in our research has material consequences for developing policies that are gender expansive and supportive of furthering possibilities for people currently invisibilized (also Stewart 2018).

Second, I was left with a yearning for more engagement by the authors with the tradition of and current offerings by Black fem(me)(inist), queer, and trans* scholars. Much of the intersectional, gender-troubling work recommended by the authors of this volume is already at hand in the scholarship of such as Saadiya Hartman, Christina Sharpe, Tourmaline, and Che Gossett. I encourage readers to read these scholars alongside and in conversation with Henderson and Nicolazzo.

Starting with Gender in International and Higher Education Research is a necessary text for anyone hoping to engage gender in research, policy, or practice within and beyond postsecondary education. Graduate students to established researchers would benefit from *Starting with Gender* as a troubled and contested framework nonetheless essential for deinscribing oppression in institutional systems and structures.

D-L Stewart is professor in the School of Education, cocoordinator of Student Affairs in Higher Education, codirector of CSU Initiatives for the Race and Intersectional Studies in Educational Equity (RISE) Center, and affiliated faculty in the Center for Women's Studies and Gender Research at Colorado State University.

References

Grande, Sandy. 2004. *Red Pedagogy: Native American Social and Political Thought.* New York: Rowman and Littlefield.

Nicolazzo, Z. 2017. *Trans* in College: Transgender Students' Strategies for Navigating Campus Life and the Institutional Politics of Inclusion.* Sterling, VA: Stylus.

Sandler, Bernice. R. 1999. "The Chilly Climate: Subtle Ways in Which Women Are Often Treated Differently at Work and in Classrooms." *About Women on Campus* 8, no. 3. National Alliance for Partnerships in Equity. www.napequity.org/nape-content/uploads/R1l-The-Chilly-Climate.pdf.

Stewart, Dafina-Lazarus. 2018. Review of *No Shortcut to Change: An Unlikely Path to a More Gender Equitable World*, by Kara Ellerby. *Teachers College Record*, February 22. www.tcrecord.org/Content.asp?ContentId=22287

Trans* Cinematic Embodiment
Spectator and Screen

NICOLE ERIN MORSE

Lana and Lilly Wachowski
Cáel M. Keegan
Chicago: University of Illinois Press, 2018. 180 pp.

Part of the University of Illinois Press's Contemporary Film Directors Series, Cáel M. Keegan's monograph on Lana and Lilly Wachowski far exceeds the series' goals, offering not only a detailed filmography, one of the most extensive interviews with Lana Wachowski to date, and a thorough critical analysis—it also provides a compelling contribution to current discussions about the relationship between trans* and cinema. Through Keegan's close readings of the Wachowski sisters' films, he articulates a theory of trans* cinematic embodiment that is crucially necessary for contemporary research at the intersection of trans* studies and cinema and media studies.

Following Susan Stryker's 2000 essay "Transsexuality: The Postmodern Body and/as Technology," as well as Stryker's current work on the cinematic afterlife of Christine Jorgensen, scholars and artists have examined the relationship between trans* and the cinematic as an issue that exceeds questions of representational politics. Instead, they explore a more complicated question: is there an ontological, phenomenological, and/or epistemological connection between the technology of cinema and trans*? While provocative, this question risks turning both trans* experience and cinema into metaphors of unmoored flexibility and fluidity, which is a role that postmodern theory has all too often required trans* figures to play. Alternatively, this argument can become reductive and even spectacularizing, equating cinematic suture with the surgical processes associated with medical transition. Instead, Keegan turns to the spectatorial

TSQ: Transgender Studies Quarterly ∗ Volume 7, Number 3 ∗ August 2020
DOI 10.1215/23289252-8553286   © 2020 Duke University Press

experience created by the Wachowskis' films and uses incisive, passionately written close analysis to explicate the sensorial and material possibilities that these films—and the trans* cinema they herald—illuminate.

In Keegan's monograph, trans* and cinema are not linked by an ontological metaphor of suturing/surgery but instead by their effects on our ways of engaging the world. His approach to trans* cinema studies "treats cinema *as if it were gender itself*—disrupting, rearranging, and evolving the cinematic sensorium in the same manner that trans* disrupts, rearranges, and evolves discrete genders and sexes" (6). Keegan's theoretical insights build on his prior research on trans* cinema and continue his efforts to connect spectatorial experience with alternative, radical, and resistant forms of knowledge production. This is crucial when examining the Wachowskis' work, given that decades passed between their rise to fame and the time when each woman publicly came out as transgender. Though Keegan does discuss some of the ways that *The Matrix* can be read as a trans* allegory (29–30), he focuses on developing a retrospective method that does not seek to uncover the intentions of trans* authors within the work but rather strives to examine and unfold "a mutually constitutive process by which I and the work have *become trans** together, over time" (6). Through attending to process, becoming, sensation, and spectatorial engagement, Keegan's approach exceeds ontological determinism.

Keegan's attention to spectatorial experience is particularly powerful in his analysis of one of the Wachowskis' lesser-known films, *Bound* (1996). Credited to the Wachowski "Brothers," *Bound*'s tale of lesbian desire has not been fully integrated into the canon of queer cinema. In Keegan's account, *Bound*'s significance extends far beyond its creators' identities, however, and his close reading reveals "one of the most radical depictions of queer women's sexuality ever to emerge from Hollywood" (9). Reading this film as a neo-noir, Keegan evocatively details how the film formally interrogates the boundaries of identities, the gender binary, and the structure of the cinematic gaze (17). In closing this analysis, Keegan also suggests that *Bound* offers the possibility of critically exploring the relationship between racialization and queerness through the femme character of Violet, played by mixed-race actor Jennifer Tilly. However, in asserting that Tilly's appearance positions Violet as "a set of tremulous potentials" that mean she "remains unfixed," Keegan risks substituting the ambiguously racialized figure for postmodernity's trans* figure—trading one spectacularized representation of postmodern flexibility for another.

Throughout his compelling analysis of the trans* cinematic possibilities within the Wachowskis' work, Keegan gestures to the long-standing criticisms of the directors' approach to race. As he notes, "theorizations of trans* that forget the materiality signaled by race threaten to unravel into totalizing deconstructions" and within *The Matrix*, specifically, "the elevation of a postracial trans∗ aesthetic often requires negative performances of black immanence" (41). This "postracial trans∗ aesthetic" that Keegan identifies within the Wachowskis' work risks reinscribing trans∗ as whiteness and raises crucial theoretical and methodological questions for scholars examining the phenomenological and material implications of reading trans∗ and cinema together. Though Keegan does not pursue this provocation as far as he might, his attention to the sensorial and material—traced vividly through his method of close reading—is a necessary approach for scholars working to account for how race and gender intersect within trans∗ cinema.

Nicole Erin Morse is assistant professor of multimedia studies and program director of the Center for Women, Gender, and Sexuality Studies at Florida Atlantic University. Their work on trans and queer cinema and media has been published in *Jump Cut*, *Feminist Media Studies*, *Porn Studies*, *TSQ*, and elsewhere.

Printed and bound by CPI Group (UK) Ltd, Croydon, CR0 4YY

28/01/2025

14634120-0001